LADY GRISELL BAILLIE
MISTRESS OF MELLERSTAIN

LADY GRISELL BAILLIE
MISTRESS OF MELLERSTAIN

LESLEY ABERNETHY

Matador
9 Priory Business Park,
Wistow Road, Kibworth Beauchamp,
Leicestershire LE8 0RX
Tel: 0116 279 2299
Email: books@troubador.co.uk
Web: www.troubador.co.uk/matador
Twitter: @matadorbooks

ISBN 978 183859 367 4

British Library Cataloguing in Publication Data.
A catalogue record for this book is available from the British Library.

Printed and bound by CPI Group (UK) Ltd, Croydon, CR0 4YY
Typeset in 11pt Baskerville by Troubador Publishing Ltd, Leicester, UK

Matador is an imprint of Troubador Publishing Ltd

To the memory of
my mother and father
Laura and Ronnie Webster

CONTENTS

FOREWORD

The archives at Mellerstain document the affairs of the Earls of Haddington dating back to the 16th Century. The books of accounts, and bundles of letters and maps provide a compelling insight into the domestic and political lives of my ancestors.

Whilst sections of the archive have been put into the public domain, much of this material has remained private and unpublished, but when Lesley Abernethy, one of the charming and knowledgeable tour guides at Mellerstain House (and my teacher at Coldstream Primary School), proposed to us that she write a historical biography of my ancestor Grisell Baillie, we were delighted to open those archives to her.

The lifetime of Grisell Baillie (née Hume) marks a particularly colourful period in Scottish history, in which the family became fatally embroiled. In the 17th Century religious authority and political power were still inseparable, and the Covenanters, whose ranks included the Baillies and Humes, fought against the Anglican and subsequently Catholic monarchy, for the spiritual independence of the Scottish Presbyterian Church. In the 18th Century Grisell's family found their friendships divided by the Jacobite uprisings, but remained loyal to the Hanoverian succession. Against this noisy backdrop, Lesley has been able to distinguish Grisell's remarkable story.

As a child, Grisell's bravery in the face of religious persecution marks her out as a heroine of Scottish history. Her prudence and determination in safeguarding her family's survival and developing her husband's restored estates, and her shrewd oversight in the first phase of building Mellerstain House, are the achievements of a unique woman of her time.

George Haddington

ACKNOWLEDGEMENTS

I am grateful to Lord Polwarth and the family of Scott of Harden for their kind permission to publish several quotations from the National Records of Scotland series GD158 (Papers of the Family of Hume of Polwarth), and to Shepherd and Wedderburn LLP for permission to publish from GD206/6 (Papers of the Hall Family of Dunglass). I am indebted to the National Records of Scotland for permission to publish from GD206/2 (Hall of Dunglass), RH15/15 (Papers of Sir Andrew Home, Lord Kimmerghame), GD1/1209/1, (Account Book of Dame Grisell Ker), GD1/649 (Transcript of the Diary of George Home of Kimmerghame) and Conjoined Processes of Separation CC8/6/167

In addition to the above unpublished material, printed sources most frequently referred to are:

Marchmont and the Humes of Polwarth (Margaret Warrender 1894)

The Household Book of Lady Grisell Baillie (Ed. Robert Scott-Moncrieff 1911)

Memoirs of the Lives and Characters of the Right Honourable George Baillie of Jerviswood and of Lady Grisell Baillie (Lady Murray of Stanhope 1822)

Observations on the Historical Work of the late Right Honourable Charles James Fox (George Rose 1809)

Scottish Lifestyle 300 Years Ago (Helen and Keith Kelsall 1993)
The Lockhart Papers (George Lockhart of Carnwath, 1702-45, published 1817)

Electronic resources provided access to Kirk Session Records (www.scottishdocuments.com) and to Old Parish Records (www.scotlandspeople.gov.uk). Historical Tax Rolls were accessed at https://scotlandsplaces.gov.uk/, and Westminster Rate Books at www.findmypast.co.uk

All quotations marked with an asterisk * are from newspapers printed in London, England, and part of the Burney Collection, accessed digitally via the National Library of Scotland.

All photographs are the work of George Haddington, with the exception of Plates 1a and 7 (Ian Abernethy), and Plate 5 (George Holywell), to whom my thanks are due. Plate 27b is my own, as are any mistakes in this work or misinterpretations of the available evidence.

I would like to thank the unfailingly helpful staff of the National Records of Scotland in Edinburgh, the National Museum of Scotland and the Scottish Borders Heritage Hub in Hawick.

Kristina Bedford of Ancestral Deeds gave unstinting advice and encouragement and my husband Ian showed enormous tolerance of my obsession with a woman who lived three centuries ago.

Most of all, my thanks are due to George, Earl of Haddington and his mother, Jane, for giving me privileged access to the private archive of letters, accounts and other documents held at Mellerstain, from which the majority of the original material in this book derives.

INTRODUCTION

Lady Grisell Baillie has for over two centuries had a place in the literature of Scotland as a 'Scottish heroine'. Her story, or part of it, has been endlessly re-told since first appearing in print in 1809 when it formed an Appendix entitled 'Lady Murray's Narrative' in a work by George Rose, *Observations on the Historical Work of the late Right Honourable Charles James Fox.* (This work was not as unrelated to Lady Grisell as the title might suggest as it is a defence of her father Sir Patrick Hume). Lady Murray, Grisell Baillie's elder daughter, had committed her thoughts to paper at Mellerstain in the Scottish Borders on 12 December 1749, entitling her 76-page narrative 'Facts relating to my mother's life and character'. Writing at Oxford in 1739, she had written a similar 25-page memorial of her father, George Baillie, 'Plain facts relating to my father's character, of which I could give many more.' Being aware that her affection for her mother might result in a too biased account, Lady Murray says, 'I will therefore set a guard upon myself, to keep strictly to truth, and relate facts which speak for themselves.' Relying largely on remembered conversations, a number of Lady Murray's 'facts' prove to be inaccurate in the light of documentary evidence, but as Lady Grisell Baillie's first biographer, with a lifelong personal acquaintance of her subject, her account is nevertheless invaluable. After its first obscure appearance in print in 1809,

Lady Murray's memoir appeared as an independent work, published in Edinburgh in 1822 by Thomas Thomson, Deputy Clerk Register, with the somewhat unwieldy title: *Memoirs of the Lives and Characters of the Right Honourable George Baillie of Jerviswood and of Lady Grisell Baillie by their daughter Lady Murray of Stanhope.*

One year before Thomson's edition of 1822, Joanna Baillie, who claimed a doubtful distant kinship, had written the first of many romanticised versions of Grisell's story in her *Metrical Legends of Exalted Characters.* Perversely, she names her heroine 'Griseld', not the 'Grisell' (with variant spellings, and rhyming with 'drizzle') that friends and family called her. Throughout the nineteenth and twentieth centuries, Lady Grisell's name became familiar in many guises from articles in children's penny papers, to fictionalised accounts of her life and plays for schoolchildren to act out, all stressing her youthful heroism and selflessness. Scholars and social historians have pored over the detail of seventeenth- and eighteenth-century life revealed in the publication by the Scottish History Society in 1911, of extracts from her numerous account books which appeared under the title *The Household Book of Lady Grisell Baillie 1692-1733.*

Each of the publications mentioned above gave only snapshots of particular features of her life; she has been pigeon-holed in print as a 'Youthful Heroine', 'Meticulous Housekeeper' and 'Scottish Songwriter', ignoring many aspects of a truly remarkable and forceful personality. Those who encountered her in her lifetime might have added to the descriptions above: estate manager, politician, landscape gardener, building supervisor, homemaker, traveller, letter-writer, patroness of the arts, educator, needlewoman, devoted wife and indefatigable nurturer and defender of her extended family. The detail of Lady Grisell's life as revealed in her own words and those of her contemporaries also sheds light on a long period of history encompassing the events characterised as the Restoration, the Killing Times, the Glorious Revolution, the Darien Scheme, the Union of 1707, the South Sea Bubble of 1720 and the Jacobite Rebellions of 1715 and 1745, all of which had direct impact on the lives of Lady Grisell and her family.

A NOTE ABOUT NAMES

Repetition of names over several generations is problematical. The most frequently-mentioned people are:

Lady Grisell Baillie (1665-1746) – referred to throughout as 'Grisell'

George Baillie (1664-1738), husband of Grisell, – referred to as 'George Baillie'

Grisell (1692-1759), elder daughter of Grisell and George Baillie – 'Grisie' or 'Lady Murray'

Rachel (1696-1773), younger daughter of Grisell and George Baillie – 'Rachy' or 'Lady Binning'

Thomas Hamilton (1721-1794), eldest grandson – 'Tamie' or 'Lord Haddington'

George Baillie (Hamilton) (1723-1797), second grandson – 'Grandson George' or 'George'

Grisell (1719-1811), eldest granddaughter – 'young/little Grisie', 'Miss Hamilton' or 'Lady Stanhope'

Sir Patrick Hume (1641-1724), Grisell's father – 'Sir Patrick', 'Lord Polwarth' then 'Earl of Marchmont'

Although a married woman usually adopted her husband's title if he had one, it was the custom in Scotland for a woman to continue to be known by her maiden surname.

There are variant spellings of the name 'Hume', i.e. 'Home',

'Hoome' etc, but all are pronounced 'Hume'; likewise, Carre and Ker(r) have identical pronunciation.

I have used the contemporary word 'Holland' for places in modern-day Netherlands.

MONEY

Money expressed in numerals is written, for example, £14:11s10d, meaning fourteen pounds, eleven shillings and ten pence. Currency at the time had twelve pence in a shilling and twenty shillings in a pound.

SPELLING

With the intention of letting the voices of the seventeenth and eighteenth centuries 'speak for themselves', wherever there are direct quotations from letters, documents or other literature, spelling, capitalisation and punctuation (or its absence) have been left as they were in the original, with the occasional [clarification].

Chapter 1

꧁ꙮꙍꙮ꧂

CHILDHOOD AT REDBRAES

1665-1686

On Christmas Eve 1665 George Holiwell, minister of the kirk of Polwarth near Greenlaw in Berwickshire, (Plate 1a) finished his lengthy sermon, said a closing prayer and hastened to Redbraes, (Plate 1b) the home of the local laird, Sir Patrick Hume. Mr. Holiwell had received a message that the laird's young wife Grisell Ker (Plate 2) had been brought to bed of a daughter, and speed was of the essence in getting to Redbraes to christen the child, as the couple's first daughter and a son had died unbaptised, and a second daughter, named Christian, had died just over a year ago, aged fifteen months. The cradle had since been occupied by a healthy boy, now one year old and named Patrick for his father and grandfather; his new sister was named Grisell for her mother and grandmother. Having returned to his manse, he carefully noted the event in the parish records, though in handwriting less well-formed than that of his predecessor David Robertson, whom he had replaced two years earlier:

Redbraes de[cembe]r 24 1665 Grissell Hume
A daughter borne to the laird of Polwart & baptized the same day
after sermon her name is Grissell witnesses Ro't ker of Craillen
hall & Jo'n Ker of West Nisbett

Sir Patrick, her father, (Plate 3) had likely been laid in the same cradle under the same roof at his own birth on 13 January 1641. That roof was an impressive one, capping a substantial building with a central tower flanked by slightly smaller towers on either side. Patrick's mother, Christian Hamilton, recorded the births of her children in her Bible; all except for Julian, Patrick's eldest sister, were recorded as taking place at Redbraes. Julian had been born at The Mains, the family's previous house very close by, so we may conclude that Redbraes was a new building when Patrick was born. Later in the century, Sir Patrick would pay tax on seventeen hearths, so the household must have been an extensive one, with an appropriate number of servants to keep it running smoothly under the direction of Grisell's mother.

Patrick's father, also called Sir Patrick, was no 'bonnet laird', having been created a baronet in 1625, and his own father, yet another Sir Patrick Hume of Polwarth, had served as Master of the Household to James VI, so the infant Grisell had a distinguished pedigree, traceable back to the Earls of Dunbar in the thirteenth century. Grisell's parents Sir Patrick Hume and Grisell Ker had been married on 29 January 1660. The marriage had almost certainly been arranged by the couple's parents years earlier. Sir Patrick's father had died when his son was only seven years old but, according to the custom of the landed classes at the time, young Patrick had possibly been earmarked as a suitable husband for Grisell Ker, daughter of Sir Thomas Ker of Cavers, even at that tender age. At a later date, when it appeared both parties had survived the rigours of childhood disease, protracted negotiations often took place regarding the terms of the marriage settlement and, if these were concluded to the satisfaction of both families, the marriage would take place. Patrick's mother Christian Hamilton married again in 1654 to Robert Kerr, who was to succeed as 3rd Lord Jedburgh in 1670. While Hume could be said to be the most prestigious family name in Berwickshire at that time, it was the Ker(r) name that largely held sway in neighbouring Roxburghshire, so Patrick's mother would have appeared to be making an advantageous match, had it not been for the fact that her new husband had to be released from a debtors' prison by her paying his very substantial debts, reducing the Polwarth inheritance for her children and grandchildren.

It was very unusual at that time for a lady such as Grisell Ker to nurse her children herself. Accordingly, a wet nurse would have been brought into the household until an infant was weaned, or sometimes the child would be taken to live with the nurse's family if she had numerous children as well as her own baby. This seemingly socially desirable failure to breastfeed an infant robbed the natural mother of the contraceptive advantages of breastfeeding; having married young, Grisell Ker had possibly 20 pregnancies between 1660 and 1686.

No doubt on Christmas Day 1665, the day following baby Grisell's birth, there would have been celebrations fêting the safe arrival of the newest member of the family and Grisell Ker's survival of the immediate traumas of childbirth, though new mothers often succumbed to infections in the weeks following a birth, so all the family could do was hope and pray for a happy outcome for both mother and child. However, despite it being Christmas Day, it was unlikely to have been marked by any other festivities. Little Grisell's grandmother Christian Hamilton, now wife of Robert Kerr, may have marked the day as a holy day in the Christian calendar at her home near Jedburgh, as she was a devoted Episcopalian, but even as a youth Sir Patrick had rebelled against his mother's religion, preferring the Presbyterian religion, the chief faith of Scotland since 1560 when acts were passed outlawing the saying of mass and refusing to acknowledge the power of the Pope. The Presbyterians claimed God as the only head of the church; no monarch, Pope or bishop could or should come between a man and his God. While the Catholics clung to their church hierarchies, rituals, elaborate robes and Latin language, the reformed church in Scotland worshipped in the vernacular, with Bible readings and prayers in English, a sermon preached by the minister, and singing of metrical psalms by the congregation.

Religious differences were of profound importance to the people of seventeenth-century Scotland, and these differences would have a huge impact on Grisell's childhood and youth. A large majority had embraced the ideas of the reformed church, and were alarmed by Charles I's attempt to impose the Anglican prayer book on Scotland, culminating in the 1638 Confession of Faith or Covenant, professing loyalty to the King but equally, loyalty to the Presbyterian way of worship. In communities all over Scotland, people had added their signatures to copies of the document, of which some fifty examples still survive today.

Following Charles I's execution in 1649, the Scots' form of worship seemed safe under Cromwell, but 1660, the same year as Sir Patrick Hume and Grisell Ker's marriage, saw the restoration of the monarchy, with Charles II letting Scotland be governed by his Privy Council, and in the hands of his Secretary for Scotland, John Maitland, Earl of Lauderdale, who was for twelve years a de facto regent. Two acknowledged Covenanters, declared to be enemies of the King, who were put to death after the Restoration were the Earl of Argyll, who had actually crowned Charles II at Scone in 1651 before the King's flight into exile in the face of Cromwell's army, and Archibald Johnston of Wariston. Johnston of Wariston had co-authored the National Covenant, and had later accepted a post from Cromwell, two now treasonable offences, and was hanged in Edinburgh on the 22 July 1663. (Archibald Johnston will reappear in the story as father of Rachel, wife of Robert Baillie, and mother of Grisell's husband George Baillie). The Covenant had been declared illegal in 1662, the year after James Sharp had been appointed Archbishop of St Andrews, and the reinstated Privy Council had decreed that the Kirk was to revert to the way it had been governed in 1633, by bishops, and that all ministers had to have their positions reconfirmed by the bishop and the patron of their own church, which in Polwarth's case was Sir Patrick.

It was in the two years after Johnston of Wariston's execution that Grisell and her elder brother Patrick were born, and at the same time their father Sir Patrick's political career began to gather momentum. Shortly before Grisell's birth he had represented Berwickshire at the Conventions of Estates [parliament] which sat in August 1665, and other political appointments followed thick and fast. In 1667 he again sat in the Conventions of Estates, and was appointed Commissioner of Supply for the county. In May of 1668 he was commissioned as Captain of the Horse in the Berwickshire militia, and appointed Excise Commissioner in November of the same year. Meanwhile, his family had increased with the births on 29 April 1667 of a son, Thomas, who died aged 18 months, and a daughter, Christian on 7 May 1668. Sir Patrick represented Berwickshire again in Charles II's second parliament 1669-74, and in 1671 and 1673 was appointed a Highway Commissioner for Berwickshire. Four more births had taken place at Redbraes by this date: a son, Robert was born on 10 July 1669; a daughter Julianne (9 November 1670) and a son Thomas (15 June 1672) who both died before their second birthday, and another daughter, Julian had been born on 16 August 1673.

Sir Patrick's public appointments must have necessitated frequent and occasionally prolonged absences from Redbraes, leaving his wife Grisell Ker in sole charge of managing the ever-increasing household, with its five surviving children and a number of servants, both indoor and outdoor. In 1673 and 1674, Sir Patrick had spoken out against the way Maitland of Lauderdale was ruling Scotland, and in September 1675 he was summoned before the Privy Council for objecting to soldiers being garrisoned with certain Berwickshire gentlemen, and was declared to be a 'factious person… incapable of all public trust'. At Redbraes another small son, Alexander, born on 1 January 1675 was thriving, and Sir Patrick's wife had suffered the miscarriage of a daughter in August, but Sir Patrick was not to see Redbraes for some time as he was imprisoned in the castle in Edinburgh at the beginning of September, being transferred at the end of the month to Stirling Castle, where he remained until February 1676, when the Privy Council received a letter from the King authorising his release. Sir Patrick's 'cell' once he had moved to Stirling Castle may have been similar to that of his friend Henry, Lord Cardross, who writes to him on 24 November 1675 from his prison in Edinburgh Castle, excusing himself for not having written more often. 'I am hardly master of one quarter of ane hour by reasone of our having only one roome which is our bedchamber, our dining roome, our drawing roome, the roome wher my wiefe reseaves her visits, the roome wher I receave my visits and does anay bussiness. Judge, I pray you, wher I can doe anay thing, the chamber being almost constantly full of women and frequently of men, which makes me often neglect my bussiness.' Cardross also commiserated with Sir Patrick on the loss of his only brother, Alexander, a colonel in the Russian army, who had died in Moscow aged 30.

Grisell was almost 10 years old when her father was first imprisoned. As the eldest girl out of the brood of small siblings, she must already have been of great practical help to her perpetually pregnant mother, but perhaps now her moral support was necessary as well. She maybe did not fully understand the danger her father and his friends were in. Lady Murray says: 'In the troubles of King Charles the Second's time, she began her life with many afflicting, terrifying hardships; though I have often heard her say, she never thought them any.'

It is probably at this time that Grisell first showed the heroism for which she became famous. Sir Patrick's good friend and fellow Covenanter Robert Baillie (Plate 4) was in prison in Edinburgh, (from June to December 1676) and Sir Patrick wished to get a message to him. Knowing that any adult visitor would be carefully scrutinised, Sir Patrick entrusted to his young daughter the task of delivering a letter to Robert Baillie. Grisell's elder brother Patrick might have seemed a more obvious choice as messenger, but Sir Patrick and Grisell Ker recognised more suitable qualities in their eldest daughter. We have no knowledge of Grisell's means of transport for the journey of some forty miles from Redbraes to Edinburgh, but she managed to get into the jail and exchange information with Robert Baillie, and arrived back unscathed with his reply at Polwarth, no doubt to the great relief of both parents. Grisell was still only 10 years old. At around this time, another baby brother, Andrew, had been born on 19 July 1676. Grisell's trip to Edinburgh had further significance in that it is thought that this was the first time she met Robert Baillie's son George, her future husband. The Redbraes family increased again on 4 November 1677 with the birth of Anne, another sister for Grisell, bringing the number of surviving children to eight. Sadly, Grisell Ker suffered the miscarriage of a son in September 1678.

Sir Patrick was imprisoned again some time before that date as he petitioned the King in September for an improvement in his conditions of confinement, having fallen ill in prison in Dumbarton, but it was not until the following 6 February (1679) that the King wrote to the Privy Council sanctioning his removal to the presumably more salubrious prison in Stirling Castle, and granting permission for his wife to be in the room with him. Here Sir Patrick and presumably also Grisell his wife, remained until 17 July when another letter from the King, signed by Lauderdale, ordered his release, with the reason given that, 'the occasion of the suspicions and publick jealousies which we had at that time being now removed'. During Sir Patrick's imprisonment an army of Covenanters had defeated Government troops at the battle of Drumclog on 1 June, but lost a battle at Bothwell Brig on 22 June. Around 1,300 Covenanters who survived that battle were imprisoned in the Inner Yard of Greyfriars Kirk in Edinburgh. Fortunately for the authorities, who had no means of accommodating such a sudden and large number of prisoners, some 1,000 of them gained their freedom by signing an oath for the King's peace:

> *I being apprehended for being at the late rebellion; and whereas the lords of his majesty's privy council, in pursuance of his majesty's command, have ordained me to be set at liberty, I enacting myself to the effect underwritten: therefore I bind, oblige, and enact myself in the books of the privy council, that hereafter I shall not take up arms, without or against his majesty, or his authority. As witness my hand...*

Unlike the Covenanters, Sir Patrick and his wife at least had the benefit of a roof over their heads during their imprisonment.

For close on six months, with both parents in prison, the household at Redbraes must have been entrusted to the care of servants, but Lady Murray is silent on the matter. Grisell, at 13 and Patrick, at 14 years old, may have helped to look after, and educate their six younger siblings. We know comparatively little of Grisell's education. When her father was at home, along with her brothers and sisters she received some tuition from Sir Patrick, whose own good education had been secured by his mother Lady Jedburgh. George Holiwell was minister of Polwarth from 1664 until his death in 1704, and must have been a figure who loomed very large in Grisell's childhood. Margaret Warrender documenting her own ancestors in *Marchmont and the Humes of Polwarth* in 1894 notes that George Holiwell is described on his gravestone as 'Pedagogue to Patrick, Earl of Marchmont'. (This inscription is now largely illegible, and may have been difficult to read even at the end of the nineteenth century as Warrender says that Holiwell's father was a periwig maker in Duns whereas that was actually Holiwell's son, Holiwell's father being a baillie and periwig maker in Selkirk). In addition to Holiwell having been Sir Patrick's own tutor, appointed as a youthful graduate of Edinburgh University, it is probable that Sir Patrick employed him as teacher of his large family, including Grisell. Patrick's sons would of course have been schooled in the Classics, as befitted gentlemen, though the education of Grisell and her sisters would have been considered complete in the way of academic subjects once they could read, write and do some arithmetic.

George Holiwell's manse was reasonably substantial, with five hearths, affording room for the numerous family he eventually had, and space to accommodate visiting ministers from other parishes. The majority of his parishioners in Polwarth lived in single-roomed dwellings thatched with heather. George Holiwell (Plate 5) had been Sir Patrick's choice as minister, as it was the prerogative of the laird to 'present' the minister. Holiwell was assisted by the Polwarth Kirk Session, a committee of elders, in reinforcing the Kirk's draconian grip on the population of the village and surrounding farmsteads. Anyone in the parish who was thought to have behaved immorally or to have profaned the Sabbath was summoned to appear before the Session and, if guilt was admitted, had to show public repentance in the kirk the following Sunday. Fornication was a frequently-mentioned sin but other, to modern eyes trivial, transgressions required penitence, as these extracts from Polwarth Kirk Session minutes in 1657 demonstrate:

Jan 18th
Compeared [appeared in response to a summons] Katharine Hume & confessed that lately upon the sabbath day she had carried in some cabbage to her daughter in Dunse. Ordains for the next sabbath day to give public evidence of her repentance.

Jan 25th
Katharine Hume did publicly upon her knees confess her sin in profaning the sabbath and promised amendment. William Jeffray, Robert Sanderson, James & George Holiday delated [reported] for going to the Ice upon the sabbath day.

Feb 1
Compeared Robert Sanderson, William Jeffray, George & James Holidays & confessed that going forth to take the air on the sabbath after both sermons they walked a turn or two upon the ice & rolled some stones upon it which they found lying there. They were rebuked for spending the sabbath unprofitably & exhorted hereafter to make greater conscience of sanctifying the holy sabbath.

Carrying cabbage was deemed to be work and rolling curling stones constituted play, neither of which was permitted on the Sabbath. Parishioners, including the laird's family, were required to be in attendance for both sermons every Sunday, and it was expected that family prayers were to be said in every house on a daily basis. Throughout the week the minister would ride around his parish visiting the sick, christening babies and catechising children. The Church of Scotland had approved the Westminster Shorter Catechism in 1648, aimed at educating children in the tenets of the Reformed Faith. It is a series of 107 questions, to which Grisell and her older siblings would have been expected to give the correct answer. When asked the first question, 'What is the chief end of man?', they would chant "Man's chief end is to glorify God, and to enjoy him forever."

The community of Polwarth, consisting of cottages huddled higgledy-piggledy around a village green, numbered perhaps 200 souls at the time of Grisell's birth, with an equal number scattered over the rest of the parish. Many of the inhabitants relied on Sir Patrick's estate for work as house servants, farm servants and foresters. Polwarth was equidistant from two larger towns, those of Dunse (as originally spelled) and Greenlaw, but was self-sufficient for most needs including shoes and clothing, as the community included weavers and a number of shoemakers or 'souters'. The half-mile walk from their cottages to the kirk, passing the manse, would be a pleasant enough walk in the summer, but less so in the snow or mud of winter. The Redbraes family too were almost a mile from the kirk, but would have had the advantage of horses and ponies to transport them. Polwarth Church records note the christening on 4 January 1682 of another son, named George, for Sir Patrick and his wife Grisell Ker.

From the year 1682 Grisell and her story might have been lost to Scotland forever. Sir Patrick was not alone in feeling unhappy with the way Scotland was being governed. Some 36 Scottish noblemen and gentlemen were willing to subscribe to a plan to set up a colony in South Carolina, where their religious freedom would be guaranteed. Sir George Campbell of Cessnock and Sir John Cochrane of Ochiltree were appointed commissioners to put this plan before King Charles, who approved it. Politicians who supported the King at this time were known as the Court Party, with those in opposition as the Country Party, whose chief motivator was Lord Shaftesbury. The subscribers, described as 'undertakers' were to subscribe 10 pounds each per 100 acres and another 10 pounds sterling if need be for charges, before the first of October 1682.

Among the 36 subscribers to the Carolina project were Lord Haddington, Sir Patrick Hume and Robert Baillie. Throughout the 1670s, staunch Presbyterians, headed by William Dunlop and Henry Erskine, Lord Cardross, had had dreams of establishing a settlement overseas where there would be no threat of persecution for their Covenanting ideals. The way had been paved for such a settlement in 1663 when King Charles II had granted a charter to eight English noblemen, including Lord Shaftesbury, in a territory which had been named 'Carolina' in 1629 after his father Charles I. This charter deemed them 'Lords Proprietors'. The Lords Proprietors were anxious to have the territory well populated as a deterrent to other would-be colonisers, namely the Spanish, so offered inducements of land, religious freedom and political representation to any future settlers. Meetings had taken place between the intending emigrants and the Lords Proprietors, but plans were stopped in their tracks by the revelation of the Rye House Plot, a supposed conspiracy to kill King Charles II and his brother the Duke of York, the future James II and VII, on their way back from the races at Newmarket on 1 April 1683. The plot had failed because a fire in the town of Newmarket meant that King Charles and his brother returned to London earlier than expected after the races were cancelled. There were known connections between the alleged plotters and the 'undertakers' of the Carolina project, and it was rumoured that the Carolina project had merely been a front to plan the assassination. Whether any genuine plot had actually existed, or whether it an excuse for Charles II to get rid of a large number of known enemies is a fruitful subject for debate.

In the aftermath of the plot, 11 men and one woman were executed, and a similar number were imprisoned and fined. Robert Baillie of Jerviswood and Mellerstain, great friend of Grisell's father, was arrested in London on 26 June 1683 on suspicion of involvement in the assassination plot. He denied any knowledge of such a conspiracy, but refused to answer questions about rumoured uprisings to be led by the Duke of Monmouth, King Charles' illegitimate son, in England, and by Archibald Campbell, 9th Earl of Argyll in Scotland. Baillie was kept shackled in the Gatehouse Prison in Westminster, as a result of which his health rapidly declined. His wife, Rachel Johnston, (Plate 6) petitioned the King to have her husband released on bail, without success, but he was moved to Scotland at the end of October 1683. He languished in prison for almost another whole year until he received a summons in September 1684 to appear before the Privy Council on a charge of treason. Robert Baillie declared himself too ill to be moved and so the Clerk Register was sent with questions to be put to him under oath, without his having to leave his prison cell. An English Puritan minister named Roger Morrice kept a diary from 1677-1691 which he called his *Ent'ring Book*, in which he notes that Baillie refused to answer on the grounds that 'he was not bound to accuse himselfe'. For refusing to answer, Baillie was fined the enormous sum of 6,000 pounds, probably the value of his entire estate.

News of Robert Baillie's ill health and impending summons in that summer of 1684 must have reached Sir Patrick at Redbraes where Grisell's little sister Jean, born 22 March 1683 and christened in Edinburgh four days later, was now toddling round unconcerned about the political troubles and dangers surrounding her family. Hearing that he too was about to be summoned, Sir Patrick decided that he must escape from Redbraes, but feared being apprehended by some of the soldiers garrisoned in the area. Lady Murray says that Sir Patrick 'thought it necessary to keep concealed; and soon found he had too good reason for so doing; parties being continually sent out in search of him, and often to his own house, to the terror of all in it.' Having put about the story that he had fled abroad, Sir Patrick went into hiding less than a mile from his own house, in the family burial vault in Polwarth Kirk. According to Lady Murray, none knew of his hiding place except Grisell, her mother and one trusted servant, the house carpenter Jamie Winter, who had carried a folding bed at night-time to the vault to make Sir Patrick's hiding place more tolerable. Margaret Warrender reports that 'The bed is still [1894] preserved at Marchmont, and is of black walnut, in good preservation, bearing the date 1660. It folds up, and the four short legs also fold down with hinges when not required, but have strong springs to keep them erect when in use. The whole goes into very little space.' (If it still exists, the bed's current whereabouts are unknown).

Sir Patrick's concealment in the vault gave rise to the most famous episode of heroism in young Grisell's life. For the space of about a month, according to Lady Murray, Sir Patrick was sustained by nightly visits from Grisell, bringing food, and staying to cheer him with news of his family, and perhaps telling him of further searches of the house and questioning of the servants about the whereabouts of their master. The servants' loyalty was not doubted, but the authorities of the time were not above using unscrupulous methods, including torture, to extract answers. Lady Polwarth's later 'Compt Book' shows her to have been a careful housekeeper, so precise account would have been taken of the quantity of certain foodstuffs which had been used on any day. The only way to procure an extra daily portion of food without arousing the servants' suspicion was for

Grisell to surreptitiously transfer items from her own plate to her lap. Alexander, now nine years old and known to the family as 'Sandy', was mystified when Grisell, knowing her father's fondness for sheep's head, had secreted the whole head from the dish of broth on the table, leading Sandy to exclaim, "Mother, will ye look at Grisell; while we have been eating our broth, she has eat up the whole sheep's head!".

Lady Murray has more details about Sir Patrick's stay in the vault, including the fact that on the first night, the minister's dogs had barked so much as she neared the kirk that she feared discovery. The next day Lady Polwarth sent for Mr. Holiwell and incited him to hang all his dogs, on pretence of a mad dog roaming the district, rabies then being endemic. There is no mention of whether the Redbraes dogs suffered the same fate. The Reverend Grimwood, minister of Polwarth, writing in the 1930s, tells us that the entrance to the vault, before the rebuilding of the church, was through a door at the bottom of a flight of steps at the west end of the church, obscured when the tower was built in 1703. This being the family's private burial vault, it seems likely that only Sir Patrick had the key. Lady Murray says of Grisell, 'She at that time had a terror for a churchyard, especially in the dark…but when engaged by concern for her father, she stumbled over the graves every night alone, without fear of any kind entering her thoughts, but for soldiers, and parties in search of him'. To light her way, Grisell carried a small lantern, that Warrender describes as being 'of very rude make'. It is three-sided, made of wood with a natural branch for the handle. The candle-holder and pierced top are of tin, and the door hinges of leather. The sides are rebated, to house thin sheets of glass to protect the candle flame from the wind. Margaret Warrender knew the lantern well as it was still at Marchmont in her lifetime, and it was she who gifted it to the National Museum of Antiquities (now the Museum of

Scotland), where it remains on permanent display in the section devoted to the history of the Covenanters (Plate 7).

Having completed her terrifying journey through the dark wood to Polwarth Kirk each night, Grisell is said to have communicated with her father through a small grating in the east end of the church, which admitted only a little light. The vault, over 50 feet long, runs the whole length of the church; looking through the grating, it is impossible to see the further end. For fear of discovery, Sir Patrick had no candle, and kept his mind occupied by repeating the Latin verse paraphrases of the Psalms, first published by George Buchanan in 1565, and which Sir Patrick knew by heart. Lady Murray says that she remembers seeing her father, just two years before his death at the age of 84, asking Grisell to take his copy of Buchanan's *Psalms* and to choose one at random for him to repeat. Having no Latin, Grisell could not understand what he was saying, but could visually check the words as he spoke them.

Confinement in the damp, dark vault was only a temporary solution, likely to be injurious to Sir Patrick's health, so Grisell and Jamie Winter began making another place of concealment at Redbraes, in a ground floor room usually unused and kept locked. A hole was made 'under a bed which drew out' by Grisell and the carpenter scraping the earth away using their bare hands for fear of making a noise, the earth from the excavations being carried in a sheet on the carpenter's back and out through the window. At his own house, Winter made a box to line the hole, large enough to take a bed for Sir Patrick to lie in, and provided with holes for ventilation, which he installed in the hiding place that had been dug out. Lady Murray continues, 'When it had stood the trial, for a month, of no water coming into it…her father ventured home, having that to trust to.' If this trial month is added to the time, possibly several weeks, that it took for the carpenter and Grisell to dig the hole, presumably working for short periods at night to avoid suspicion from long absences, Sir Patrick's confinement in the vault must have been longer than the month Lady Murray estimates. Alternatively, it may be that the place of concealment at Redbraes had already been begun earlier in the summer if it had become apparent that a warrant for Sir Patrick's arrest was inevitable in the near future.

Lady Murray continues, 'After being at home a week or two, the bed daily examined as usual, one day, in lifting the boards, the bed bounced to the top, the box being full of water'. Sir Patrick seems to have taken this as an omen that he should stay at Redbraes no longer. There is further confusion here in the timing of events. Sir Patrick himself says 'I had gone off the country September 11th 1684', and David Hume of Crossrig says of him, 'Polwart fled in the harvest', which also makes the month of September seem likely. However, Lady Murray says that Sir Patrick's hiding place under the floorboards at Redbraes having become flooded, a further incentive for him to leave was the news, brought by a carrier from Edinburgh, that the previous day, 24 December, Robert Baillie had been executed. Lady Murray also says that Grisell 'worked night and day, in making some alterations in his clothes for disguise', making Sir Patrick's likely departure around 27 December. This version of events is contradicted by the existence of a letter, written by Sir Patrick after he had reached Ghent on 29 December 1684, so Lady Murray must be mistaken in thinking that her grandfather was at Redbraes when the news of Robert Baillie's execution reached there. Despite Holland being a place of relative safety, Sir Patrick does not write under his own name, but signs his first letters from there 'Peter Pereson', with subsequent surnames assumed while in exile there being Wallace, Sinclair and Walton, always with the forename 'Peter', synonymous with 'Patrick'.

Having made the decision to flee Redbraes, Sir Patrick had to take one more trustworthy person into his confidence and this was his grieve [the usual term in Scotland for a farm steward or manager]. Lady Murray names him as *John* Allan, but a gravestone inscription in Polwarth kirkyard reads, 'Lyes interred the body of *James* Allan grive to Sir Patrick Hume of Polwarth Baronet and Baillie of the Barony of Polwarth who died 27.12.1695 in the 63rd year of his age.' Lady Murray says that Allan 'fainted away when he was told his master was in the house and that he was to set out with him on horseback before day, and pretend to the rest of the servants that he had orders to sell some horses at Morpeth Fair.' Allan was to ride ahead, with Sir Patrick following at some distance behind. At some point Sir Patrick must have missed the way and got lost, as he found himself beside the Tweed, and spent a long time searching for a suitable place to ford the river. Having got across and rejoined the agreed road he found Allan overjoyed to see him, as he had been intercepted by a party of soldiers who had been to search Redbraes again, and hearing horses were gone from the house, had set off in pursuit. They questioned Allan, who Lady Murray says, 'was too cunning for them, that they were gone back before my grandfather came up with him.' It was decided, after this narrow escape, that it would be safer to go by less-travelled roads, and after a couple of days Sir Patrick sent Allan back to Redbraes to give the news that he had evaded the search party and was on his way to London. It was at this point that Sir Patrick began to masquerade as 'Dr. Wallace', a surgeon. Although his own study had been law, he must have acquired a basic medical knowledge somewhere as Lady Murray says, 'He could bleed, and always carried lancets.'

During these last months of 1684, Grisell Ker must have struggled to maintain some sense of normality for all her children in the Redbraes household. Her eldest son Patrick had been taken as a hostage for his father on 24 September, when William Hastie, an officer of the circuit court, had arrived at

Redbraes to arrest Sir Patrick and, finding he was not there, took away Grisell's elder brother in his place. Young Patrick, now aged almost 20, was not released until December. He had written a plea to the Privy Council, saying, 'that he is a poor afflicted younge boy wanting now ane father to care for him and all means of subsistance, on[e] of tenn sterving children, and that therefor the Councill would be please to sett him at liberty that he may be in some condition to help and serve his diconsolat muthar and the said children', and on the 13 December the Privy Council had suggested Patrick might be released if Lord Jedburgh, Sir Patrick's stepfather, would provide surety of £5,000 sterling. Lord Jedburgh either wouldn't or couldn't produce this sum, so young Patrick petitioned the Council again on 16 December, and the Council ordained that he should be set free on a caution of £2,000 sterling. There would have been more anxious moments when George Holiwell, the minister, was summoned to the Sheriff Court in Jedburgh in October 1684 and questioned under oath, but he denied all knowledge of Sir Patrick's whereabouts, either truthfully or otherwise.

As well as Sir Patrick's absence, the news of the execution of Robert Baillie on a charge of High Treason must have cast a very long shadow at Redbraes. After his lengthy imprisonment, Robert Baillie had been summoned to trial on the 23 December with only a few hours' notice instead of the legal 15 days allowed for the defence to prepare a case, and was so ill he had to attend his trial in his nightshirt. The jury had debated from midnight for three hours then retired to sleep until the 'Guilty' verdict was announced at 9 o'clock on the 24 December. The execution was to take place between 2 o'clock and 4 o'clock that same afternoon, in case Baillie should die before the authorities had the chance to execute him. In the *Complete Collection of State-Trials for High Treason* there is a footnote to the effect that 'This great Expedition was occasioned by the Prisoner's bad state of Health who they feared might avoid his Execution by a natural Death.' Robert Baillie's 20-year old son George, Grisell's future husband, was said to have witnessed his father's execution. Whether or not he remained to see the unspeakable horror of his father's head mounted on a spike at the Netherbow Port in Edinburgh and his body quartered and the limbs despatched to be displayed at the tolbooths of Jedburgh, Lanark, Ayr and Glasgow is not known. [The tollbooth was a building encompassing town hall, court house and jail in old Scottish burghs]. The piece that was sent to Lanark was only briefly on the tollbooth just a mile from Baillie's house at Jerviswood as a group of young men 'headed by a certain yeoman named William Leishman, came and stole it away for burial.' In gratitude for this act of kindness the Baillie family later gave a bursary for Leishman's son to attend college, which he amply justified by eventually becoming Principal of Glasgow University.

January 1685 may have seemed a little less bleak, with young Patrick returned to the household, and another letter received from 'Peter Pereson' in Rotterdam, whose handwriting would have been immediately recognised, even if the name was unfamiliar. Young Patrick, Grisell, Christian and Robert, aged between 15 and 20 would have fully understood the reason for their father's absence and shared their mother's anxiety, but perhaps shielded their younger siblings aged 11, 9, 8, 7, 3 and 18 months.

As all the North Sea British ports were being watched, Sir Patrick's route to Holland had not been direct. William Lindsay, Earl of Crawford, whose estates were also forfeit, wrote of the impossibility of leaving Scotland by sea: 'Masters of ships and skippers are so straitly sworne to give up the names of all such as goe with them', as ordained by a Privy Council proclamation of September 1684. Accordingly, Sir Patrick had made his way south through England and 'so soone as I got upon the continent

I stayed but short in France, but spent some weeks in Dunkirk, Ostend, Bruges and other towns in Flanders and Brabant wher I traversed before I came to Brussells.' Lady Polwarth may have been hoping her husband might find lodgings in some suitably obscure place, and then send for his family to join him, but all such hopes were dashed with the announcement of the death of King Charles II on 6 February 1685. Charles was succeeded by his brother the Duke of York, known as James II in England and James VII in Scotland. There had been attempts to exclude James from succession to the throne, as he was a Catholic, but these had failed, and many people feared that his marriage to Mary of Modena might yet provide a living child to continue a Catholic monarchy.

Sir Patrick had tried unsuccessfully to meet up with the Duke of Monmouth, Charles II's illegitimate son, since arriving in Holland, and now travelled from Utrecht to Rotterdam, where a number of Presbyterian Scottish nobles were gathered. They were shortly joined by the Earl of Argyll, by Sir John Cochrane and his son and 'other gentlemen', whom Sir Patrick does not name as, at the time of writing the narrative addressed to his wife, their lives might still be in danger. At a meeting on 17 April 1685 in Amsterdam, it was agreed 'to declare and undertake a war against the Duke of York and his assisters for restoring and setling of the true religion and the native rights and liberties of the three kingdoms.' The Earl of Argyll was to lead the Scottish arm of the two-pronged attack, with the Duke of Monmouth promising to set sail for an invasion in the south of England within a very few days of Argyll setting out for Scotland.

A number of letters had reached Redbraes from 'Peter Pereson' in Holland, the last dated 30 April 1685. Sir Patrick set sail with Argyll two days later, but the expedition was ill-planned, and the thousands of men Argyll had said he could call upon in Scotland failed to materialise, and even those most loyal to him began to disperse by the middle of June. Argyll himself was captured, and executed in Edinburgh on 30 June. After the abortive attempt to overthrow James II and VII, Sir Patrick once again found himself a fugitive in his own country. Initially sheltered by David Montgomerie of Lainshaw [Langshaw], near Kilwinning in Ayrshire, whose estates were also forfeit on account of his supposed involvement in the Rye House Plot, it was there that he wrote a narrative of the failed expedition. A false report of Sir Patrick's death was put about, so that he would not be searched for, though King James had issued a proclamation on 24 June, offering a reward of 1,800 merks to anyone apprehending Sir Patrick or any other of 'that hellish crew'. It seems that several women bravely took the risk of harbouring a fugitive, as, in a letter of 19 August to his wife, he says, 'I will never be able to recompense the kindness of Lady Eleanor Montgomerie, the Lady Baldoon, the Lady Dunlap, the Lady Lanshaw and the Lady Ralston, Dunlap's sister & Miss Jean Montgomerie, Langshawe's daughter.' Letters written by Sir Patrick between 8 July and 22 August have new pseudonyms, 'Peter Wallace' and 'Peter St Clare'. A letter of 25 July is written from Dumfries, but after this Sir Patrick must have returned to Ayrshire as on 19 August James Boyle, Provost of Irvine, signed a pass permitting 'Peter Wallace, surgeon' and also 'James Scott, wright at Irvine' to go to Ireland.

Although Sir Patrick had made good his escape by sea, Patrick junior again lost his liberty in London as a hostage for his father, but he does not seem to have found it any great hardship, and remained indefatigably cheerful. He was 'placed under charge of a messenger', but apparently not confined to quarters, as he reported to his mother on 1 April 1685 that he had purchased presents: 'I have bought three pair of silk gloves for you & Grisell & Cirst [his sister Christian] & a pair for my

Ant [probably his father Patrick's sister, Julian]…and a wig to Richard [Julian's son]'. He speaks of 'Peter Brown', the Polwarth gardener, at whose marriage in 1675 he had been a youthful witness. Young Patrick may have been physically imprisoned during the rising of May-June as in a letter of 4 July, he wrote, 'I am in verry good health and verry good company…I find myselfe cut out to be made a prisoner of, for I take verry well with it, though it be verry hard I should be made a publick hostage of, that now since Argil is taken and our business put to a verry good close. I must yet stay till the divelry that Munmouth hath raised be ended also, or he taken, for they will not now let me out upon bail.' Monmouth's 'divelry' had begun later than he had promised to Argyll, as he had not landed with his invasion force until 11 June, at Lyme Regis, but his campaign too was doomed to failure, culminating in defeat at the battle of Sedgemoor on 6 July, followed by Monmouth's execution nine days later. The Privy Council gave orders on the 18 August 1685 to the captain of the guard to set young Patrick free.

When news of the executions of Argyll and Monmouth reached Redbraes, it must have struck fear into the hearts of Grisell and her mother, as Sir Patrick had been so closely connected with Argyll's expedition. It seems likely that Sir Patrick sailed from Irvine to Dublin, and thence to Bordeaux, as letters between 14 November 1685 and 26 March 1686 are all written from that city. [Ten days should be subtracted from the dates of letters written from the continent, as Britain was still using the Julian calendar whereas many countries in Europe had changed to the Gregorian]. The arrival at Polwarth of a letter from Sir Patrick must have been a cause for much rejoicing, though their tenure of Redbraes was now precarious, as on the 22 May 1685, the Government had passed a sentence of forfeiture of the Polwarth estates; the income from rentals of land, food from the farm and the very roof over Grisell's head were all to be taken away, leaving the family destitute. Sir Patrick wrote to his wife on 15 January 1686, telling her to be of good heart, and asking that the children be kept 'merry & cheerfull… for lost estates can be recovered againe, but health once lost by a habit of Melancholy can never be recovered.' Some letters were taking two months to reach their destination as, writing on 17 January, Sir Patrick told of his joy at receiving the letter written by his wife on 15 November. That letter must have told of some illness in the family, as Sir Patrick replied, 'I thank god the poxe [smallpox] have done no hurt.'

Fortunately, the necessity for the family to leave Redbraes was not immediate. An Edinburgh writer [solicitor], John Trotter, had been appointed as the King's Chamberlain for the estates of Polwarth and also of the forfeited Berwickshire estates (named as 'Mellarstanes') of Robert Baillie, and on 29 January 1686 the Privy Council issued Trotter with instructions on how the estates and their tenants were to be managed. Among these instructions, Trotter is to 'maintain houses and mills customarily repaired by the master, Lady Polwarth furnishing glass for the windows at Redbraes and Trotter paying for lead and workmanship'.

A year on from the first notice of confiscation a warrant from King James confirmed that the estate of Polwarth was to be given to the Earl of Seaforth, providing he adhered to certain conditions, namely that he paid any debts due out of the estate, that he paid any debts owing to Lady Hilton, Sir Patrick's aunt, whose husband had been murdered by another Hume family member, William Home, brother to the Earl of Home, in December 1683. The warrant also demanded that Seaforth should pay Lady Polwarth's jointure, the money which would have been due to her if Sir Patrick were dead. A certain sum had been fixed as part of the marriage contract between Sir Patrick and Grisell Ker, and apparently an additional amount had been granted at a later date, in total amounting to 3,000 merks. [The merk was a unit of account, equal to two-thirds of a pound Scots, so the jointure was worth £2,000 Scots, or £166 sterling, per annum]. Further to these conditions, the Earl of Seaforth had to pay the King 2,000 pounds to take possession of Polwarth. The granting of Lady Polwarth's jointure had apparently only been done as a result of the efforts of Grisell and her mother. Lady Murray says: 'My grandmother and mother went to London by sea, to solicit an allowance for her and her ten children, where they long attended; and even though assisted by many good friends, from whom they met with much kindness and civility… all she could obtain for herself and them was about L150 a year.' The king's letter granting the jointure does not appear in the register of the Privy Council until 3 September 1686, almost two years after Sir Patrick's leaving Redbraes.

HM letter (Windsor, Aug 21) announcing decision to allow their jointures to wives and relicts of rebels, and ordering payment of jointure still owing for 1684 and 1685 to Lady Polwarth, as she and her numerous family are reduced to great straits.

Throughout a childhood and adolescence dogged by religious and political upheaval, under a régime that sanctioned torture and summary executions, with frequent absence of a father and occasionally of both parents, the one constant in Grisell's life had been Redbraes, on whose lands her ancestors had lived for centuries. Now, in the summer of 1686, it seemed that the connection with Redbraes was to end and that Grisell and the entire family faced a dangerous and uncertain future.

Chapter 2

~ɔℚℓ~

EXILE

1686-1689

In less arduous times, a young woman of Grisell's class might have expected, approaching her twenty-first birthday, to be already married to the man chosen for her by her parents. Her dowry or 'marriage portion' was an important part of the agreement, but no less important was alliance with a family perceived to be of equal, or superior status. However, since the time Grisell was less than 10 years old the lives of her parents Sir Patrick Hume and Grisell Ker had been so turbulent that it is unlikely much thought was given to finding a suitable marriage partner for Grisell, or indeed her younger sisters. Now, in the summer of 1686, with landless and penniless Sir Patrick in Geneva, and his wife and family still living in a house they could no longer call their own, all thoughts must have been directed towards reuniting the family in a place of safety.

The supposed surgeon 'Peter Wallace' had lingered in Bordeaux for four months, perhaps hoping to find clients among the extensive community of Scots merchants who traded out of that port, but he had arrived there in November 1685, immediately after King Louis XIV had signed the Edict of Fontainebleau. This Edict revoked the Edict of Nantes of 1598, which had granted significant rights and freedoms to Protestants in France, but after the revocation Protestants were now suffering persecution, which may have prompted Sir Patrick to leave France. Between 13 May and 2 July 1686 Sir Patrick's letters are starting their journey to Scotland from Geneva, then an independent republic. In a letter of the 17 May he wrote to his wife: 'Our religion is now banished from France, all forced to change, & when changed yet cannot get out of the Kingdom, especially the women and children, and now their greif and complaint is, that they had delayed to fly in the beginning while they might… out of a fancie that such things could never come to passe as have since.' While apparently speaking entirely about the plight of the French Protestants, Sir Patrick is giving a warning that perhaps his wife and family should leave Scotland while they still can, as he continues, 'I wish others may take a lesson if the case draw near them.'

A letter of 12 June 1686 hints at some family tragedy, and suggests that a female child has died. In order to confuse anyone who might intercept his letters, he always refers at this time to his children as his 'brothers' and 'sisters', and writes, 'I could heartily have redeemed the life of my dear sweet sister with my owne, yet what you write doth confort me enough, god preserve the rest, I cannot write much on the subject: I only beg that you will cherish the rest with gentlenes & care, as I would desire to do if I were by them especially the two eldest…'. There is no female child unaccounted for; the known family consists of four boys, Patrick, Robert, Alexander and Andrew, and five surviving girls: Grisell, Christian, Julian, Anne and Jean, but young Patrick had described himself as 'one of tenn starving children', and in troubled times a christening may have gone unrecorded.

Sir Patrick signs off affectionately, 'I assure you nothing but the grave when it comes to be my bed as tibbies will cut off my love for you, for I am vowed yours'. 'Tibby' is a common diminutive in Scotland for 'Elizabeth', so that may have been the dead child's name. Another mystery is the fate of Grisell's brother George, christened at Redbraes on 1 January 1682. He appears not to have survived long, but his death is not recorded in the Polwarth parish registers.

In anxious times, the interval between a letter being sent and its arrival in the hands of the recipient must have seemed interminable to the divided family. Lady Polwarth had written to her husband on 29 May, assuring him that she has received his letters of 13 and 17 May, a 12-day journey at least for the letters, and Sir Patrick's reply to his wife's letter of 29 May is not written until 22 June, a gap of over three weeks. In this letter, addressed to 'Mrs Grisell Drummond', he again hints at the sad news, writing, 'I owe you much for this letter which has been so great paines to you'. Lady Polwarth seems to have told him what a great support her eldest daughter has been to her after the loss of the child, as Sir Patrick writes, 'what you tell me of my Dearest G H [Grisell] & her good heart, gives me a joy unexpressible pray give my service to her & her sister [Christian] & tell them to deal lovingly and tenderly with the rest for love of me & to mind mee alwise when they looke upon them.' He continues about financial matters, saying that he expects some money from 'my cussen Mr Broune…whereby I may goe into Holland', and signs off, 'I am with all my heart My Dearest Love yours wholly & unchangably Peter Wallas.'

Grisell's eldest brother Patrick had preceded the rest of the family to Holland. George Baillie, who had begun studying at the University of Franeker in Friesland in the north of Holland in 1682 before returning to Scotland towards the end of 1684 when his father Robert Baillie of Jerviswood's execution was threatened, had gone back to Holland with the intention of serving in the army of the Prince of Orange. Writing from London on 20 April 1686, young Patrick is looking forward to meeting up again with George Baillie 'for I resolve to be very merry with him all this campagne, but I find I shall have little or no fighting…I waite now for his majesties pass I hop to be in Rotterdame the beginning of the next week.' Lost luggage appears not just to be a peril of modern travel, as early in May and again at the beginning of June, Patrick is lamenting that trunks sent from Scotland have still not arrived.

For Sir Patrick and his wife, worry about the family is not limited to the younger members, but extends to young Patrick the eldest of all, now 21 years old. An alarming rumour has been circulating that he intends to go to Hungary, presumably as a soldier. He writes to his mother on 14 June 1686, denying the rumour, saying it is the first he has heard of it, but hinting that he thinks his parents have over-reacted: 'I wonder as much to see you look on Hungary as going to Hell'. Young Patrick may not have been entirely truthful to his mother, as Sir Patrick writes to his wife in July, 'I have heared from him of his intention & have also stopt it, I assure you he will goe no way till we meet, which I hope shall be very shortly.'

A letter of 28 August originated in Frankfurt when Sir Patrick must have left Geneva and been making his way north towards Holland. Many of the letters written once he had reached Holland, probably in the month of September 1686, are still written with the intention of being deliberately obscure. He was now in a place of relative safety, but a fugitive living under an assumed identity, so no risks could be taken with the naming of names, and references which were very obvious to the original recipient of letters from this period are unclear over three centuries later. As well as writing under various pseudonyms, Sir Patrick also addresses the letters to fictitious names, to confound any Government spies who might intercept the letters.

The earliest existing letter in Grisell's own hand is addressed to her brother Patrick, and written on 6 November 1686. Grisell has just disembarked from a ship in Scotland, and may have been to visit her brother Patrick and her father, who are now together in Holland. She writes, 'We are this afternoon landed hear and have had a very good passag as you may know by the swiftness of it', which suggests that her brother knew exactly when she had set out on her journey. She asks to be remembered to 'Mr Sincklar' [her father], and threatens her brother that if he laughs at the imperfections of her letter-writing she will never write to him again, betraying the affectionate, teasing nature of her relationship with the brother just a year older than herself. Patrick, on 4 December, reveals in a letter to his mother that he is to be a volunteer in the Prince of Orange's own guard, but that George Baillie is to stay in Utrecht all winter. Utrecht and the seat of the Prince's court in The Hague are some forty miles apart, not an insurmountable distance for young Patrick to visit his father and his friend, to exchange news and, apparently, to go shopping, as Patrick proudly announces early in February that, 'Geriswood [George Baillie] and I have provided ourselves verry well with nightgowns'. This may seem a curious occasion for such satisfaction, but a 'nightgown' was not a garment for sleeping in, but a robe resembling a kimono or dressing gown, often made of rich fabric, which a gentleman would wear in his own house, more comfortable than his coat and waistcoat, while also serving to preserve those expensively tailored garments from excessive wear. Although the military life obviously suits Patrick, he says on 4 February, somewhat regretfully, 'I am to study law and history for all my sodgery with Geriswood this summer.'

Grisell Ker receives some of the same news from Sir Patrick.

Writing to her on 7 February 1687, he tells her he has received her letter of 20 January, and 'Mons'r Hume [his son, Patrick] also shewed mee some from his Mother'. He is glad to hear that 'the Lady has got her jointar', and imparts the news that, 'Hume is a musketeer in the prince's guard', though without pay, and that he is resolved to follow his study at the 'Colledges of Utrecht'. Sir Patrick makes pretence of also being a student, and says, 'I am very ernest to have my brother Robert [in reality his son Robert, aged 17] over as soon as possible', and speaks of 'the two young boys' [Sandy, now 11, and Andrew, 10] and 'my sisters', meaning his daughters. He is anxious that his wife and family should all join him but acknowledges that the fact that 'shee can possesse stil her house, may probably be a hinderance.'

One month later Sir Patrick, in a message supposedly from 'Geriswood' to his mother, is entreating 'the Lady' [his wife] to travel to Holland, bringing her sons and daughters, but 'putting the youngest with some friend'. Little Jean at three years old is apparently considered too young to travel, and possibly nine-year old Anne as well. Sir Patrick is hopeful that his wife will not be put out of the house, but if she is, he recommends she should 'give a quiet pension to the gardener to stay and take all the care he can both of the house yards and planting'. This suggests that Sir Patrick did not view his forfeiture as a permanent loss, but was hopeful of coming into possession of his estate again at some time in the future. On a more mundane note, he requests 'if the Lady come over tell her to bring the rupture girdle with her', as those to be had in Holland are inferior in design.

The following week a letter of 14 March 1687 repeats much of the same advice, perhaps because of the uncertainty of letters reaching their destination, and happily reports that 'I saw your friends here, Jeris and Hume [George Baillie and young Patrick] they are very well as can be'. By 4 May, Sir Patrick is getting impatient for his family to join him for financial as well as personal reasons. Once again pretending to be 'Geriswood', he says, 'He has taken a house for the whole family for a year which now he must keep and pay for …there is much more money spent now than would serve if all were together'. Scarcity of money would have been a fairly new problem for Sir Patrick since leaving Redbraes. He has managed on relatively little while on his journey and in the past few months in Holland, but accommodating an exiled family, and a large one, would not be inexpensive. In this long letter he gives details of the house he has rented, which consists of 'cellar, ladner [larder] Kitchen, peet house and roomes for drying of cloathes & servants beds; a dining roome; & five chambers & a litle garden for taking the air privatly, so he thinks she would furnish these roomes with nine or ten beddings'. He reveals that the house is in Utrecht, which he describes as 'both convenient and cheap living', and that he has bought some larger items of furniture, 'so she needs not send over tables, timber of beds, chaires, pots or pans & the like troublesome hardware, but Hangings, curtaines, blankets, sheets, naperie and packing ware as much as she pleases; with what silver plate, good pewter (for it is dear here), knives, looking glasses, or any other but grosse hard ware that is ill to pack & apt to break.'

The reason for the delay in the family's setting out for Holland becomes apparent in the next letter of 11 May, when Sir Patrick has learned that there has been a lot of illness in the family. 'I hear that some of my friends have been sick, &, which went nearest me that you have had a feaver, I wonder no friend was so kinde as to advertise me'. He says to his wife, referring to her as 'the Lady', '..ther can be no hazard in her coming to live here with her Children; who can take it ill that shee come with them to where her son is setled and in a way of living to help to get the rest educated', and also says that 'if great inconvenience follows upon it she can stop it by returning againe.'

We learn from a letter written on Friday 26 May 1687 by Grisell to her brother Patrick at The Hague that Sir Patrick's anxious wait for his wife to join him is nearly at an end. 'Geriswood's mother [Grisell Ker] desires you to shou him, that she, his three brither [Robert, Alexander and Andrew] & second sister [Christian] will goe off from this abute the 8. or 10. of June wt'out faile his eldest sister [Grisell herself] cannot conveniently come at this time which is not a little trouble to her'. 14-year-old Julian, 10-year-old Anne and 4-year-old Jean appear not to be included in the party about to embark for Holland. After a little message from her mother to her father concerning money, Grisell then sets to teasing her brother about the frequent letters passing between himself and a girl whose initials she gives as 'E:M:', having complained bitterly in the same letter that she, Grisell, has not had a letter from him for three months. At the end she says, 'James Winter your frind [the Polwarth house carpenter] has him kindly remembert to you.' Although this letter is still headed 'Polwart Hous', Grisell reveals that 'we are all very busie making readie for our flittin [moving house] which will be on Thursday first', so on the first of June, 1687, the family will finally leave Redbraes.

Grisell appears to have remained in Scotland for several weeks after the rest of the family departed for Holland, as she writes on 15 July from Newton, her aunt Julian's house near Gifford in East Lothian. Julian was Sir Patrick's elder sister who had been widowed after only a year of marriage, leaving her with an infant son, Richard. Julian was a very capable manager and oversaw the Newton estate well during her son's minority, but there were undoubtedly many visits to Redbraes so that Richard could enjoy the company of his cousins, one of whom, Robert, was his exact contemporary. Grisell airs various grievances in the course of this letter, the first of which is young Patrick's slowness in writing to her. Although Patrick is a year older than herself,

Grisell appears to take on an almost parental role regarding her brother's behaviour and welfare. It seems there had been a story circulating that Patrick had taken part in a drunken affray during which his landlord had been stabbed. Having received no letter from Patrick, Grisell had been obliged to seek out someone 'new come from Holland', who had told her that there was no truth in the rumour that Patrick was involved. Although relieved, Grisell is unhappy that she did not hear it from Patrick himself, 'the account did not please me thinking alwise if it had not been treu you had writtin yourself'. She reports that, 'I have done all the business I had to doe' and urges Patrick to ask her brother Robert, whom she refers to as 'Robi', to 'writ all he would have done hear'. Robert too receives her censure as he did not write to her to tell her the rest of the family were safely landed; Grisell had had to rely on a report from someone else who had seen them after they reached Holland. 'Robi' had been tasked with asking Patrick to do Grisell's 'commission', possibly organising a sea crossing for herself and Julian, and Grisell is anxious for an answer. 'I am just wateing for a word from you…I will assure you if you writt not soon, I will not wate on it', saying she will take the first available crossing.

The voyage Grisell was about to undertake may be the one described in detail by Lady Murray in the memoir of her mother. According to Lady Murray, Julian had been left at home when the rest of the family departed for Holland, as she was too ill to travel. Lady Murray says, 'My mother returned from Holland by herself, to bring her over, and to negotiate business, and try if she could pick up any money of some that was owing to her father', but it would seem from the letter of 15 July 1687 that Grisell had in fact remained behind with the ailing Julian and her two youngest sisters, rather than travelling to Holland then coming back for Julian. Whatever the case, the details of the awful journey were deeply etched in Grisell's memory, and no doubt had had numerous re-tellings. Lady Murray says that Grisell 'had agreed for the cabin bed' and had taken plenty of food for the voyage. Once aboard ship, she discovered that several other women had also been promised the cabin bed. Grisell and Julian did not argue, but lay down on the deck, using a bag of books they were taking to Sir Patrick as a pillow. Soon afterwards, the captain came in and ate all of their food 'with a gluttony incredible', then turned two gentlewomen out of the bed which, having stripped off his clothes, he occupied himself. Lady Murray reports with some satisfaction that the captain 'did not long enjoy the effects of his brutality; for a terrible storm came on, so that his attendance and labour was necessary to save the ship; they never saw more of him till they landed at the Brill'. 'The Brill' [Brielle], not being the intended destination as they had been blown off course, was some twenty miles distant from where young Patrick and his father were waiting for Grisell and Julian in Rotterdam and, according to Lady Murray, 'It was a cold, wet, dirty night'. A gentleman also seeking refuge in Holland befriended them and carried their 'small baggage', while Grisell carried Julian, still weakened by illness and having lost her shoes in the mud, on her back 'the rest of the way'. Twenty miles of piggyback in the dark and rain is inconceivable. It was possible to get direct to Rotterdam from Brielle by boat, so it is to be hoped that 'the rest of the way' in reality was only the journey from one vessel to another. Having finally been reunited with the rest of the family at the house in Utrecht, Grisell 'felt nothing but happiness and contentment'.

Lady Murray states that, 'They lived three years and a half in Holland' but, as we have seen, discounting the period in 1685 while planning Argyll's invasion, Sir Patrick did not arrive in Holland until September 1686, and his wife until June 1687. Sir Patrick kept a very low profile and rarely left the house, though 'the well-wishers to the Revolution' knew the real identity of 'Dr

Wallace'. Lady Murray says that a quarter of the family income went on the rent for the house which was not a small one except by comparison with Redbraes, but that they could afford no servants apart from 'a little girl to wash the dishes', so many of the household tasks became Grisell's responsibility. 'She went to the market, went to the mill to have their corn ground, which it seems is the way with good managers there, dressed the linen, cleaned the house, made ready the dinner, mended the children's stockings and other clothes, made what she could for them, and in short did everything.' Lady Murray goes on to paint a kind of 'Grasshopper and the Ant' scenario. While Grisell worked her fingers to the bone, her sister Christian, at 19 two years younger than Grisell, 'diverted her father and mother and the rest, who were fond of music. Out of their small income they bought a harpsichord, for little money, but it is a Rucar [Ruckers], now in my custody and most valuable. My aunt [Christian] played and sung well, and had a great deal of life and humour, but no turn to business. Though my mother had the same qualifications, and liked it as well as she did, she was forced to drudge; and many jokes used to pass between the sisters, about their different occupations.'

The assertion that 'my mother had the same qualifications' is almost the only suggestion that Grisell played a musical instrument. Music was obviously very important to the family, and Christian had a special talent, but there is no specific mention of Grisell being skilled at the keyboard though she 'also diverted herself with music'. Lady Murray tantalisingly says, 'I have now a book of songs of her writing when there [in Holland]; many of them interrupted, half writ, some broke off in the middle of a sentence.' This book appears not to have survived, and Grisell's reputation as a song writer rests on just two examples, only one of which is complete. (See Appendix 1). Professor John Veitch in *The History and Poetry of the Scottish Border* (1894) writes: 'Is it vain now to inquire as to what has become of this MS book? Its recovery, if that were possible, might be an unspeakable gain to Border and Scottish song.'

Letters between the separated family members have been a great source of information, but once the family is reunited, correspondence between them ceases, and it is only possible to glean details of their life in exile from Lady Murray's account. Life in clean, orderly Utrecht must have been in great contrast to either the countryside surroundings of Polwarth or the crowded tenements of Edinburgh whose streets were renowned for their filth. Grisell's daily routine began at an early hour: 'Every morning before six, my mother lighted her father's fire in his study, then waked him;...then got him...warm small beer with a spoonful of bitters in it... Then she took up the children, and brought them all to his room, where he taught them every thing that was fit for their age; some Latin, others French, Dutch, geography, writing, reading, English &c; and my grandmother taught them what was necessary on her part.' Grisell Ker's laboriously printed handwriting does not suggest much in the way of an academic education, so probably she was passing on the traditionally female skills of needlework and cookery. Her eldest daughter seems to have fared a little better, as Lady Murray says, 'my mother, when she had a moment's time, took a lesson with the rest, in French and Dutch'.

As if doing the cooking, cleaning, shopping, laundry and mending for a family of nine were not enough, there were often guests to be fed as well. Lady Murray says, 'The professors and men of learning in the place came often to see my grandfather: the best entertainment he could give them was a glass of alabast beer, which was a better kind of ale than common'. [Allerbest, Dutch word meaning 'very best']. Grisell told her daughter Lady Murray a famous anecdote of how Andrew her brother, a boy of eleven in 1687, had been sent to the cellar to draw some beer for the guests and returned upstairs with not only the beer but the tap of the barrel in his hand. He ran downstairs as fast as he could once Sir Patrick had enquired what he had in his hand, but it was too late to save the contents of the beer barrel. 'This occasioned much mirth, though perhaps they did not well know where to get more'. Other visitors were no doubt various members of the exile community, such as Gilbert Burnet, the Dalrymple family, Fletcher of Saltoun, Pringle of Torwoodlee and Sir John Swinton of that Ilk, all of whom had been close friends or associates in Scotland.

Despite the unaccustomed privations, Lady Murray says that Grisell 'always declared it the most pleasing part of her life… many a hundred times I have heard her say, she could never look back upon their manner of living there, without thinking it a miracle: they had no want, but plenty of everything they desired, and much contentment.' The exiled community relied on being sent money from friends and relatives in Scotland, but sometimes the chain of supply broke down, or expected payments were late, causing a certain hardship and no little embarrassment. An incident etched in Grisell's memory concerned a collection of money for the poor of Utrecht. A bell was rung in the street to tell people the collection was taking place, so that they could come to their doors with their offering. There was only a single coin of very small value in the Polwarth household, and it was passed from person to person, as all were too ashamed to go to the door with it, until Sir Patrick said, 'Well then, I'll go with it; we can do no more than give all we have.'

Keeping up appearances was especially important to young Patrick in his position as a musketeer in the Prince of Orange's guard. Lady Murray says of her mother, 'Her constant attention was, to have her brother appear right in his linen and dress: they wore little point [needle lace] cravats and cuffs, which many a night she sat up to have in as good order for him as any in the place; and one of their greatest expenses was in dressing him as he ought to be'. There is no written mention anywhere of Grisell's own clothing or personal appearance at this time. The earliest known portrait of her (Plate 8) is attributed to the artist David Scougall so, if the attribution is correct, must have been painted before his death in 1685, and probably in the period 1680-82, when she was aged fifteen or seventeen, before the household became too troubled. The portrait shows a young girl with light brown hair drawn back from her face and falling in a single long ringlet over her shoulder, and wearing a white décolleté chemise draped with a green velvet cloak, which was fairly standard portrait attire for the time, but probably doesn't reflect the way she ordinarily looked.

Lady Polwarth had brought the family silver with her from Scotland, and another way out of financial difficulties was to pawn some of it, or 'put it in lumber' in the parlance of the time. Lady Murray reports that it was able to be redeemed and 'brought with them again to Scotland', and that they 'left no debt behind them'. However, it is likely that the family was deeply indebted to relatives who had remained in Scotland. One very useful go-between in financial matters was a merchant named Andrew Russell, whose papers from the period survive. From them we learn that George Baillie was drawing bills on his mother after his father's arrest in 1683, that young Patrick sent a bill to his aunt Lady Newton [Sir Patrick's sister] in October 1686, that Grisell's younger brother Robert wrote a bill in November 1687 to another relative on his mother's side, Lady Galashiels. Even after Lady Polwarth's arrival in Utrecht, both young Patrick and Robert continued to draw bills on their mother who in turn passed them to relatives for payment. Andrew Russell's factor in Edinburgh wrote in 1688 that all previous bills on Lady

Polwarth had been paid by Lady Hilton of Huttonhall, Sir Patrick's aunt Sophia.

Despite every appearance of lying low and devoting himself to his family and their education, Sir Patrick was eager for news of what was happening in Scotland. In February 1687 King James had issued a Declaration of Toleration in Scotland, whereby moderate Presbyterians were to be allowed to worship in private houses, as were Quakers, and all laws previously passed against Roman Catholics were rescinded, allowing them to take public office and worship as they pleased. However, field preachers and those attending conventicles were still to be prosecuted 'to the utmost severity'. The Declaration of Indulgence was then issued in England in April 1687, but many Anglicans objected as the King had assumed sole power to overturn acts passed by Parliament. A modified version of the Indulgence appeared in Scotland in June 1687, giving Presbyterians the same rights as Roman Catholics. Many Presbyterians accepted this version, with the exception of the Covenanters. The English Indulgence was re-issued in April 1688, and the Scottish one in May, but many were still unhappy with the assertion in all the documents that the King's power was absolute. People of all religious persuasions who were against a Catholic monarchy were alarmed by the birth on 10 June 1688 of King James' son, James Francis Edward Stuart, who ousted his Protestant half-sister Mary as heir to the throne. When this news reached Sir Patrick in Utrecht, his zeal for rebellion would have been re-awakened, but probably even before hearing of the royal birth, Sir Patrick had addressed a very long letter (amounting to 26 pages of printed transcript), to Sir William Denholm on 15 June. The letter warned the Presbyterian clergy that they should not accept the Indulgence, as it would be 'a great and very dangerous error and mistake', on account of the Indulgence being a front for the 'popish plot'. Much of the letter is devoted to extolling the virtues of the Prince of Orange. Perhaps for the first time in four years, Sir Patrick feels confident in signing the letter with his own name. 'I will not whisper in the dark, as many of our opposites do, but avow both my argument, and my advice upon it, by setting my name to it.'

On 30 June 1688 seven English peers wrote to William, Prince of Orange, requesting his assistance, and offering support if he should mount an invasion. Once the letter reached the Dutch court, news of it would have travelled fast to the Scottish exiles, so Sir Patrick probably knew of it in the second week of July. Although Grisell had enjoyed the life the family had lived in Holland, there must have been considerable excitement at the prospect of a return to Scotland, tempered with apprehension at the danger her father was likely to put himself in yet again, to fight for his religion and principles. The Prince of Orange immediately began military preparations and increased his navy, initially under pretence of preparing in case of war with France, and of fighting pirates threatening Dutch vessels, but on 10 October he showed his true colours by issuing a declaration of his intention to invade Britain. For some days William's ships were prevented from sailing by a series of westerly gales, but finally on 19 October a huge fleet of 50 men-of-war, 25 frigates, many fire-ships and 400 transport vessels carrying 4,000 cavalry and 10,000 foot-soldiers set sail from Hellevoetsluys.

Among those on board the ships were Sir Patrick, young Patrick and George Baillie. Around midnight the wind changed direction and a great storm blew up, causing the fleet to be dispersed, and several ships lost. Lady Murray continues the narrative: 'They [Grisell Ker and family] soon heard the melancholy report of the whole fleet being cast away or dispersed, and immediately came from Utrecht to Helvoetsluys, to get what information they could. The place was so crowded by people from all quarters, come for the same purpose, that her mother, she [Grisell] and her sister [Christian], were forced to lie [sleep overnight] in the boat they came in; and for three days continually to see come floating in, beds, chests, horses &c. that had been thrown over-board in their distress. At the end of the third day, the Prince, and some other ships came in; but no account of the ship their friends were in. Their despair was great; but in a few days was relieved by their coming in safe, but with the loss of all their luggage, which at that time was no small distress to them'. George Baillie was so grateful for his deliverance from the storm that he fasted one day a week for the rest of his life.

The fleet was rapidly repaired and made ready to sail again by the first of November and this time had safe passage, landing at Torbay in Devon on 5 November. News of the safe arrival of the fleet, carried on board some other vessel, would have taken five or six days to reach Utrecht. Grisell, having come so close to losing her father, her favourite brother and, as we shall see, her lover less than a month earlier, should have been ecstatic to hear that all were safe, 'yet, when that happy news came, it was no more to my mother than any occurrence she had not the least concern in; for that very day, her sister Christian died of a sore throat, which was so heavy an affliction to both her mother and her, that they had no feeling for anything else'. The task of writing to Sir Patrick to tell him of the death of Christian may have fallen to Grisell; the miles between the family in Utrecht and Sir Patrick, wherever he was, must have seemed very great when the news reached him eventually. We know where Sir Patrick was from 26 November to 18 December as he left a diary of his march from Exeter to London in the wake of the Prince of Orange, reaching London on 15 December. Three days later 'the King went under the Prince's guards to Rochester' to sail for France and lifelong exile, and London extended a warm welcome to William, Prince of Orange. 'About noone the

Prince entered Westminster with great acclamation & tokens of joy among the people & ringing of bells and bonfires at night.'

After the loss of Christian, the family, now no longer needing to keep a low profile, perhaps moved from Utrecht to The Hague, seat of the court of William and Mary, as Lady Murray says: 'When all was settled in England, the children were sent over to Scotland, and my grandmother and she [Grisell] came over with the Princess'. Princess Mary sailed from Brielle on a yacht named *Mary*, and arrived at Gravesend on 12 February 1689. The fleet included several other yachts, both Dutch and English, and a number of transport vessels. The Princess then travelled from Gravesend to London by coach, and as part of her retinue, Grisell and her mother may have made a similar journey. Mary set about establishing her household at Hampton Court. The Countess of Derby, Groom of the Stole and Mistress of the Robes, received a salary of £1,200 (an enormous sum for the times), five ladies of the bedchamber were each to receive £500 per annum, and maids of honour, of whom six was the usual number, received a salary of £200. Although this amount was greater than the annual sum the entire family had subsisted on over the last two years, Grisell refused Princess Mary's offer of becoming one of her maids of honour. While ladies of the bedchamber performed many useful practical tasks, the function of maids of honour could perhaps be described as decorative companionship. They joined the Princess at her needlework, read to her, accompanied her to chapel and on walks in the Palace grounds.

Lady Murray is in no doubt that Grisell would have fulfilled such a position admirably. 'She was offered to be made one of her maids of honour, and was well qualified for it; her actions show what her mind was, and her outward appearance was no less singular. She was middle-sized, well made, clever in her person, very handsome, with a life and sweetness in her eyes very uncommon, and great delicacy in all her features; her hair was chestnut, and to her last had the finest complexion, with the clearest red in her cheeks and lips, that could be seen in one of fifteen.' So suitably qualified, with the prospect of bringing honour to her family with a position at court, and a salary that could alleviate her parents' hardships, why, then, did Grisell refuse Princess Mary's offer? Again, Lady Murray is in no doubt. 'She declined being maid of honour and chose going home with the rest of her family. Having her union with my father always in view, their affection for one another increased in their exile; though they well knew it was no time to declare it, neither of them having a shilling; and were at no small trouble to conceal it from her parents, who could not but think such an engagement ruinous to them both especially when, in the midst of their distress, there were offers pressed upon them, from two gentlemen in their neighbourhood... with whom they thought it would have been happy to settle their daughter at any time. She earnestly rejected both, but without giving a reason for it, though her parents suspected it; and it was the only thing she ever displeased or disobeyed them in'. A further reason for Grisell's rejecting the chance to be a maid of honour may have been the reputation for debauchery at previous royal courts, particularly that of Charles II, though Queen Mary's court proved to be a much more sedate and respectable affair.

The coronation of William and Mary took place in London on 11 April 1689. It is likely that Sir Patrick and his family were living in lodgings in Edinburgh at this time, still in straitened circumstances, but with hope of regaining the Polwarth estates in the near future. It was presumably on the strength of this that the two other suitors presented themselves for Grisell as they could look forward to her bringing a sizeable marriage portion to the union, even if not immediately. The suitors, one of whom was a relative, John Ker or Carre, a widowed father of three looking for a second wife, must have been able to offer Grisell a good degree of financial security. George Baillie had hopes of soon regaining the estates of Jerviswood in Lanarkshire and Mellerstain in Berwickshire, but as yet had nothing to offer a wife. In addition to his being the son of Sir Patrick's great friend Robert Baillie, George had been a mainstay of Grisell's family while in exile. 'Her parents were ever fond of my father, and he always with them; so great an opinion had they of him, that he was generally preferred to any other, and trusted to go out with my mother and take care of her, when she had any business to do. They had no objection but the circumstances he was in; which had no weight with my mother, who always hoped things would turn out at last as they really did; and if they did not, was resolved never to marry at all.' Grisell's parents were unaware that they were setting the wolf to guard the sheep when George Baillie acted as Grisell's chaperone, as we know from a note on a scrap of paper, in Lady Murray's handwriting, that the young lovers had become secretly engaged in June 1684, even before Sir Patrick's flight and Robert Baillie's execution.

The first parliament of William and Mary in Scotland opened on 6 June 1689, when Sir Patrick sat as member for Berwickshire, and he was appointed Commissioner of Supply for the county in June 1690, and is known to have attended the Privy Council on 56 days in 1690, so was politically very active, though we know little of his family circumstances at the time. Formal confirmation of Sir Patrick being restored to his lands and estates came on 22 July 1690 and, as a mark of his favour with King William, he was promoted to the peerage, becoming Lord Polwarth on 26 December 1690. As an extra mark of royal approval, Sir Patrick was granted an addition to his coat of arms, an orange surmounted by a crown.

George Baillie, having been a staunch supporter of the Prince of Orange since his exile in 1685 and during the 'Glorious

Revolution' that brought William to the throne, had every right to expect that some Government post might come his way, and was appointed Commissioner of Supply for Berwickshire and Lanarkshire in 1689, and Commissioner of Militia in the same year. On 28 June 1690 he was formally restored to his estates of Jerviswood and Mellerstain. There may not have been great rejoicing at regaining what was his rightful inheritance, and knowing that his father was innocent of the crime for which he lost his life in such cruel circumstances, but being in possession of his estates, and of modest remuneration for his appointments, must have given him hope that he might now be considered a suitable marriage partner for Grisell, whom he had no doubt would accept his proposal if the approval of her parents could be obtained.

With possession of his estates came the responsibility of paying his mother's jointure and maintaining his younger siblings. Mindful of the fact that Government salaries were not always paid promptly, George Baillie immediately set about raising some cash from the sale of standing timber at Jerviswood. A contract was drawn up on 11 August 1690 at Lanark for the sale of the 'Back and Fore Woods of Jerviswood' for 2,000 merks. The contract was to last for five years 'with a further extension if on account of troubles in the country the sale of wood is prevented through want of markets'. Having endured uncertainty and traumatic events for most of his life, 25-year old George Baillie seems unwilling to believe that his recent good fortune is likely to last.

Chapter 3

ꝏꝏꝏ

BRIDE AND MOTHER

_1690–1699_

The marriage contract between George Baillie and Grisell was signed in Edinburgh on 7 August 1791 in front of no fewer than 18 witnesses who all signed the document, including Grisell's parents, with Sir Patrick offering a tocher [dowry] of 12,000 merks. The couple were married at Redbraes on 17 September, probably by the minister George Holiwell who had officiated at Grisell's christening in 1665. Having been obliged by the decrees of Charles II to embrace Episcopalianism in 1663, Holiwell was reluctant to abandon it when it was outlawed in 1691, but fortunately the administration was now much less draconian. Lady Anne Purves, in an appendix to Margaret Warrender's book, says, 'An allowance was granted to such of the Episcopal Clergy who took the Oaths to continue in their Kirks without being obliged to subscribe to the Confession of Faith… Mr Hollywell, Episcopal Minister of Polwarth, continued in his Kirk on taking the Oaths.'

No official written church record of Grisell's marriage

survives, as the parish registers of Polwarth for the years following 1688 are lost, but Grisell herself noted in the blank pages of an almanac, 'September 17th, 1691 which day I was maried'. The tenants of Sir Patrick's estate and the Polwarth villagers undoubtedly joined in the celebrations in some way, and Grisell and her new husband possibly continued an old tradition described by Mr. Robert Home, minister of Polwarth in 1793, almost exactly a century after Grisell's wedding. 'In the middle of the village there are two thorn trees, at about six yards distance from each other, around which, it was formerly the custom, for every new married pair, with their company, to dance in a ring; from hence the song of "Polwarth on the Green". But this custom has fallen much into disuse, there not having been above 2 instances of it these 20 years.'

George Baillie was now in possession of both his estates, at Jerviswood in Lanarkshire, and Mellerstain in Berwickshire. Because Jerviswood had been the first estate bought by George Baillie's grandfather (also named George Baillie), in 1636, as the laird George Baillie was referred to, according to the custom in Scotland at the time, as 'Jerviswood', and his wife as 'Lady Jerviswood'. It might therefore have seemed logical that Grisell would go off to live in Lanarkshire, were it not for the fact that George Baillie's widowed mother Rachel Johnston and her younger children were still living in the house at Jerviswood, presumably having had to quit it for a couple of years in the way that Grisell's mother had had to leave Redbraes. Mellerstain estate, whose sale had been finalised in 1643, was therefore destined to become the home of Grisell and George Baillie. By comparison with her childhood home at Redbraes, the dwelling house then existing at Mellerstain fared very badly. Only a re-used door lintel and a few dressed stones incorporated into a later cottage standing on the same site now remain of the tower house that Grisell had become mistress of, but there are one or two written clues to tell us what it may have been like. Andrew Hay of Craignethan, writing in his diary on 10 November 1659, was not impressed by the house at Mellerstain, even 30 years before Grisell became its châtelaine. He wrote: 'We cam be Eccles and Stitchell, and at lenth cam to Mellerstane wher we met with Jerviswood [Robert Baillie] who took us in and we took a drink with him. It is ane old melancholick hous that had had great buildings about it.' To be described as old in the decade after Robert Baillie's father had bought the estate, it seems likely it was not built by him but by the Haitlie family who had previously possessed Mellerstain for many years.

The house is often referred to in Grisell's accounts as 'Mellerstain Tower', and may have been similar to nearby sixteenth-century Smailholm Tower, which still stands. The 'great buildings' spoken about by Hay were possibly separate kitchens, laundries and storerooms that the tall, narrow structure of a tower house could not accommodate, but which improving standards of living in the seventeenth century demanded. The Hearth Tax reveals that Mellerstain Tower had thirteen hearths, some of which were probably in the additional buildings. Sir Patrick's cousin George Home, writing in his diary some forty years later than Andrew Hay on 16 September 1700, though having favourable first impressions of the surroundings, is rather scathing about the house: 'It seems to be a good country for grass, and corn and peats. The trees grow well in the court yards. They have but ane old tower with but one room off a floor, about 5 stories high, but it looks very ruinous. There has been much building about it, but the stone is much wasted, being bad.' Further evidence of Mellerstain Tower's similarity to Smailholm Tower comes from Grisell herself, writing in her account book in 1719, describing remedial works to the tower's battlements: 'taikeing down the Batlement and weight of Mellerstaine tour head and slating it & finishing all about it besids timber £17:8s8d'. A stout rope usually formed a handrail in the spiral 'turnpike' stairs of tower houses and in October 1701 Grisell pays 16 shillings 'For tows [ropes] to the stair of Mellersteans'. This is the first mention of repairs to Mellerstain, a whole decade after her marriage, but the repairs that year were extensive as the total cost was £767:18s4d. No new stone is included in the bill, but numerous loads of lime and payments to masons suggest complete re-pointing, and 'sclating [slating] the roof of the Tower' cost £12. The tower house appears to have been completely reconfigured internally, as £9 was paid for 'putting up the partition in the [great] hall', and huge amounts of timber, both 'dails' [planks] and 'trees' [beams] suggesting all the floors were renewed with the aid of 4,500 'flooring nails'.

The advancing political career of Grisell's husband, and also that of her father, meant that neither household spent a lot of time in the 1690s at their country estates in Berwickshire, but were often in lodgings in Edinburgh, conveniently near to the Parliament. Grisell's first house was in 'Wariston's Land', in the High Street, close to St Giles', which had belonged previously to George Baillie's maternal grandfather Archibald Johnston, Lord Wariston, and was now in the possession of George Baillie's uncle James Johnston. When Grisell's first child was expected in October 1692, she did not stay among the noise and filth of the High Street for her confinement, but went back to her childhood home. She wrote, 'October 26th 1692 my daughter Grisell was born at Polwarth'. George Baillie had been elected to parliament in 1691 as MP for Berwickshire, in place of Sir Patrick, who was now Lord Polwarth, but he did not attend until 1693, when he was nominated to the Commission for Building Kirks and also appointed Receiver-General.

Not long after baby 'Grisie's' birth in 1692, Grisell began keeping what became known as her *Household Book* when extracts from it were published in 1911 by the Scottish History

Society. The *Household Book* was in fact a large number of notebooks and ledgers, with daily outlays scribbled down and later totalled, with the amounts for various different classes of expenditure later being transferred to larger Day Books. There is also in existence an account book or 'Compt Book', commenced by Grisell's mother in 1694. It is easy to assume that Grisell began keeping her accounts following her mother's example, but given the fact that no previous books written by Grisell's mother are known, it was perhaps the orderly-minded and meticulous Grisell who persuaded her mother that she should keep accounts, especially as Sir Patrick was busy with political matters. Grisell's mother noted the expenses down, but made no attempt to total any of them. Perhaps with an eye to posterity's interest, Grisell had her mother's Compt Book annotated and indexed after her death, writing on the flyleaf, 'Compt-Book of Dame Grisel Kar Countess of Marchmont Begun in Anno 1694 Pairtlie wryten in her own hand Pairtly filled up from her Notes And the rest added since the 11th October 1703 being Munday when the Lord took her at four of the Clock in the afternoon.'

Little Grisie was probably christened at Polwarth very soon after her birth by Mr. Holiwell before being taken to Edinburgh when her mother was able to travel. Having acted so frequently as surrogate mother to her siblings in her childhood and youth, motherhood would have come naturally to Grisell as she added that role to those of wife, housekeeper, estate manager and dutiful daughter. Sir Patrick, now grandfather to his first grandchild writes to Grisell at the beginning of December, 'My Heart, I am glad you are so well recovered as my wife writes. & that your child prospers, I wish the continuance & that you may have joy of her'. When little Grisie was fifteen months old a second child, named Robert after his executed grandfather, was born, as noted in the parish registers of St Giles', Edinburgh 'on tewsday 23 Jan'y last in the morning'. Robert's christening took place on Sunday 4 February 1694, with 'Patrick Lord Polwort, Patrick Home the Master of Polwort, Capt James Baillie, Dr Andrew Kirton doctor of medicine' as witnesses. The 'sundries' account has an entry for 4 February when 'Mr Will Liviston' was paid £9 [Scots] 'at my childs christining'. George Baillie now had a son and heir to perpetuate the family name and inherit his estates.

Having known very little regarding the minutiae of Grisell's life before 1692, with the commencement of the account books there is a wealth of detail, some of it self-explanatory, some of it puzzling, after the passage of three centuries. Grisell was writing for herself, not an audience, though her careful editing and annotation of her mother's Compt Book suggest she may have had an inkling that future generations might be fascinated by the accounts which, to her, were quite mundane, and essential to a well-run household. Grisell's handwriting is, by and large, clear and readable. Some unfamiliar-looking words have to be read aloud to become clear; spelling was only to become fixed and standardised during the course of the eighteenth century, and Grisell sometimes spells the same word two different ways in one sentence. In preparing the extracts for publication as *The Household Book of Lady Grisell Baillie* in 1911, Robert Scott-Moncrieff transcribes his selection of pages under certain headings, as did Grisell herself when transferring accounts from her notebooks to the Day Books. 'Housekeeping', 'Sundries', 'Household furniture' and 'Servants' are among the most frequent headings at this early point in her marriage. Although Scotland adopted sterling currency in 1707, some people continued to keep their accounts in pounds Scots for many years. Grisell writes in her Day Book, 'I begine to count sterline money January 1710 all the accounts befor that is Scots money'.

From being a near destitute single man in 1689, by 1695 George Baillie found himself the possessor of two estates and a salary of £300 sterling as Receiver-General. He had a wife and two children, with a third on the way, and was gaining respect in his political career as a 'man of profound, solid judgment' (as described by George Lockhart) in his own right, as well as being respected because his father Robert Baillie and grandfather Archibald Johnston of Wariston had been martyrs to the Presbyterian cause. Additionally, his uncle James Johnston had become joint Secretary of State for Scotland in 1692, and his father's cousin Gilbert Burnet had been appointed chaplain to King William, so the star of the wider family was in the ascendant.

One valuable contemporary source to shed light on the comings and goings of the Baillie family at this period is the diary of George Home, Sir Patrick's cousin, a frequent visitor to Polwarth House, and to the Edinburgh lodgings of Sir Patrick and of George Baillie. George Home records details which might otherwise have been lost, and sometimes makes surprising revelations about the everyday lives of his friends and acquaintances. On 2 June 1694 Home reports that 'I went to Polwart house and finding my Lord My Lady Jeriswood and his Lady &c were Gone to the fishing at Greenlaw I went on and stayd wt them till they came home and supped wt my Lord'. (In May 1699 Ladies Marchmont, Jerviswood and Polwarth are again said to be at the fishing, and obviously had success in the Blackadder Water as on their return they 'had some troutes drest for them').

At the beginning of August 1695 George Baillie had had to leave his wife and family in their increasingly well-furnished lodgings to accompany the Secretary of State on a prolonged trip to London; his absence in London was to be a frequent occurrence for the next two decades. Lady Murray says her mother had 'some hundreds of his letters, he having been often at London, absent from her for many months at a time, and never missed writing one single post'. Unlike his wife's clear script, George Baillie's handwriting is much less well-formed, and often appears to have been written in haste, making his letters difficult to read. While Grisell, in a permanent family home, was able to keep her husband's letters, George Baillie in temporary lodgings with his uncle Secretary Johnston, kept very few of his wife's.

A letter in November 1694 from the reputedly 'morose, proud and severe' George Baillie to Grisell over 10 years after their secret engagement leaves us in no doubt that their marriage was a love match. 'D[ear] H[eart], I have yours of the 13th and am glad you are in such a good humour as to send me kisses qch [which] I like beter than all those I might have here tho I will assure you I never either gave or got any save those in publick company since I left you however I hope you will take my returne of kisses qch is all I can do at this distance and I wish from my heart I were with you my life'. He also misses his little daughter, saying, 'I long to hear Grisie chatter'. Alarming news about Queen Mary is contained in George Baillie's letter of 27 December 1694. 'She is taken both with the small pox and a purpy feaver [purple fever] and is so ill that there is small if any hopes of her recovery unless by a miracle... she has been twise bled and blistered and now all they do is to give her cordialls'. The Queen died the following morning, and George Baillie reported, 'I never saw such a consternation amongst people as this day at court whither I went to know the manner of her death and she died as she had lived most Christianly...it seems to be a judgement upon the nations for their sins'. There is no evidence that Grisell herself maintained any connections with the court of Queen Mary once she had declined the position of maid of honour, but nevertheless the death of the Queen, Grisell's near contemporary, must have been keenly felt. Queen Mary was 32 years old; Grisell had just passed her 29th birthday. A year later Grisell's accounts show the purchase of a personal memento of the Queen: 'For a ring wt the Quins hair £9'.

Grisell is still busy feathering the marital nest in Edinburgh in the first few years of her marriage. One item in the accounts from 1697 mentions a piece of furniture still in existence: 'For bustin [cotton fabric] (to) the big chair 14 shillings' (Plate 9). The amounts 'Deburst for Howshold furnitur' include not just 'furniture' in the modern sense but many items of household linen, cushions and bed hangings, kitchenware and tableware, and not only of a basic kind as several accounts show payments to goldsmiths for '6 spons 6 forks, etc'. By contrast with her Edinburgh lodgings, Mellerstain Tower at this period although largely rebuilt in 1701 was probably still sparsely furnished. The building at George Baillie's other estate of Jerviswood was in better condition than Mellerstain had been, being a typical L-shaped laird's house of the 1630s rather than a sixteenth century tower house, but the interior had very few home comforts, according to the inventory drawn up by George Baillie's mother Rachel Johnston in November 1694, where the purple chamber contained just 'a very old bed all brok', and her tableware included 'three win glasses two of them wanting [missing] the foot'.

Whenever her husband was in London on Government business, Grisell was left in charge of his Scottish affairs, household, financial and even political. Having assisted her mother with the running of Polwarth estate during the periods her father was away from home, Grisell had already served an apprenticeship in estate management. There were teinds [tithes to be paid to the Kirk] to be collected, the schoolmasters in Mellerstain 'toun' to be given their salaries, and the stipend of the minister of Earlston, in whose parish Mellerstain lay, to be attended to, as well as the cess [land tax] to be paid. The accounts also show payment of a new tax, the Poll Tax, which was instituted in Scotland in 1694 to pay for the army and navy, as King William had committed Britain to fighting expensive wars in a coalition aiming to curb the ambitions of Louis XIV of France. Every person over 16 was taxed according to their means, with only the very poorest exempted from paying the minimum six shillings. The 1694 return notes that 'Jeriswood' was 'valued in the country' and that his household included his wife and two children as well as three named males and three unnamed 'servant women', amounting to a tax of over 30 pounds. The Poll Tax was collected again in 1695 and twice in 1698.

February 1696 saw the birth of a third child for Grisell and George Baillie. Their daughter Rachel was christened in Edinburgh on Sunday 23 February, the official witnesses being Grisell's father, her brother Patrick, Captain James Baillie and Mr James Kir(k)ton, minister. Tragically, just five days after this joyful event little Robert, always referred to by Grisell in the Household Book as 'my Robin', died and was 'buried by his grandfather Robert Baillie in the Grafreers [Greyfriars] churchyard 3 quarters from Mortons stone'. Two small entries in the accounts give little idea how grief-stricken the household must have been. On 28 February Grisell notes the expense of 17 pounds and 8 shillings 'for my childs dead linen', and a payment in April 'to a man in Gray Frirs for keeping up my childs grave'. 'Robin' had just passed his second birthday. A portrait of a small boy holding a black bird is almost certainly a memorial to Grisell and George Baillie's young son, probably painted by John Scougall whose studio in Advocate's Close was just a short distance away from their lodgings in the High Street, and who probably had known the child in life (Plate 10).

In the intervening days between Rachel's christening and Robin's death, on 26 February the general subscription book had opened for 'The Company of Scotland Trading to Africa and the Indies', later referred to as the 'African Company' or the 'Darien Scheme'. George Baillie was among the 79 subscribers on the very first day, and one of the larger subscribers, pledging £1,000 sterling. The eventual failure of this venture was to have consequences not just for the investors but for the future of the entire Scottish nation.

With daughter Grisie aged 4 and the babe in arms 'Rachy' to care for, Grisell would have had plenty to distract her from her grief at the loss of her son. Despite having servants including a cook, 'Nany Christie', she took steps to improve her own housekeeping skills, spending over 15 pounds in April 'to lairn cookry from Mr Addison'. As the only servant kept while the family was in exile in Utrecht was the little girl to wash the dishes, Grisell must have been well used to cooking for a family, and on very little means, but perhaps her elevated status in Edinburgh society necessitated a more refined style of cuisine if she was to be entertaining the highest in the land. Somewhat surprisingly, in view of his status as a fugitive only a decade earlier, the highest in the land, in political terms at any rate, was her father, as Sir Patrick was appointed Chancellor of Scotland at the beginning of May 1696.

When little Robin had died, he was buried without great ceremony the following day, but when George Baillie's mother Rachel Johnston died in 1697, the funeral on the first of February was a grand and public affair, and 'the expence of my mothers funerals' came to over £800 Scots. Apart from the more obvious elements of 'dead linen', coffin, hearse, church, church officers, and grave digger, money had to be spent on sending letters out to invite people to the funeral, donations to the poor and tips for servants. The guests were to be regaled with 'plumkake' and 'bisket' and £130 worth of wine and sack which came from George Baillie's apparently well stocked wine cellar. The greatest expense of all was the payment of over £210 to 'the herralds for her scuchens'. Funerary escutcheons or 'hatchments' were lozenge-shaped boards painted with the arms of the deceased, and which were displayed on the coffin or the deceased's house, sometimes both, and often later transferred to the church. 'Rachel, Lady Jareswood' was laid to rest in Greyfriars beside her grandchild Robin and husband Robert whose remains, interestingly, are recorded in the register of interments as having been buried on 26 October 1688, almost four years after his death, but just a week after William of Orange first set sail with his invading fleet. The funeral party at Lady Jeriswood's burial may well have had company in the kirkyard as 213 interments are recorded at Greyfriars in the month of February 1697, around seven per day. The diarist John Evelyn wrote on 7 February 1697 (in London), 'Severe frost continued with snow. Soldiers in the armies and garrison towns frozen to death on their posts.' The £14:10s paid for 'brecking the ground' may have been very well earned by the gravediggers.

The burden of organising her mother-in-law's funeral may well have fallen on Grisell rather than on George Baillie as Rachel Johnston's death came only weeks after George Baillie had a very serious, potentially fatal, illness. In a letter of 21 November 1696, James Hamilton of Pencaitland wrote: 'the laird of jeriswood Gn'l receaver of the Kings rents is Lying dangerously ill & feared he may dye.' Life must have seemed so precarious in those days, when a multitude of diseases could carry off people, old or young, without warning. Grisell had already lost a number of young siblings to unknown causes, and her sister Christian to a 'sore throat'. Her soldier brother Robert had died of a fever in 1692 and her small son Robin just earlier in the year, so Grisell must have been immensely thankful when it appeared that her husband would recover from his illness. It may be that this illness was the origin of George

Baillie's subsequent lifelong struggles with deafness, for which he frequently sought treatment.

During George Baillie's illness, Edinburgh society was rocked and divided by the case of Thomas Aikenhead, a 20-year old student who had been found guilty of blasphemy, and was sentenced to death even though he was a first offender and the statute under which he was tried said blasphemy was punishable by death only on the third offence. An appeal to save his life was made to the Privy Council, whose members were of equally divided opinion whether Aikenhead should live or die. Sir Patrick had the casting vote, and declared that the death sentence should be carried out. Thomas Aikenhead was hanged on 8 January 1697, and was the last person to be executed for blasphemy in Scotland. It seems hardly credible that the Sir Patrick who condemned the youth Aikenhead was the same man who had written such tender letters to his wife, and cherished his own children so dearly a decade before. He himself had suffered so much for his sincerely held religious beliefs and perhaps, in sending Aikenhead to his death, saw himself as defending the one true religion. It has also been suggested that, with rumours of his elevation to an earldom already in circulation, that Sir Patrick's motive was political, as he sought his own advancement. Grisell's thoughts on her father's harsh decision are not recorded. On 23 April 1697, Sir Patrick was made Earl of Marchmont. Grisell, as the daughter of an earl, could now use the courtesy title, 'Lady Grisell Baillie'.

George Baillie appears never to have made any decisions with a view to personal advancement, but only regarding what he believed to be the right course for his country. George Lockhart said of him: 'In King William's time he had gained a great reputation by standing so stiffly by the interest of his country; but being of a rebellious race, he never had the least thought of serving the Royal Family; and tho' he joined with the Cavaliers and Country parties, in opposition to the Duke of Queensbury and the Court measures, yet he always favoured the Hanoverian succession.' George Baillie's opinions at this time had begun to diverge from those of his father-in-law, Sir Patrick, posing a problem of divided loyalties for Grisell, though there seems to have been no animosity between her husband and her father despite their political differences. Deafness was proving a great hindrance to George Baillie, though he was apparently still hopeful of a cure, and one of the remedies he tried was sweating in the salt pans. Salt was produced by evaporation of sea water in various places along the Scottish coast where coal could be easily got, and in March 1698 he writes to Sir Patrick from Maitland Pans, 'Being resolved to make use of the pans as long as time will allow I cannot wait upon your Lp [Lordship] this day but shall do it the morrow if your Lp will be pleased to send out your coach that I may be in before sermon'. George Baillie apparently did not attend the 1698 session of parliament, probably because he could not hear or contribute to the political debates. No doubt Grisell and her two small daughters had to make some concessions to his deafness within the household, but George Home, reporting on 6 January 1699 on the arrival of Grisell and her husband from London by coach says, 'They look well enough, but Jeriswood is still somewhat deaf. He has a silver instrument like a trumpet he puts to his ear to cause the air beat his ear more strongly but I did not see him make use of it.'

However distressing and inconvenient George Baillie's deafness seemed, Grisell had more serious ailments in the family to worry about in January 1699 as Grisell's younger sister 'Annie', Lady Anne Hall, was dangerously ill. Reminding us of the perils of seventeenth century living, George Home says, 'This morning my Lady Marchmont [Grisell's mother] told me she, L[ady] Anne, past a worme a Span [22cms] and more long wch I wish may produce some change for the better'. (Grisell tried to protect her own family from the debilitating effects of intestinal worms as evidenced by the purchase in 1706 of 'worm seed' [artemisia santonicum] costing four shillings). Sadly, Lady Anne died on the 24th of the month, 'much regrated by all that knew her: the pleasantest spryghtliest Young Lady I ever knew'. Annie was just 21 years old, and had been married to Sir James Hall for less than two years, having given birth to a short-lived son, John, in February 1698. It had been agreed for some years previously that she should marry a Mr. Hepburn of Humbie, and that her elder sister Julian should marry Sir James Hall, who seems to have changed his mind which of Sir Patrick's daughters he wished to marry when the marriage settlement came to be finalised. Julian obviously felt slighted, and reacted by eloping in January 1698 with Charles Bellingham, a man of no fortune and doubtful reputation, as he and his brother had previously been imprisoned for highway robbery. In taking such drastic action, Julian was in effect cutting herself off from the rest of her family, angering and distressing her parents in particular. Annie must have felt partly responsible, having married Sir James Hall, and 'before she died got My Lady her mother and Lady Julian reconciled, and My Lo: Chancellor promised her the same'. A month after Annie died, Sir Patrick kept his promise of reconciliation by purchasing a post at Dumbarton for Charles Bellingham. Sir Patrick was intent on also showing forgiveness by inviting Bellingham to Annie's funeral, but Grisell's brother Patrick was less forgiving, declaring that he [Polwarth] would not attend if Bellingham were there.

Just a month later in February 1699, family tensions were again heightened, this time by Grisell's brother Andrew whose choice of a future wife was upsetting his parents. George Home casts Grisell in the role of peacemaker: 'I entreated Lady Grizell to speake to My Lord [her father] to deal a litle more kindly wt Andrew wch I thought the best way to bring him off this foolish Intrigue'. The lady in question was a young widow, Lady Mangerton [Manderston], whose mother Lady Hilton had been very helpful when the family was in exile in Holland, and to modern eyes might have seemed an ideal choice to whom a debt of gratitude might be paid, but to Sir Patrick she was far from ideal as she would have been able to bring only a small amount of money to the marriage. To avoid scandal the lovers used to meet at the house of another young widow, Lady Douglas of Cavers, who had a large jointure from her deceased husband. Despite having married for love herself, Grisell moves from peacemaker to matchmaker, on seeing a financial advantage for her brother. Lady Anne Purves says: 'Lady Grizel Baillie thought her [Lady Douglas'] Jointure would be of use to her Brother, proposed it to her Father, and carried on the Matter with such Activity (which was her way when she took a thing in hand) that Sir Andrew was over-persuaded, and had not the Courage to own his Engagements'. Lady Douglas proved very demanding in terms of what she wanted from the marriage settlement, and Sir Patrick was obliged to give 5,000 merks more than he had offered at first.

Amid her grief for the loss of her sister Annie, concern for her brother Andrew's marriage prospects and anxiety about her husband's deafness, Grisell had young Grisie, now aged 6, and Rachy, aged 2, to care for and educate. We know exactly what her daughters looked like at this date as Grisell had recently commissioned a double portrait of them (Plate 11) from John Scougall. The small girls are sumptuously dressed, both sporting 'fontange' headdresses, the very height of fashion, which it is to be hoped were only worn for the purposes of the portrait rather than everyday wear for small children. Already in the accounts we can note expenses laid out on Grisie's education, with the seemingly curious fact that in 1696 a quarter's dancing lessons cost £20:12s, but a reading master received only £2:18s for a quarter's teaching 4-year-old Grisie to read.

Grisell's parents, as the Lord Chancellor of Scotland and his Lady, were entitled to lodgings in the abbey at Holyrood, to which they moved in April 1699. Though somewhat out of town, Sir Patrick had a coach to transport him up the hill, and it is unlikely that neighbours would cause much trouble, as they frequently did in the crowded tenements of the High Street. George Home complains numerous times: 'Last night our neighbours above keept such a work and noise that they keept me waking towards 3'. On another occasion, 'Yesternight, or rather this morning my neighbour Sir James came in very drunk... I could not get rest for his bawling. About 2 in the morning came fiddles, and serenaded some young lady at Dr Trotter's, who lives in the stair'. It was probably improved financial circumstances rather than noisy neighbours that had caused George Baillie and Grisell to move from Wariston's Land at a cost for the 'flitting' of £11 in May 1696, and in September 1697 they appear to have quit the noise and dirt of the High Street for a house at the Dean, about a mile distant, as Grisell records a bill for £20 'To take our furnitur to the Dean & bring it in again'. For whatever reason, the stay at the Dean was brief and the family took up lodgings again close to the Parliament and the social amenities offered by the High Street. Probably much political discussion and manoeuvring took place not in any official building, but in the places where gentlemen went to meet socially. George Home makes many mentions of 'the coffee house', and 'the new chocolat house', and eating houses run by Stephen Cuthles and a Frenchman named Pascal, as well as various inns. The interval between the two sermons on a Sunday was also a great opportunity for dissemination of news and gossip, particularly for women, who did not frequent the generally male-only preserve of the coffee house. On Sunday 13 August 1699 the rumours circulating among the church-goers were alarming, suggesting that the settlement at Darien had been abandoned. Five ships had left Scotland the previous summer for Darien, in central America, carrying 1200 people and the hopes of the Scottish nation for increased prosperity that the new colony would bring. Many Scots Lords and lairds, particularly in the lowlands, had welcomed King William's deposing of James II, but William nevertheless remained mistrustful of the Scots and had insisted that clan chiefs in the Highlands make a pledge of loyalty. The chief of the McDonalds' failure to do so on time had given William the excuse to sign the order that resulted in the massacre of Glencoe in 1692. Now in 1699 King William, not wishing to provoke the hostile Spanish who were already settled in nearby areas, had issued a proclamation that English and Dutch colonists in the Americas and the Caribbean were not to trade with the Scots at Darien. News travelled very slowly, and two other ships had set out some months after the first ones, not realising that many of the original settlers had died of disease, and King William's new proclamation meant the survivors had little chance of obtaining food to replace their failed crops. Failed crops were also an issue in Scotland itself in 1699, as the harvests had been very poor in 1695, 1696 and 1698 because of cold, wet summers, which became known as 'the ill years'. Consequently, export of grain from Scotland was forbidden, as sections of the population were starving.

The rumours about Darien must have been worrying to George Baillie both on a national and personal level, as he had invested £1,000 of the family finances in the venture, no doubt with Grisell's approval and encouragement, but that same weekend in August brought family sorrow when Grisell suffered a miscarriage, or as George Home put it, 'My Lady Marchmont was gone to Ed [Edinburgh] Lady Grizell having parted with child'. Sadness at the loss of the child may have been softened by thoughts that Grisell was still only 33, and hope for a son and heir was not yet extinguished, but that autumn must have seemed very bleak to George Baillie, with not just personal sadness but the confirmation of the abandonment of Darien and of the great loss of life there. The streets of Edinburgh were thronged with starving beggars, a scarcity of horse fodder was causing many ill-fed animals to succumb to a widespread fatal disease which was sweeping the country, and hope was fading for any improvement in his deafness, making him wonder if he could continue in public life: 'My Lord [Sir Patrick] told me that he had heard from Jeriswood who was mightily discouraged at the continuing of his deafnesse so that he begun to weary of his place.'

In October the African Company had petitioned the King to hold a parliament to discuss Darien, but King William had replied, 'The parliament shall meet when we judge that the Good of the Nation does require it'. Not content with this, the Country Party began collecting signatures for a further petition or 'national address'. George Baillie must have been somewhat cut off from the current political events as he seemed not to know about this second petition, and Grisell, ever protective of her husband's interests, is determined that he should not find out. 'I found L.G. [Lady Grisell] not pleased S.J.H. [Sir J Hume] should desire Jeriswood to signe the addresse, and wisht his friends should doe their endevour that the paper should not be brought to him, wch if it should be she knew he would signe it'. As Grisell had feared, the King was angry that a second petition for the same cause should be got up when he had given what he intended as a final answer to the first one, which 'ought to have given intire Satisfaction to all our Good Subjects'. On speaking to George Baillie about it, George Home says, 'he had not heard of the Kings letter', which seems to imply that he [Baillie] was relying on Grisell to keep him abreast of political news, but that she was quite selective about what she told him.

As the year 1699 drew to a close, Home says, 'My Lady Marchmt desired me to come back to dinner this being Christmisse day & Lady Grizells birthday'. Grisell's birthday was always celebrated on Christmas Day, and even the epitaph carved on the family mausoleum says she was 'buried on her birth-day, the 25th of that month'. However, we have seen that the meticulous Mr. Holiwell christened her on Sunday 24 December 1665 'after sermon', so her birthday should have been celebrated on Christmas Eve. It is possible that once she married George Baillie the 24th of December was dedicated to remembering his father Robert, as that was the date of his execution, and celebrations on that day did not seem fitting, so were always put off until the following day.

Despite the wealth of detail in George Home's diaries he regrettably never tells us what was served when he dropped in so frequently on the Marchmont or Jerviswood households for dinner. Some menus or 'Bills of Fair' (sic) exist from the time of Sir Patrick's residence in Holyrood Abbey, but these were for lavish formal dinners whose main purpose was probably political rather than social. Family dinners enjoyed by George Home were likely to have been much less elaborate but in accordance with the general fashion of the day, when dinner consisted of two courses, each of a number of dishes laid on the table at the same time, with a smaller offering between the two courses which was known as the 'relief'. Lady Marchmont's menu for 28 August 1698 is almost entirely meat, with 'pottaige' (soup), 'rost mutton', 'gellie', 'a dish of tarts', 'rost hens', and 'portigall eggs' [Portugal eggs, a visually spectacular dish], being common to both courses, which also each included a 'sellet' [salad] which would have been at least partially composed of vegetables. The 'relief' in between the courses was one dish with eight wild fowl and six chickens, and another with six more chickens and 14 pigeons. There are 'lobesters' in the first course and 'friedd skaite' in the second, being the only foods from the sea. Each course on this occasion had 17 dishes named, allowing plenty of choice to cater for guests' individual preferences, though 'roast mutton in blood', 'cold bark pudding' and 'pigeon compost' sound less than tempting to the modern diner.

Although any formal dinners given by Grisell were likely to have been similar to her mother's in the dishes offered, Lady Murray asserts that her mother's lovely complexion 'might be owing to the great moderation she had in her diet, throughout her whole life. Pottage and milk was her greatest feast, and by choice preferred them to every thing; though nothing came wrong to her that others could eat. Water she preferred to any liquor; though often obliged to take a glass of wine, always did it unwillingly, thinking it hurt her, and did not like it'. We are not told who the guests were, nor how many were present to partake of Lady Marchmont's dinner described above, but they got through 18 bottles of claret, seven of sherry, two of gin and four of port. Lady Anne Purves is more forthcoming about what was offered for a family dinner at Polwarth, citing Lady Wedderburn who shared 'a plain Leg of Mutton' eaten al fresco beside the 'round pond', an ornamental feature which Sir Patrick had had made just to provide work for Polwarth villagers during the time of scarcity. Oatmeal was selling at eight shillings a peck, a very high price, and Sir Patrick 'caused a large Cauldron to be filled with porridge and carried out in washing Tubs to the work people', setting an example of charitable giving that his daughter Grisell was to follow all her life.

Chapter 4

~◈~

EDINBURGH BEFORE THE UNION

1700–1707

The new year, and new century, should have brought hope for an improvement in Scotland's fortune, but only a month of 1700 had elapsed when a dreadful fire broke out on 3 February in the Mealmarket in Edinburgh, just as people were going to bed. George Home gives us an eyewitness account, and was himself a victim as his lodging, which was in a building 13 storeys high not counting garrets and cellars, was burnt down. Home had seen the fire was likely to reach his tenement and had prudently, with the aid of his own footman and that of Grisell's brother Andrew, removed many of his belongings to a safer place, and lost only 21 ells of linen he had intended for some new shirts. Sir Patrick, as Chancellor, was kept busy giving orders and mobilising the city authorities, especially when the Parliament House itself was threatened. It was saved, says George Home, 'by building up the windows with the flag stones of the Close, and covering them with horse dung'. The fire raged for two whole days, and the glow in the sky was visible to Sir Patrick's neighbours many miles away in Berwickshire. A large area of the city was destroyed, and many people lost possessions and documents. Despite the fire, the General Assembly of the Church of Scotland took place the following week as planned, and George Baillie attended as Commissioner for the Building of Kirks. George Home was still lodging with different friends in turn, as accommodation was hard to find with so many having lost their homes.

The fire provided a temporary distraction from the Darien failure which was still uppermost in many people's minds as it involved an estimated loss of between a quarter and a half of the wealth of the Scottish nation. George Home reports on 19 February on news in 'the Gazette', by which he must mean the *London Gazette*, an official Government-produced newspaper, the *Edinburgh Gazette* having only appeared for a few months in 1699 before ceasing publication. 'I bought the Gazette, which has the Parliament's address and the King's answer. In it he proposes to take away the difference between the two nations, that there may be ane union.' The idea of a union between Scotland and England was to occupy the great political minds for the next seven years, and George Baillie was in the forefront of the group aiming to bring that union about.

The family moved again in 1700 to a house, probably in Foulis Close, owned by Sir James Foulis of Colinton, where they were to remain until 1707. Besides supporting her husband in his political life and organising the household finances, Grisell devoted much of her energies to her daughters and their education. Smallpox was rife in Scotland and England in the seventeenth and eighteenth centuries, and, as can be seen from the fact that the Queen had died of it in 1694, was no respecter of privilege. A large proportion of the population was likely to suffer from it at some stage in their lives. Those who survived were scarred for life, though contemporary portraits never give any indication of this. In *The Songstresses of Scotland* there is an unsubstantiated comment from 'an old servant', describing Grisell in old age as 'a little woman marked by small-pox', suggesting Grisell herself had survived the disease at some time. In August 1700, George Baillie and Grisell's hearts must have been struck with fear, as George Home reports that both Grisie and Rachy had had smallpox, but were recovering. Although there must have been some anxious weeks, relief would have followed when their daughters seemed likely to recover, and, once recovered were safe from smallpox for the rest of their lives. Grisell did purchase cosmetics to improve the complexion, though she doesn't say if for her own use or her daughters'. In January 1705 she spends four shillings 'To Tarter ston for taking of[f] Freckels', and in January 1707 she lays out 16 shillings 'For a bottle Queen Hungary water', a herbal astringent which she must have been impressed with as another bottle is purchased at the same price in April.

Another little understood but very prevalent disease was tuberculosis. Grisell's 'most dearly beloved' brother Patrick, having found a liking for soldiery in William of Orange's army in the 1680s, continued his military career. He was at home on leave in 1696 when he met two cousins from Ireland who had been invited to spend some time in Scotland; they attended the Chancellor's New Year's Eve Ball, and young Patrick fell in love with one of them, Elizabeth Hume, known in the family as Betty. His regiment was soon ordered to Flanders, but the following December Patrick and Betty were married in the Tron church in Edinburgh. Young Patrick was now Sir Patrick, Lord Polwarth since his father's elevation to the earldom, so his bride became Lady Polwarth. It is possible she was already in the early stages of tuberculosis, though Lady Anne Purves attributes the cause of her illness to getting a soaking from a large wave when sitting with her back to the sea at Dunglass. On 9 June 1701 George Home reports that both Dr. Stevenson and Dr. Abernethy were at Polwarth House to treat Lady Polwarth, and had advised that travel might do her good. George Home expresses no sympathy for Betty, but only for her husband. 'However, I pity my Lord Polwarth, who must be obliged to trudge about'. Writing from Edinburgh in September to his brother Andrew, Lord Polwarth says, 'My wyfe continowes ill & become very weak. Ther is nothing left us except trifling with Asses Milk'. Lady Polwarth died at Holyrood Abbey on 11 December 1701, leaving young Patrick heartbroken by her loss after only four years of marriage.

On 13 March 1702, George Home notes in his diary that he received a letter from Grisell's brother Andrew. 'He tells me the King had got a fall at hunting, but was thought almost well; but a little after he took some fits of ane ague which brought him so low that his physicians acquaint the Council of England they thought him in great danger: that ane express was come to my Lord Chancellor about it on Wednesday morning'. The King had died on Sunday 8 March, so it had taken three days for the news to reach Sir Patrick in Edinburgh. The King had died at 8 o'clock in the morning, and George Home writes that 'The Queen [Anne] was proclaimed at one in the afternoon… and was yesterday [13 March] proclaimed Queen of Scotland. God knows what change this may produce. I know we have lost a King under whom we lived easily, and peaceably.'

Grisell's brother Patrick remained in a distracted state and poor health for a long time after the death of his young wife, but Grisell and her father were anxious that he should marry again. Margaret Warrender says, 'He [Patrick] made no secret that he married solely to please his family'. Grisell and her father selected a beautiful young woman, Lady Jane Home, eldest daughter of the 6th Earl of Home, who was known as 'Bonnie Jean o' the Hirsel'. Judging by the date of her parents' marriage [1680], Jean was possibly up to 20 years younger than Patrick, and the Hirsel family was a more prestigious one than the Marchmont family, so from Jean Home's point of view the marriage at the beginning of April 1703 was a strange one, but proved happy, though childless. Having no children of his own, Patrick didn't understand parental pride, as we see from a letter he wrote in February 1704 to his brother Andrew, in which he criticises modern mothers for the way they dress and feed their offspring and for their excessive 'fondness upon their children as if there were not or ever had been any such Creature'.

After Patrick's wedding, there was further cause for rejoicing later in the same month when Grisell's youngest sister Jean, referred to as 'Jani' in her mother's Compt Book, and now aged 20, was married to James Sandilands, Lord Torphichen, whose family seat was at Calder House in West Lothian, already famed at that date as the place where John Knox openly celebrated the first reformed communion in 1556. The marriage was to be a long and happy one, blessed with seven sons and three daughters. Grisell gives out a generous £29 'For drinkmony [tips] to the fidlers at Jean's Mariadge'.

While Sir Patrick had been in lonely confinement in the vault of Polwarth kirk in 1684, he may have vowed to himself that at some future time, in gratitude for his place of sanctuary, he would rebuild the kirk, which was in a state of disrepair. In 1703 that time had come. The walls were rebuilt and a fine tower bearing Sir Patrick's coat of arms was added. The renovation seems to have been intended for a number of years as the bell which originally hung in the tower, and which was the gift of Lady Marchmont, was commissioned in 1697, but appears, from its inscription, not to have been cast until 20 years later. 'Given to the Kirk of Polwarth by Lady Grizel Kar Countess of Marchmont 1697. R.M. [Robert Maxwell] Fecit Edr. 1717'. Grisell made her own contribution to the renovated kirk by embroidering a green velvet valance for the pulpit, which is still in existence and on display at Mellerstain House.

Grisell's mother had been in poor health for some time, and in the summer of 1703 she could no longer hide the seriousness of her condition, so at Sir Patrick's insistence she left Polwarth House for Edinburgh, to be closer to medical assistance, though the word 'assistance' may not be accurate if Lady Anne Purves' account is correct: 'Lord Marchmont found it [her illness] out, and applied to the Physicians in Edinbro', who gave her Mercurial Vomits, which threw the Cancer through her Blood'. Lady Murray describes the scene at her grandmother's deathbed: 'She had her judgment to the last; her children were all round her bed; my mother was in such agonies of grief, she had hid herself behind the curtain of the bed, that my grandmother, in looking round to them all, did not see her, and said, "Where is Grisell?" upon which she came near her; she, taking her by the hand, said, "My dear Grisell, blessed be you above all, for a helpful child you have been to me".'

Sir Patrick wrote a moving elegy to his wife in her own Bible, which he gave to Grisell, but must have been writing also with an eye to posterity, as Grisell obviously did not need any description of her mother's appearance. 'Grisell Lady Marchmont, her book. To Lady Grisell Hume, Lady Jerviswood, my beloved daughter. – My Heart, in remembrance of your mother, keep this Bible, which is what she ordinarily made use of. She had been happy of a religious and virtuous education, by the care of virtuous and religious parents. She was of a middle stature, of a plump, full body, a clear ruddy complexion, a grave majestic countenance, a composed, steady, and mild spirit, of a most firm and equal mind, never elevated by prosperity, nor debased or daunted by adversity. She was a wonderful stay and support to me in our exile and trouble, and a humble and thankful partaker with me in our more prosperous condition; in both which, by the blessing of God, she helped much to keep the balance of our deportment even. She was constant and diligent in the practice of religion and virtue, a careful observer of worship to God, and of her duties to her husband, her children, her friends, her neighbours, her tenants and her servants; so that it may justly be said, her piety, probity, virtue, and prudence were without a blot or stain, and beyond reproach. As, by the blessing of God, she had lived well, so by his mercy, in the time of her sickness, and at her death, there appeared many convincing evidences, that the Lord took her to the enjoyment of endless happiness and bliss. She died the 11th of October 1703, at Edinburgh, and was buried in my burying-place near the Canongate Church, where I have caused mark out a grave for myself close by hers, upon the left side, in the middle of the ground.'

The rhythms of life in Grisell's own household carried on unbroken through political happenings and family celebrations or sorrows, for the sake of her daughters. In 1701, when Rachy was five, a man called Porterfield is paid £18 'to perfite Rachy in reading'. The accounts also reveal that Grisie's musical education is thorough and varied. 'Grisie's quarter with Crumbin', at £19:7s indicates she is having harpsichord lessons from Henry Crumden, and in January 1702 £14:4s is paid 'to Grisie's singing master Krenberg' [Jakob Kremberg]. By 1707 Grisie has added the 'violl' [viol da gamba] to her musical skills, and 'Sinckolum' [St. Colombe] is paid £12 for teaching her. Several keyboard instruments are mentioned in the accounts, namely the spinet, the virginals and the harpsichord, all of them strung with thin wire strings which needed to be professionally tuned on a frequent basis, and with delicate mechanisms needing repair. Public concerts had only begun to be given in the 1690s in Edinburgh, but by 1702 money is being laid out 'To Grisie to goe to a consert'. Sometimes Grisie and Rachy were treated to a personal music recital, 'Thomson the violer playing to the bairns' costing £2:18s. In January 1703 there is mention of 'Thomson Grisie's writing master', and a 'french gramer' and 'ane arithmetick book' are purchased, more evidence of the diversity of Grisie's and Rachy's education. It was not, however, all work and no play, for the same month sees spending 'For little Dutch toys to the childrin', and the girls are to be diverted by a pet as in April the expense of 'bringing the Parit [parrot] from Glasgow' is noted. (Late in 1704 the parrot must have made at least one bid for freedom as amounts of 10 shillings and 14 shillings are spent 'For finding Parrit'). A feathered friend is also bought to enhance the garden as 14s 6d is paid 'For pecok [peacock] cariing'. In November 1705 Edinburgh received a strange and wonderful visitor, when Grisell spent 14 shillings 'For seeing the Elifent', a female Indian elephant that had been touring Europe since the 1680s and which had, incredibly, been kept in a tenement in Fishmarket Close while it was on display in Edinburgh.

The Council upon ane petitione given in by Abraham Sever Dutchman grants liberty to the petitioner to expose his elephant to all persones within the toun and suburbs upon his payment of ane gratification to the kirk thesaurer [treasurer] for the use of the poor.

Although now over 15 years distant, Grisell's time in Holland may still have been in her mind when in April 1705 she purchased a 'waffill yron', surely an unusual commodity in Edinburgh at that date, if not quite so exotic as the 'elifent'.

To assist in Grisie's and Rachy's education, a governess by the name of May Menzies was engaged in the summer of 1705. As several eighteenth and nineteenth century writers have described, the position of governess was a strange one in a kind of no man's land between the family and the domestic servants, but May Menzies almost became one of the family, remaining in their service for the rest of her life, subsequently caring for Grisell's grandchildren. Lady Murray says of her:

'She was always with us when our masters came, and had no other thought or business but the care and instruction of us; which I must here acknowledge with gratitude, having been an indulgent though exact mistress to us when young'. Grisell herself said of her, 'I could trust my life to her honesty'. In a letter dated at Edinburgh 16 August 1705, Grisell gives May Menzies directions for a daily timetable for Grisie, approaching the age of 13: 'To rise by seven a clock and goe about her duty of reading, etc. etc., and be drest to come to Breckfast at nine, to play on the spinnet till eleven, from eleven till twelve to write and read french. At two a clock sow her seam till four, at four learn arithmetic, after that dance and play on the spinet again till six and play herself till supper and to bed at nine'. One tangible reminder of May Menzies remains to be seen at Mellerstain House in the form of the embroidery now known as the 'Mellerstain Panel' (Plate 12). Grisell's accounts reveal a purchase costing £4:16s in July 1705 of 'worsits' [woollen thread] for the 'petipoint pice'. May Menzies obviously came from a line of skilled needlewomen, as the pattern book of motifs for the embroidery, also still on display at Mellerstain, had belonged to May Menzies' grandmother, Katherine Logan. The book is inscribed, 'this book doth appertain to Katharin Logan Julie 27 1635'. The tent stitch embroidery using both woollen and silk threads was completed in 1706 and bears the initials 'GB', 'RB' and 'MM'. Grisie and Rachy were aged 14 and 10 respectively, and the fineness of the embroidery, with its 24 stitches to the linear inch, is testament to their already very skilled needlework. All the motifs on the work are contained in May Menzies' pattern book, except for a hound chasing a hare at the bottom margin. It seems likely that one animal was Grisie's own creation, and the other, her sister's.

In the parliamentary sessions of 1700 and 1701 George Baillie had voted consistently against the Court Party, and so was dismissed from his post as Receiver-General. His correspondence for the period 1702-1708 was published in 1842 as it is historically important, shedding light on the political thinking leading up to the Union with England in 1707. George Baillie was a leading member of a group named the 'Squadrone Volante', whose other chief players were John Hay, 2nd Marquess of Tweeddale, John Ker, Earl of Roxburghe, and George Baillie's father-in-law Sir Patrick, Earl of Marchmont, together with the Duke of Montrose and the Earls of Haddington and Rothes. The Squadrone had agreed on a cipher so that, should letters between them be intercepted, they would be unintelligible to anyone outside the group, as all names and various other nouns were represented by numbers. George Baillie had been made a member of the Scottish Privy Council in 1704, but Tweeddale's Government was dismissed in 1705, to be replaced by the Court Party, with the Country Party in opposition. However, the Squadrone refused to re-join the opposition, and held the balance of power, voting with the Government to push the Union through in 1707.

In the male-dominated world of the early eighteenth century it was unthinkable that a woman should be involved in politics but, as we have seen, Grisell was certainly a behind-the-scenes promoter and guardian of her husband's career. George Baillie pays her a back-handed compliment in June 1705 in a letter to the Earl of Roxburghe, suggesting she would be a better treasurer than the one intended for the post: 'I had almost forgot to tell you that, for certain, Forfar is to be of the Treasury. Our Government will, at this rate, turn a jeast: they had better put my Lady ther.' It is also apparent that Grisell acted as her husband's secretary as in June 1706, Secretary Johnston tells George Baillie to 'Write by an unknown hand: your wife's is as well known as your own.' According to George Home, Grisell took part in a more public political act in February 1704 when

David Baillie, son of Robert Baillie's brother George, was tried and convicted of a libel against the Marquess of Queensberry. His sentence was to be transportation to the West Indies, but prior to that he was to suffer the indignity of being pilloried at the Tron in Edinburgh's High Street, enduring a barrage of whatever the public could find lying in the nearby gutters. It seems Grisell and others had attempted to spare him this by freeing him on his way to the Tron, as Home says: 'I was told the women followed him and cutt bitts of the ribband with which his hands were tied behind his back and yt [that] L.G.B. [Lady Grisell Baillie] should be among them.' This implies that the women, including Grisell, were following on foot, which would also be unusual as ladies of status rarely walked anywhere in the city, as demonstrated by regular amounts for [sedan] chair hire in Grisell's accounts. Unlike the leather shoes of the less well-off who habitually walked, avoiding the filth in the streets as best they could, the footwear of élite ladies was totally impractical, being made of delicate fabric, often silk (Plate 13a, 13b). Early in their marriage George Baillie and Grisell had purchased a 'chariot', a small carriage to seat two people, but for short journeys within Edinburgh a chair was much more convenient.

During this pre-Union period, Grisell continued to run the household in Edinburgh or Mellerstain while George Baillie devoted his energies to politics in London. A letter addressed in 1707 to 'The Honobl Geo: Baillie of Jerviswood at his Lodging in Queen Street Westminster next door to ye Lamp on the Right Hand' tells us he was very conveniently situated close to Parliament Square, but equally near to the royal court and open green spaces of St. James's Park. We are reminded that at this period the monarch still took a very active part in government as the Earl of Roxburghe writes, 'On Wensday the Queen being in the house [of Commons] at first on the Throne, and after it being cold on a Bench at the fire...'. Sometimes the court was less conveniently situated to George Baillie's lodgings as he writes to Grisell in September 1704, just having returned to London from Scotland, 'I have been this day taken up wt buying cloaths and other necessaries in order for Windsor to morrow to waite upon the Queen.'

In a letter of 25 January 1707 from George Baillie's uncle Secretary Johnston, using the Squadrone's cipher, Johnston is advising that Baillie should visit Bath for the sake of his health. 'I think your own illness should bring you to goe to the Bath, for it all comes from your stomack, which is the part the Bath waters certainly help; and I am still for your bringing your daughter [Grisie] hither, if you be not for marrying her quickly, which usually makes for a sickly wife and sickly children'. It appears from this that there had already been discussion of marriage plans for 14-year-old Grisie, who would have been seen as a good 'catch': attractive, accomplished and daughter of a wealthy and influential father, albeit without a title. As early as 1696, there is expenditure of over 1,000 pounds Scots 'To my jurnay to the Bath', but this need not necessarily mean that George Baillie went there for his health on that occasion, as the court often spent periods at Bath. The town was to increase in popularity throughout the eighteenth century, when a visit to Bath was an essential part of the social calendar of the aristocracy. There is still concern for George Baillie's health in September 1707 as a letter from the Earl of Roxburghe, using the Squadrone's cipher, indicates. '183 [James Johnston] tels me he has offer'd you his house at Twitnam [Twickenham] where you may be as retir'd as at Mellerston in case your illness continue'. It seems Grisie did visit the Johnstons at Twickenham in November 1707, unaccompanied by either parent as Grisell writes to her there with an avalanche of advice about how to behave towards her hostess, when to stand and sit in a (presumably Anglican) church service, not to fraternise with the servants, not to be idle, not to make unnecessary expense in fire or anything else, and 'be sure ye burn all your letters as soon as you have read and consider'd them', which last advice Grisie happily did not comply with.

George Baillie's presence in London that Autumn may have been especially necessary as on the first of May 1707 Scotland became part of 'Great Britain', and the first parliament of this United Kingdom was to sit on 1 October, 1707.

1a Polwarth Kirk

1b Redbraes Castle

2 *Grisell Ker by John Scougall 1696*

3   Sir Patrick Hume c1690 by John Scougall (?)

4 Robert Baillie style of Gerard Soest

5 *George Holiwell, minister of Polwarth 1664–1704*

6   Rachel Johnston 1696 by John Scougall

7   *Grisell's lantern 1680s in the National Museum of Scotland*

8   Grisell c1680 by David or John Scougall

9 'The big chair' 1690s

10 Robin 1696 by John Scougall (?)

11 *Grisie and Rachy 1698 by John Scougall*

12a   The Mellerstain panel 1706

12b   Gilt table purchased 1721

13a and b   Grisell's shoes 1730s

14   *Lord Binning by William Aikman 1717*

15 *Grisie, Lady Murray by William Aikman*

16   *Lady Mary Howard 1725 by Maria Verelst*

Chapter 5

∿

DIVIDED HOUSEHOLD

1707–1714

Once the centre of political action for Scots moved from Edinburgh to London in 1707 there were frequent and long periods when George Baillie was absent from the household, in lodgings in London and only able to communicate by letter. Grisell was, of course, more than capable of running the household in Scotland, but George Baillie must have regretted not seeing his daughters growing up. It had apparently been decided that to maintain two Scottish households, when one in Edinburgh was no longer necessary for George Baillie's career, was too great an extravagance, and that Mellerstain should become the family's main residence. In June 1708, it cost £19 'For bringing pairt of the Furniture to Mellerstaine'.

To George Baillie, one of life's essentials was books, and there are regular purchases of volumes noted in Grisell's accounts, and also payments to bookbinders, as books at the time were often supplied unbound, enabling the purchaser to personalise them with his own binding. Some of the titles which still grace the shelves of Mellerstain library today are specified in the accounts, others unnamed. In 1703 'Jaillot's Maps' had cost £130 and three volumes of 'Mazerays Historie', £80. Sometimes the quantity bought was too great to name individual works, as in 1708 'For books bought from Andrew Bell in pairt £360'. We learn that the move to Mellerstain entailed shipping four cartloads of books. 'To expence of the Cart 3 times to Ed[inburgh] for books £4:11s' and 'To expence of another Cart wt books £1:9s'.

Although there had been regular visits to Mellerstain, the family must have had to make considerable adjustments to living there on a permanent basis. In Edinburgh there had been ready access to foodstuffs in the markets, music masters available and concerts to go to, fashionable fabrics and dressmakers to make them up, and the society of similar families who could be met with on a daily basis. Now foodstuffs that could not be supplied by the estate were bought in bulk, and Grisie and Rachy, aged 15 and 11, would have to make their own entertainment. Other services provided in Edinburgh were also lacking as we see in 1708 that £12 is paid 'To one in Kelso to teach George Lamb to shave'. George Lamb's usefulness had also been increased the previous year when he was given writing lessons. The girls could get healthful exercise riding round the estate as there is mention of 'Rachy's powny' and a new 'powny' being bought for Grisie at £40. The girls would have had to master the art of riding side-saddle, as females did not ride astride at this period. There was the excitement of the various local fairs where there was entertainment, and trinkets to be bought, as well as the more serious business of buying and selling beasts and foodstuffs. £8 was spent at Kelso fair, with an additional £2 for a boatman, £2:18s for the pipe and drum and £1:12s for fiddlers, who were prevailed upon to come and play at Mellerstain for two days for an extra £5:16s. Mellerstain had fairs of its own as a warrant from Charles II in 1681 had granted permission for the laird to hold two fairs annually on 12 July and 6 October. Some goods such as candles and soap could be bought in Kelso or Greenlaw, both about seven miles distant from Mellerstain, and neighbouring estates might have surplus, such as when Greenknowe, a couple of miles away in Gordon, supplied a stone [14 pounds] of cheese for £1:14s. Other seemingly simple purchases required more effort, when the cost of two new spades is increased by the gardener having to go to Berwick to get them, necessitating an overnight stay. Curiously, it seems to have been thought cheaper to send goods such as barrels of herring by sea from London than to obtain them in Scotland.

Every winter, the household was deprived of George Baillie's company as he went to London 'and staid as long as the Parliament sat. He strictly observed his attendance in Parliament, and blamed those who made a bustle to get in, and then absented themselves upon any pretence; which he never did upon any account, but when his health necessarily required it'. Lady Murray also tells us she always looked forward to her father's return, and to the presents he brought. 'When he went to London every year to the Parliament, and we in Scotland, he would restrain himself in necessary expenses, to bring all of us something he thought we would like, and was useful to us; and would have his trunk opened to give us them, before he took time to rest himself, and shewed a pleasure in doing it I can never forget.' She apparently lost one of her father's earlier presents, as reported in a letter from her Uncle Patrick [Lord Polwarth] to her Uncle Andrew in 1703. 'You must buy for Gris: Bailly which I shall allow [pay for] a little case about 5 or 6 inches long, with a silver spoon & fork & a knife, she has lost, that her father brought her from London, this is a mighty secreat'. (At this date cutlery would be provided by the host if dining in a private house, but in public eating places or when travelling it was still best to take a personal set of cutlery). With ready access in London to fine merchandise, George Baillie was often given commissions by his wife and daughters. As he reveals the price, it is to be hoped that a quantity of fabric is a commission, not a gift: 'I bought yesternight as much muslin with Indian flowers the prettiest thing can be as will be two combing cloaths [dressing gowns] for you it cost me eleven shillings the yeard.'

Efforts to make dilapidated Mellerstain Tower more habitable as a permanent residence began to be made in October 1707, when almost £242 was spent 'For repairing Mellerstaine Tour and other work there' and in 1708 £653:13s was spent on 'Repairing Mellerstain Tour and office howses', and a new home farm was constructed: 'For building and all expences of Mellerstain Mains £886:10s'. Stone walls are built to make an enclosed park, and tenants are compensated with £74:10s for land lost to stone walls and cart roads and for 'eaten corns'. Innovations in farming by John Cockburn of Ormiston in East Lothian, such as giving tenants longer leases and larger parcels of land rather than runrig strips had impressed other landowners, notably Grisell's brother-in-law Sir James Hall and her brother Patrick, and these influences are bound to have reached Grisell at Mellerstain too. Various 'bagnios' or bath houses had been available in Edinburgh, and patronised by Grisell and her family, but the tower house at Mellerstain offered no such conveniences, which were obviously sorely missed as another major expenditure in 1708 is 'For the expence of building the Bath & House £782:11s'. This was a substantial, stone-built and slated building, with a corn loft above it, all properly drained with a sluice. In addition to the skilled masons and quarriers, work by the day labourers at fivepence per day cost £39:10s, equating to 9,000 days' work. It is generally said that despite the emphasis placed on outward appearance, personal hygiene in the eighteenth century was sadly neglected, but the building of the bath house and regular purchases of soap and 'wash balls' suggest that cleanliness was a priority for Grisell. The kitchen facilities are also improved at this date, probably in a separate building from the tower house: 'For Building the two ovens setting the copper and boyler in the Kitchen & chimny £18'. Grisell now has the means to bake bread and other goods, and hot water in quantity. She seems also to be aiming to be self-sufficient in dairy produce, as four milk pails, a butter dish, a skim dish and a little cog are purchased. Repairs are also carried out to Earlston Church, and to Langshaw, a tenanted property with a mill, near Galashiels, where major works seem to have been necessary, though at Jerviswood only the 'pigion House' needs a little money spending on it.

In 1709 Grisell turns her attention to making the garden more productive, buying '34 foot glass for hote beds', so that the growing season for vegetables could begin earlier. A number of new garden tools, seeds and plants, most bought locally, feature in the accounts, though the four ounces of 'spinage sead' was obtained in Edinburgh. She may even have been a 'hands-on' gardener, as she assures her father in a letter of 6 May 1709 that she will 'take care to sett the artichokes right'. The garden as a place for leisure was the focus in 1710, with the setting up and maintenance of a bowling green requiring 237 (and a half!) days' labour at fivepence a day. Grisell also makes efforts to add refinement to the internal furnishings of Mellerstain Tower, the most expensive being 'a chimny and pannel glasses bought at London [an overmantel mirror and smaller ones] £130:14s' and 'For changing and making of New plate as pr John Campbell Goldsmith In London's account £468'. When silverware became old-fashioned or dented it was given to a silversmith to melt down and make new articles, though sadly on this occasion Grisell doesn't say what items were made by John Campbell to enhance her dinner table.

A portrait of Grisell painted in 1689 by John Scougall is

in the collection at Paxton House near Berwick-upon-Tweed, and shows her with curled hair piled high on her head except for one ringlet falling over her shoulder. Her hairstyle does not differ greatly in a portrait of some twenty years later when we can view Grisell as seen in 1709 through the eyes of Sir John de Medina, a Flemish portrait painter with a Spanish father. Medina had worked originally in Brussels, then in London, and had been persuaded by Margaret, Countess of Rothes to visit Scotland after she had rounded up sufficient commissions from her friends and relatives to make it worth his while. He set out with a large number of canvases already painted with figures of ladies and gentlemen, lacking only the heads. Having been initially reluctant to travel, Medina discovered that the only portraitist of note working in Scotland was Scougall, whereas in London there was competition from quite a number of other artists. Accordingly, around 1694 he had moved his family and studio to Edinburgh. Grisell's commissions must have been some of his last, as he died in 1710, having made such a favourable impression in Scotland that he was the last person to receive a knighthood from the Scottish parliament before its dissolution. Grisell's entry in her accounts reads, 'To Medina picture drawer for Jerviswoods my own & the two bairens's Pictures drawing £20'. Grisell must initially have been dissatisfied with the portrait of her husband as he writes to her, 'I wish you had not cause mend my picture for I thought it exceeding like and I hope you do not pretend to give me a better countenance than nature has given me.'

It does seem as if no formal marriage arrangement had been made for Grisie by her parents during her childhood. As early as December 1708, when Grisie has just turned 16, George Baillie is surprised to receive a letter 'with a proposall of marriage from Philiphaugh [John Murray of Philiphaugh] to Gris: I resolve to give my answer next post yt [that] you may be sure will be a refusall in as distinct terms as I can'. This first proposal seems to have opened the floodgates for many others, enticed by her obvious charms and 20,000 merks marriage portion. For any suitor involved in politics, Grisie's having a father and grandfather among the first ranks of politicians would have been an added attraction. In January 1709 Alexander Murray of Stanhope requests permission to write to George Baillie, and in February a suitor named only as Baird enters the fray. George Baillie writes to Grisell, 'Baird has a good estate and yet I'm not for him', and it is apparent that the responsibility of finding a suitable marriage partner for Grisie is beginning to wear him down. 'I wish with you most heartily that your daughter were well off our hand…meantime you must keep your daughter from all engagements whatsoever …therefore no visits are to be allowed but when you are present but even that must not be allowed but to such as you may think are equall match to her'. Alexander Murray's estate is discovered not to be worth as much as previously thought, Baird is dismissed as 'a weak lad', and Grisell is consulted for her opinion of 'Sir James' and his estate. It seems George Baillie is not seeking a suitable match only for his daughter 'for I must have one that can be a comrad to me otherwise I shall have no satisfaction were his estate never so considerable.'

In several other letters George Baillie reiterates that money is not his chief consideration. 'I should be glad to have it in my power to provide better for my children…they must be content with what I can give them and possibly a middle state in the world may be best for them'. Alexander Murray is proving troublesome in his persistence, but another suitor is rejected out of hand. 'I do not like the knight [possibly 'Sir James' mentioned above] after the description you give of him'. Grisie's father is also worried that the number of claimants for her hand might damage her reputation 'for the multitude of suitors will expose the girl to the town talk'. Grisell must have reported that her brother Patrick, Lord Polwarth, is still urging the case for the suitor named Baird, but we learn that Grisie does have some say in whom she is to marry as her father says, 'I will not force my child to marry someone she does not like…on the other hand I hope she'll be so dutifull as not to have a groundless aversion or to incline to any body I do not like.'

The correspondence between Grisell and her husband continues to be dominated well into the spring of 1709 by talk of Grisie's marriage. With George Baillie in London, it falls to Grisell to fend off the suitors, or at least make them keep their distance and form an orderly queue, which she was no doubt more than capable of doing by herself, and with added authority from her husband who says, 'I reason the disposall of daughters belongs more properly to the mother than the father'. However, all the months of agonising over the marriage decision might almost have been in vain as Grisie fell very seriously ill in the summer, as we learn from her grandfather Sir Patrick, Earl of Marchmont, writing to his son Andrew on 30 June. 'I have been so perplexed and disordered by the sickness of your niece Grisell Baillie, who since the 10th current has been dangerously ill of a spotted fever, very malignant, that the physicians had no hope of her recovery till Tuesday, since which time she has been somewhat better, albeit in all appearance she may come slowly out of it'. 'Spotted fever' was the name frequently used at the time for typhus, which was often spread by body lice or fleas, so perhaps Grisell's attempts at household cleanliness were in vain, though Grisie did recover.

After his marriage to Jean Home of the Hirsel, Grisell's brother Patrick had continued his military career, and in 1707 had been promoted to the rank of Colonel of his regiment, the 7th Queen's Dragoons, but his health declined after this date and by the summer of 1709 he was seriously unwell, suffering from tuberculosis, probably contracted from his first wife Elizabeth who had died in 1701. He and his wife Jean were living at Polwarth House, or Redbraes Castle as it was now designated, but alterations were going on in the Autumn of 1709 and it was thought the cold and dampness from new plaster were injurious to Patrick's health, so the couple took lodgings in Kelso. He wrote to the Queen to resign his commission, and in a letter to the Earl of Morton discussing his successor as Colonel of the regiment, Patrick writes from Kelso on 24 October 1709, 'I have been ill these two days & if it were not to answer your Lo: [Lordship's] letter I would not be out of bed'. Patrick died a month later, on 25 November, having just passed his 45th birthday. A few months later his father, Sir Patrick, on being asked to write about his son's military service, includes a general character description. 'He was a person of great probity and honesty; that he was a most dutiful child to his parents, and a good husband to his wife; that he was a faithful and steady friend, where he professed it; and that, as a soldier, he was both diligent and daring, composed and courageous, brave and benign'. Of the family who had shared his exile in Holland, Sir Patrick had now lost Christian, Robert, Anne and Patrick, as well as his beloved wife. It was perhaps fortunate that Grisell was living at Mellerstain at this time, only 12 miles from Redbraes, so could be close to her father, though her own grief at the loss of her favourite brother was also great. Lady Murray says, 'Her eldest brother Patrick, who was nearest her age, and bred up together, was her most dearly beloved'. The clothing account for January 1710 includes, 'For some small things at Kelso for my mornins [mourning] 5s 6d'.

Grisell and her daughters left Mellerstain for a visit to Edinburgh before Christmas 1709. George Baillie writes, 'I am exceedingly pleased you have got so good lodging, the lasses are in the eye of the market', indicating that after the distractions of Grisie's near-fatal illness and the death of Grisell's brother Patrick, his thoughts are turning again to finding a marriage partner for Grisie, and he is perhaps hoping that with his daughters now being visible in Edinburgh society, a completely suitable candidate might put himself forward. Alexander Murray, an advocate, has been irritatingly persistent and Baillie writes to his wife, 'I wish he would not fash [trouble] me so much', but concedes 'Murray seems to be good-natured'.

A couple of weeks later George Baillie says, 'I have had a new attack from Murray', who is anxious to be given permission to pay his addresses to Grisie, but Baillie deflects him, saying much depends on Grisie's mother's opinion, 'if it were a son possibly I might take more upon me'. On 5 January 1710, he complains again, saying, 'Murray plagues me at that rate I begin to fancy he takes me for my daughter', adding, with a rare flash of humour, 'you know if I'm a bon[n]y bride.'

Grisell had been surreptitiously asking her father the Earl of Marchmont for advice on furthering George Baillie's political career in May 1709, fearing that his disrupted education in Latin might hold him back, and saying, 'He knows nothing of my asking any advice about him but I thought he wanted it & know he would observe it'. His poor Latin did not, however, hinder him from being appointed to the Board of Trade in May 1710, at an impressive annual salary of £1000. This appointment, however, delayed his expected return to Scotland until the beginning of June, which he regrets as he is horrified by the contents of Grisell's last letter of 12 May. 'I cannot tell you how angry I am at Murray's being at Mellerstaines nor can I say that I'm well pleased at your suffering him to stay all night for surely you might have made abundance of shifts to have got him off. This forwardness of his can never promote his affair with me, but rather spoile it even tho I were half determined in his favour and you must on no account whatsomever admitt him againe'.

George Baillie fears that other possible suitors may be put off by this apparent display of favour to Murray 'and I shall be forced to give him my daughter or keep her to my selfe.'

Once the family is reunited by George Baillie's return to Mellerstain, letters between them cease to be necessary, so we cannot eavesdrop on the final marriage deliberations. Murray has been writing letters to Grisie since January all of which, even as late as July, have been returned to him on her father's instructions, but it seems there was a sudden change of heart on George Baillie's part. Lady Murray says of him: 'He was the most just and sagacious observer of mankind that was possible; and was seldom deceived in his opinion of them. This made him press me, with many arguments, to marry one he preferred to Mr Murray; but as his affection and tenderness made him unable to stand out against the tears of any one he loved, upon my answering him only with tears, he said, "Dear child, I cannot see you cry; you must do what pleases yourself; I give my consent, since you cannot follow my opinion".' George Baillie's indulgence in allowing Grisie to marry the man of her choice against his better judgment, no doubt supported in his decision by Grisell, was to have severe repercussions for the entire family up to and beyond Murray's death in 1743.

Having made the decision that Grisie was to marry Alexander Murray, not a moment was lost. In a letter of 12 August 1710, Sir Patrick writes to Jean Home, his son Patrick's widow: 'You know that Mr Murray, younger of Stanhope, son to Sir David, has long been a suitor to my grandchild, Grisell Baillie'. He goes on to describe the rapidity with which the marriage had been arranged: 'Now in end parties and friends have come to an agreement very suddenly at one meeting; and because of some uncertainty of Jerviswood's stay in this country, they are to be proclaimed thrice [have the banns read] on Sunday next, having concluded upon terms of the contract on Thursday last, and in a private way are to be married upon Wednesday'. Sir Patrick was already a little behind events as the proclamations, according to Edinburgh parish register, had already taken place on 6 August, the registers also noting that 'Alexander Murray younger of Stanhop and Mrs Grisell Baillie eldest lawfull daughter to George Baillie of Jerviswood' were married on 16 August.

If the marriage contract had only been signed the Thursday previous to the proclamation, that gave Grisell less than a fortnight to make preparations for her daughter's wedding, and to ensure everyone was suitably dressed for the occasion. May Menzies was provided with a gown and coat costing £8, but Grisie's lace headdress alone exceeded that at £10:9s9d, and 'For a sute cloathes trim'd with silver for Grisie, a sute trim'd with silk to Rachy, a skerff to each, and stokins, shoes, rubans, fans and handkerchieffs and 3 big night gouns and stays for Grisies mariage', Grisell laid out £112:8s6d. Grisell herself must have worn something she already possessed, as there is no mention of clothing for herself, and George Baillie seems to have made do with a new pair of shoes costing five shillings. Money was also spent on traditional elements of a wedding: bride's favours, a garland to break over the bride's head, and ribbon and silver tassels for the bride's garters. The fiddlers for the dancing were paid £1:1s6d, but the wedding euphoria lasted no further than the celebrations on the day after the ceremony. A 'Mr [Alexander] Hamilton' who had perhaps acted as best man to Alexander Murray, had danced several times with Grisie, causing Murray to become uncontrollably jealous. Margaret Warrender continues: 'During supper he had tried to suppress his feelings, but that on retiring to his room they had burst forth in a way very deeply to offend his wife, and to call for the immediate interposition of her mother.'

George Rose says, 'After the most patient endeavours to

soothe and cure his distempered imagination, during many months he continued to live in the bosom of this amiable family, and from which he at length made himself a voluntary outcast'. While the parliament was sitting in London, Murray was acting as some kind of assistant to his father-in-law while hoping for a Government position of his own, so was apart from Grisie for lengthy periods, and communicating by letter. While he was courting Grisie, Murray's letters were many pages long, and full of endearments, but by April 1711 his letters are shorter, filled only with bits of mundane news, contrasting with those of George Baillie to Grisell, still, after twenty years of marriage, full of yearning to be with her, and anxiety if he does not receive a letter from her at the expected interval. Having lost his little son Robin in 1696, George Baillie is impatient for a male heir, and has expressed disappointment in several letters that Grisie is not yet expecting a child. Apparently, he has never abandoned hope of having another child of his own as he writes to Grisell on 17 April 1711: 'It seems you must have a very indifferent opinion of me since you conclude it impossible for you to have any more children; I must be allowed to differ from you and cannot but think it near as probable as having them by Grisie tho I must own my selfe to be very doubtfull about it'. Grisell was probably just being realistic about the chance of any further pregnancy, given that she is now approaching the age of 46.

The parliament had risen at the beginning of June, so Murray returned to Mellerstain, though George Baillie had to stay on in London for a while. Grisell must have initially found nothing to object to in Murray's treatment of his wife, as on 5 June George Baillie writes to her: 'I'm glad you're so well pleased with him'. In September 1711, a year after the marriage, Grisell has received a letter from Grisie which must have detailed further unreasonable behaviour of Alexander Murray, and she has written a reply but says, 'I was afraid to send it in case it should be seen by others & perhaps they woud not like you should write so freely to me', implying that society would have thought Grisie disloyal to her husband for telling her mother what had happened between them. Grisell is keeping George Baillie in the dark about Grisie's letter which 'has very near falen into your father's hand', and also says, 'Poor man he knows little of the trouble that seems to be hanging over our heads'. One of the reasons for Grisell's disquiet is the fact that Murray had been keen to show Grisie a copy of *The Tatler* of May 1710, in which there was a report about a man of uncertain temper called Francis Eustace stabbing his wife to death; Grisie has not suffered any physical violence, but is terrified by the state of her husband's mind.

After her marriage, Grisie disappears from her mother's accounts for a while as her husband is responsible for his wife's expenses, but there are many items relating to clothing and education for Rachy, now aged 14. Rachy does not seem to be possessed of the same outstanding musical talent as her sister, but, back in Edinburgh for a spell in 1711, 'Mr Mcgiven' (possibly William McGibbon) is paid £1 in March 'for two moneth at the floot' and £1 again in June, which also saw the purchase of 'a flute to Rachy' costing £1:5s. Three months' lessons from 'Mr Mcgibber' are also paid for in January 1712, so Rachy must have persisted in her musical endeavours for a while at least. Her talents perhaps lay in painting, as Grisell pays for 'Materiell for Rachys painting', and 'Mr Cumin' is remunerated in January 1711 'for two Moneths teaching Rachy to paint'.

While Grisell is in Edinburgh, all her letters to Grisie at Mellerstain are full of anxiety for Grisie's situation, and advice about how she should respond to Murray's behaviour, which Grisell wishes to be kept informed about. 'Pray be most exact in writting me the leest turn he takes'. Grisell has commissioned a portrait of Murray from William Aikman, which is ready by the beginning of November 1711. 'Just this moment I have gote home his picture I was twise up the way to see it but could not find Mr Aikman within & its exceeding like'. Further comments from Grisell reveal that Murray's erratic behaviour is continuing, even worsening, as she says, 'He is so angry with you for trifles' and 'all his friends were takeing notice of it & that every one of them was mighty fond of you'. Grisell also suspects Murray of financial recklessness, and Grisie has noticed him hiding papers when she comes into the room, but her mother says, 'Take care he catch you not at my letters for that wo'd make a dale of mischieff'. May Menzies is also sending reports from Mellerstain about Murray, as Grisell says, 'I long to know what was the ocasion of the two bouts May writes of', though she concludes, 'My heart is to[o] much tyed to you to dislike him for any thing he can doe, & as it is poor man he is more to be pittied than we are.'

It seems likely that Murray's treatment of Grisie is still being kept hidden from George Baillie, as he makes no comment about it, only saying, once Murray has returned to London and is considering whether Grisie should join him there, 'If your husband brings you along with him you must by no means repine at leaving your mother behind…and I hope you know it be your Duty to forsake all for your husband'. Having now been elected to parliament in his own right, Murray is no longer under George Baillie's wing, and Baillie says, 'M: is at such a distance from me that I don't see him every day unless it is in publick places'. Grisie's continuing childlessness is still a concern to her father, though Lady Greenknowe in her home near Mellerstain must have been foretelling an heir to the estate, as George Baillie writes, 'I wish the Lady Greenknows prognostick with respect to Gr: may hold tho I confess I don't much rely upon it which makes me the more eager to have R[achy] disposed of but not to throw her away and I fear the giving her to the person you have mentioned would be little better.'

Improvements to the facilities continue at Mellerstain in 1712, with a new kitchen being built, and a new coalhouse. The milk house [dairy] is improved by being floored, and a house of office [privy] is built. This was possibly for the use of servants and outdoor workers, costing only five shillings to construct. (There are numerous purchases throughout the accounts of chamber pots of various materials for use inside the house). Grisell's use of language is interesting here, as on adjacent lines she says 'biging the Collhouse' and 'building the House of office', using the Scots word for building immediately followed by the standard English one. The accounts also reveal that perhaps the servants or nearby tenants are not to be trusted, as very soon follow the purchases of a 'Collhouse Lock' and '3 locks to servants beds', these presumably being 'closs' [box] beds. Further developments are made in the garden, 'for inclosing the Nursary', hinting at Grisell's ambition that Mellerstain should become well wooded, with trees grown on the estate, and a lot of purchased trees are planted, including 'young Trees bought by John Hope which was a perfit cheat', £2:10s sterling seeming to Grisell an exorbitant amount though she doesn't grudge the 80 days labour for the upkeep of the [bowling] Green at £1:13s8d. (Gardener John Hope was soon to be dismissed, but for drinking, not extravagance.) Purchases for the house hint at the nature of foodstuffs being consumed, with 'a chocalet stick', 'tart pans', 'suger tongs' and 'pickle jars' revealing a varied and quite luxurious diet. An expensive item at £2 in 1713 is a 'Masken fatt' [brewing vat] with another six shillings for 'a tub to draw the wort in', so Mellerstain's own brewery will soon be up and running. Diversions are also high on the list of priorities, with '2 duson bowls for the Green & 2 jacks' costing a huge £4:6s, and a 'Mavis cage' for a song thrush probably unappreciative of its luxury housing, £1:10s. Economies are made, though, when '14 porangers [porridge bowls], plates, jelly Glases etc' are bought 'at a rouping [auction]' for only 11s7½d.

A letter from Grisie at Mellerstain to Alexander Murray in London in March 1713 reveals that Murray's jealous accusations are continuing. 'I'm gri[e]ved to the heart for the groundless vexation you continue to give yourself & that there seems to be no end of it; all I can answer to it is that I have endeavourd to the outmost of my pour [power] to please you. what condisentions have I not made to make you easie but it seems all to no purpose however I hope nothing I can meet with shall be able to make me come short of that duty I owe you.' At some stage George Baillie must have been informed of the true state of relations between his daughter and her husband, and we learn from a letter he writes at the end of June to Grisell that Murray seems resolved that he and Grisie should live together in Edinburgh rather than under her parents' roof at Mellerstain. 'By no means must she decline living at Ed'r if he is bent upon it and who knows what being in a family of his own may work it may be attended by good consequences; however she shall have done her duty by making the trial and if it does not succeed we must think what is to be next done.'

We have already seen that Grisell is in the forefront of fashion in interior decoration with the purchase of expensive mirrors, and in 1713 she buys five pieces [rolls] of 'vernisht paper' and four pieces of 'stamped paper', wallpaper still being a relative novelty. It must have been deemed a good thing as 25 more pieces are bought the following year. The summer of 1713 also sees an extensive round of visiting. Friends and relations did not expect payment for entertaining visitors as they could hope for reciprocal hospitality, but it was expected that servants would be tipped generously at every port of call. From the 'drink money' [tips] left by Grisell, we can see that she visited Makerstoun, Kimmerghame [her brother Andrew's house], Stichill, Rutherford and Redbraes, before going on to Broughton in Tweeddale, seat of the Murrays, then continuing west to Jerviswood. It is reported that Grisie paid for half of the journey to Broughton and Jerviswood.

It may be during this visit to Broughton that a last attempt was made to reconcile Grisie and her husband, but as nothing had changed in his behaviour, a process of separation was initiated in December 1713 in Edinburgh. The documents for this process, which are numerous as Murray kept submitting lengthy written arguments, are still in existence, and include a letter that he wrote to George Baillie on 'Tuesday past 11 in the morning 1713', which begins 'Let me beg you Dr [Dear] Sr [Sir] that you would show this for sometime to none whatsoever'. It is a long, rambling, rather incoherent letter in which he displays what might now be termed paranoid delusions. He accuses Grisie of making 'secret signs and Gestures altogether unnatural…and answered by the persons following-by the Old Lady Greenknow, and the Laird of Greenknow, Torwoodly, Collonel Stewart, Mr William Hall, My Lady Hall, My Lady Coldingknows, not to mention others out of notions of Justice that I have'. The secret gestures he accuses all these acquaintances of include picking their teeth with a pin, 'putting their thumb or first finger on the table or holding it out in some unnatural posture often scratching their face or Neck, Resting their elbow on their own hand or scratching it – And many such like Carriadges which must appear rediculous to those who are unacquaint with such like practises and will be best believed and understood when seen'. Having concluded the letter, he begins to write again repeating the accusations, saying that it is 'to my Lord Polwarth [Grisell's brother Alexander] and Greenknows family that I lay all the blame. The Gestures I have mentioned confirm me in this belief and Collonell Stewart as I imagine has gote them from

Lewis Pringle who Was much and a great manager in Christy Wauchop's marriage, this I say only on suspicion but sure I am Collonell Stewart did nothing but sign all the time he was here.'

George Baillie, taking no notice of the entreaty not to show the letter to anyone, added it to the pile of Alexander Murray's writings already resting with the Commissary Court of Edinburgh. Unsurprisingly, the Court, having assessed the evidence, granted the separation, with aliment of £150 per annum, on 5 March 1714, ending three and a half years of emotional turmoil and uncertainty for Grisie and her parents. Although her personal safety is now assured, Grisie is in a very strange situation, shared by very few women at the time. She is still Alexander Murray's wife, as this is a separation, not a divorce, so no re-marriage is possible, and the Scots law of 'jus mariti' decreed that on marriage a woman and her moveable goods other than her clothes and jewellery became the property of her husband, and the separation did not revoke this. Many of the wider circle of the Baillies' acquaintances probably thought their applying for the process of separation was reprehensible; after all, many women were living in unhappy marriages as they had not chosen their marriage partner themselves, but just put up with it as there seemed no alternative.

Alexander Murray's letter quoted above was useful in providing evidence to the court of the state of his mind, but additionally gives clues about Grisell's close social circle in the Borders when Murray names the supposed perpetrators of the secret gestures. 'Greenknow' is George Pringle, laird of Greenknowe near Gordon and brother of the Lewis Pringle mentioned, and 'Old Lady Greenknow' is their mother Sophia, née Pringle. 'Torwoodly' is James Pringle, laird of Torwoodlee who had married Isobell Hall of Dunglass. Grisell's sister Annie had married Sir James Hall of Dunglass a year before her death, so there is a family connection there, and additionally James

Pringle, like Grisell's brother Patrick, had been imprisoned as a hostage for his father in the 1680s and for similar reasons, so there is also a longstanding religious and political connection with their Borders neighbours.

Despite the difficulties that must have been caused by the decision to petition for a separation, life had carried on as normal in 1713-14 at Mellerstain. Yet more repairs to the tower had been carried out, and more steps taken towards self-sufficiency in food, as there is mention of feeding for swine, fowls and pigeons, the purchase of a milk cow, and money laid out for carrying a bee skep [straw beehive]. Although coffee houses had been a feature of life in towns and cities for half a century, domestic coffee drinking was a more recent fashion. Fifty ounces of old silver plate was given to 'Mckinzie Gold Smith' [Colin McKenzie of Edinburgh] who was paid £6:8s3d for 'workmanship of the Silver Coffie pot and Milk pot'. Happily, both these items, which are engraved with the arms of Baillie of Jerviswood and Mellerstain, survive and are on display in the National Museum of Scotland. The coffee pot is the earliest known example of a Scottish silver coffee pot.

The account books show another round of visiting and paying drink money to servants in 1714 after the separation had been granted, and George Baillie sees a need to arm himself and his household. There are bills for powder and ball and for cleaning pistols, probably carried by him as a precaution on every journey, and the purchase of a gun and 30 swords, followed a little later by 29 guns and bagginets [bayonets], the latter obviously not for George Baillie's personal use. It may be that the buying of arms was precipitated by the death of Queen Anne on the first of August 1714. Anne's health had never been good; she suffered from gout and dropsy, and 17 pregnancies took their toll, but the only surviving child, William, Duke of Gloucester, had died in 1700 aged 11. The Act of Settlement of 1701 had established that if there were no Protestant heir to the throne descending from King William or Queen Anne, the crown of England and Ireland would go to Sophia, Electress of Hanover, a granddaughter of James VI and I. There were a number of other possible claimants to the throne, all Catholic, and it was feared that Anne's death might prompt supporters of the descendants of the deposed King James VII (Jacobites) to rise up to prevent the Hanoverian succession. The majority of Jacobites were Scots; perhaps in the autumn of 1714 George Baillie feared for his family's safety if they were alone at Mellerstain while he was in London, maybe he was tired of living apart from them for half the year, perhaps it was on account of Grisie's separation, or maybe because in October he had been rewarded for supporting the Hanoverian succession by being appointed a Lord of the Admiralty; for whatever reason, it was decided to move the household from Mellerstain to London. Sophia, Electress of Hanover, Queen Anne's designated heir, had predeceased Anne by a few weeks, so the succession passed to Sophia's son George, who reached Britain on 18 September 1714. George Baillie is keen to show his allegiance to the new Hanoverian monarch but writing to Grisell three days after the king's arrival tells of several disappointments: 'The K[ing] came to St James's yesterday. The Cavalcade was so late before it got the length of where I was to see it near the Court that I could not possibly see His Majestie so as to know him from another. This day I waited more than three hours at Court with a design to have kissed the K: and prince their hands but the Crowd was so great that I could not possibly find ane opportunity for it.' The coronation of George I took place at Westminster on 20 October.

Even leaving Mellerstain mostly furnished, moving a household to London, some 350 miles distant, was no mean feat in 1714. Five places were booked on the stage coach from

Edinburgh, presumably for Grisell, Grisie and Rachy, May Menzies and 'little Rob. Pringle', being conveyed as a favour to his father in London. George Baillie is insistent that a male servant should ride alongside, 'for I will not permitt you to travell alone'. Each seat in the coach cost £4:10s, the booking fee was 2s 6d, and only 20 pounds weight of luggage per person was allowed, resulting in an excess baggage charge of £2:7s. Food eaten en route cost £10. Two servants, long-serving Tam Youll the coachman and Katie Hearts, a laundry maid, travelled by sea much more cheaply, for £1 each, inclusive of food. 'Fraught of Goods from Berwick in three ships' was £3:8s, and carts to get the goods from the ships to the lodgings another £1:9s1d. After seven years of lengthy separations from George Baillie, made even more difficult by Grisie's disastrous marriage, Grisell and her daughters could enjoy the prospect of living under the same roof with the head of the family.

Chapter 6

_∂θℓ_

LIFE IN LONDON

_1715–1719_

Grisell had worked hard over the previous seven years to make Mellerstain a modern working estate, despite the antiquity of the tower house at its heart. The exterior of the house had been endlessly repaired, the interior refurnished, new kitchens and bath house built, surrounding land enclosed to become a park with extensive tree planting, farm buildings constructed and gardens laid out for pleasure as well as food production. Now, in November 1714, Mellerstain is to be left in the care of a skeleton staff of servants for much of the year. To judge by Grisell's accounts, the family does not visit Scotland again until August 1717, returning to London in January 1718.

Once in London, there is much for Grisell to do. At first, lodgings are taken in a house belonging to 'Mr. Broun', at £14 a month. This high rent probably meant that this was a furnished house, further evidence of this being that towards the end of June when final accounts are being settled with Mr. Broun, 10s 2d is paid 'To Mr Broun for spoyling his furnitur', though the damage can't have been too great at that price. Mr. Broun's 'furnitur' does not appear to have included tableware and kitchenware as large amounts of each are purchased by Grisell.

London society immediately offered plenty of diversions and educational opportunities. Firstly 'Mistres Taucour' and then 'Mr Dumbar' are engaged to teach French, and Rachy also has dancing lessons from 'Mr Isack' whose 'violer', 'Monsieur La fever' requires to be paid additionally, as does a harper who sometimes plays instead. (Notation for a number of dances invented by Mr. Isaac to celebrate Queen Anne's birthdays is still in existence.) Tickets to a play are quite frequently bought, which had not been a possibility in Scotland, where the Kirk and the magistrates frowned on all attempts at theatrical productions. One expensive item in Grisell's accounts is 'a watch and gold chean to Rachie from Massie', (probably Henry or Jacob Massy, renowned Huguenot clock makers), a very substantial gift at £27; perhaps precise time-keeping was felt to be more necessary in London than in Scotland. One expense that didn't feature at all while the family was resident in Scotland was losses to gambling. Lady Murray tells us a story of her father's, when he was going into exile after the execution of his father Robert Baillie: 'When in the ship going to Holland, with others in the same circumstances as himself, who had all they had to subsist on in their pockets, without any prospect where they could get more, some proposed playing dice to divert themselves. He had the luck to strip the whole company, which left them in a most destitute condition; He returned every man his money, with his advice, not again to risk their all; and this occasioned his making such reflections on the frailty of human nature, and the bewitchingness of play, as made him resolve against it, and hate it in all shapes, ever after throughout his whole life.' Despite his personal convictions, George Baillie must not have put any restrictions on his wife's gambling, as Grisell variously reports losses at cards, at dice, and in wagers, the first mention of which is five shillings lost playing cards at the Duchess of Montrose's in January 1715. Lady Murray also says, 'When we first came to London, and were of an age to relish diversions, such as balls, masquerades, parties by water, music and such like, my mother and he were always in all our parties; neither choosing to deprive us of them, nor let us go alone.'

At the end of April 1715, 18s 6d is paid 'to Chair men for removeing our goods to the new house', the carriers of sedan chairs apparently having a sideline in furniture removal. This house was in Broad Street (now Broadwick Street, Soho), conveniently close to the Navy Pay Office for George Baillie. The house belonged to a Mrs. Smith, and part of the deal seemed to be that the Baillies should repair the house, as there are sums for mending the roof, painting the house, glazing the windows and putting up shelves, but the rent is a fairly modest £44 a year. In May 1715, five beds, 12 pairs of blankets and other bedding arrive by sea, presumably from Mellerstain. Furnishing a house more or less from scratch was, however, very expensive, as the total spent on furnishings in 1715 was £559 (and fourpence-halfpenny). It must be noted that Grisell is buying from the very best makers. A number of items are purchased from 'Mr Turin', probably William Turing, and over 20 chairs, 10 stools and other items of furniture are 'made by Moor', now known as 'James Moore the Elder', who was appointed royal cabinetmaker to the recently crowned George I. A set of 12 each of knives, forks and spoons are 'all made by Platel', the renowned Huguenot silversmith Pierre Platel. Mirrors were still a luxury item, but the quantity bought is remarkable. There are '2 dressing Glasses for my self and Grisie with drawers' and 'a dressing glass to May and Rachel', suggesting that Rachy shares a bedroom with May Menzies. There are no fewer than 10 other mirrors, the most expensive at £13, including five 'chimny glasses' [overmantel mirrors] and a bookcase with looking glass doors at £7:18s, and even the female servants benefit from 'a glass to the wemens room' costing two shillings.

Providing a mirror in the female servants' room might have been designed to keep them happy, but it seems that Grisell did not succeed. May Menzies, Tam Youll the coachman, Katie Hearts the laundrymaid and James Grieve the butler who had all been servants at Mellerstain, stayed to earn their entire year's wages, but servants hired in London were a different matter. In addition to the servants named above, Grisell saw the need for a cook, a housemaid, a chambermaid and a footman to staff her household, and in filling these four roles in the course of 1715 no fewer than 15 women and four men came and went, some remaining for only a day. Grisell's exacting housekeeping standards were obviously too much for many servants to cope with. The wages she was offering seem by the standards of the day to have been fair, and included the usual 'perks' of two pairs of shoes per year for maidservants and outer clothing for menservants; living conditions were probably above average in terms of cleanliness and amenities, and food would be adequate if unexciting, but something about Grisell's management of her household was obviously not to the liking of Londoners. Even increasing familiarity with the ways of London servants doesn't seem to have improved things rapidly, as 1717 still sees a high turnover of cooks, though one did manage to remain as long as seven months. A rapid succession of servants had other drawbacks in that some might have come from households not so rigorously clean as Grisell's, bringing vermin such as bedbugs with them, as £2:19s6d had to be spent 'changing servants beds for bugs'.

From Grisell's point of view, if she was paying out good money in addition to food, lodging and items of clothing, she expected good service for it. There were no idle moments for the female servants, who, if their allotted tasks were finished, were to spin until 9 o'clock at night, at least in Scotland, though it seems unlikely that London servants were required to spin. Flax was grown at Mellerstain, harvested and processed by local labour, then spun by local women or the household servants. The resulting yarn was woven, locally or at Earlston, into cloth of varying qualities from the coarse 'hagabag' [huckaback] for towels to fine damask for tablecloths. In later years, Grisell would employ a housekeeper whose job would include management of servants, but at this time she is her own housekeeper. She seems to view servants as inherently dishonest, as all foodstuffs are to be weighed, every item of cutlery or napery counted; she has no hesitation in calling in the constables if any thieving is suspected, as was the case with two of the female servants during the first year in London. Grisell had passed on the news, in a letter to her father in December 1709, that 'Mr Johnstone [George Baillie's uncle Secretary Johnston] has a Butler run away from him with a good dale of monie & goods', so maybe her suspicions were well founded. Carelessness which caused damage, particularly if resulting from drunkenness, was likely to incur a fine, a substantial reduction in the cash wage that the servant received, and the coachman Tam Youll was sanctioned in this way, not for the first or last time. The appearance of the family's male servants seems to have taken on new importance with the move to London, with purchases of 'a sute Liveras to James Grive' at £4:10s, and coats, hats, livery suits and stockings bought for other servants. James Grieve also received 'a big Blew coat' as did Tam Youll, and it was probably he and the other coachman mentioned, 'Nicolles' who looked fine in the 'gold lace to two hats' costing 17s2d.

The housekeeping accounts demonstrate some changes in diet after the move from Mellerstain to London. At Mellerstain in 1714 there is mention of large quantities of oats to be turned into oatmeal for human consumption as well as oats for fowls, horses and swine; oatmeal seems strangely absent from the London housekeeping until 1717, when we see £8 'For 16 bolls oats at 10s made in Meall and sent to London in 1715,16 and 1717', so it seems the supply of this essential staple had been uninterrupted. Perhaps London servants are deserting their posts because they are being fed on what Samuel Johnson famously described in 1755 in *A Dictionary of the English Language* as 'a grain which in England is generally given to horses, but in Scotland supports the people'. Bread is bought from a baker named 'Arther Grumball', and beef, mutton and ham are on Grisell's family menu, as is venison: 'To wonsor [Windsor] park keeper for 2 bucks of the Kings venison £2:3s'. Life in London requires much more frequent purchases of tea and sugar, but indigo and starch for laundry, and pearl barley and shelled peas for broth are still sent by sea from Scotland. In general, the cost of bought-in goods may, surprisingly, have been cheaper in London than in impoverished Scotland, as reported by tax official Francis Philipson in July 1708, recently having moved from London to Edinburgh: 'But things are dearer than I thought of or could imagine nay dearer than London particularly Lodging and Provisions'.

Another outlay which becomes frequent after the move to London is that for newspapers, sometimes referred to by Grisell as 'news prints' or just 'the prints'. As well as the official *London Gazette*, London had an abundance of small independent newspapers, most published weekly or twice weekly at most. As well as copying unashamedly from the *London Gazette*, often called 'the public prints', some papers apparently had correspondents in far-flung places, including Edinburgh, who sent letters reporting the news from those areas, though readers were aware that they were reading 'news' that was up to a week old because of the slowness of communication. From late summer 1715 newspapers are bought very often by Grisell; the Earl of Mar had raised the standard of 'James VIII and III' at Braemar on 6 September, initiating the challenge to the house of Hanover that many had feared, and George Baillie and Grisell would have been desperate to know what was happening in Scotland. Not only were they committed Hanoverians, but they had personal acquaintance with people on both sides of the divide. On the Jacobite side, Lady Mar was a particular friend of Grisie, and Grisie's estranged husband Alexander Murray had taken up arms for the Stuart cause, probably to Grisie's further embarrassment. George Baillie's long-term friend and political ally Thomas, the 6th Earl of Haddington had joined the campaign for the Government, which was led by John Campbell, 2nd Duke of Argyll, as had Haddington's son, Charles, Lord Binning. Although Mar remained with his troops in the Scottish Highlands, the newspaper *Weekly Packet* for 22-29 October gave disturbing details about another section of the Jacobite army's march southwards into the Scottish Borders. 'They write from Berwick the 24th [October] that the Rebels remain at Kelso where they melt down all the Pewter Dishes to make Bullets of'.* Although a private letter may have already relayed the information to George Baillie and Grisell, the *Flying Post or Post Master* of 5-8 November carried worse news about the actions of the rebel army: 'Before they went from Kelso, they plunder'd the House of the Rt Hon George Baillie of Jerriswood, and broke open every thing that was lock'd. They did the like to Sir John Pringle's House at Stitchel'.* Replying as a Government official to a letter from a disgruntled fellow Scotsman who has suffered losses at the hands of the 'Rebells', George Baillie says 'I cannot I must own but be deeply affected with the desolation of that Country', but points out that a standing army of only 8,000 could not possibly defend the entire kingdom, and that the King wished 'to make the beginning of his Reign as little burdensome to his people as possible... I speak it without flattery never was there a prince that deserved the hearts of the people more than K: George.'

A week after Mellerstain was plundered, there were two battles on 13 November, in Scotland at Sheriffmuir near Dunblane and in England at Preston in Lancashire, where Government troops effectively laid siege to the Jacobite army causing their leader, the Northumbrian John Forster, to surrender. 1,468 Jacobite soldiers were captured, including Grisie's husband Alexander Murray. The battle at Sheriffmuir was inconclusive, with both sides claiming victory. Grisell's brother-in-law James Sandilands, Lord Torphichen, husband of her youngest sister Jean, was very satisfied with his own contribution to the battle: 'General William...was soe sensible of the service I had done that when wee marched off with our artillery and ammunition he did me the honour to order me with my Squadron to forme the rear guard tho my squadron was the youngest in the field'. George Baillie and Grisell would have been happy to hear, in a report by the Provost of Edinburgh, that other friends and acquaintances were also unscathed. 'No more of our great men are hurt, the Dukes of Roxburgh and Douglass, Rothes, Haddingtoun, Lauderdale and Belhaven I left standing on the field with my Lo: Duke of Argyle very saife and well'. (Despite the Provost's assertions, the Earl of Haddington had had his horse shot from underneath him and was himself wounded in the shoulder.)

Though disagreeing with their politics, George Baillie showed great compassion towards the Jacobites who were imprisoned. Lady Murray writes: 'He publicly declared himself for mercy to the poor unhappy sufferers by the rebellion; and, amongst many arguments for it, in a long speech he made in Parliament, which he begun by saying he had been bred in the school of affliction, which had instructed him in both the reasonableness and necessity of showing mercy to others in like circumstances…His private behaviour was no less singular. His house was open to the wives, mothers, sisters and other relations and friends of the poor prisoners.' Grisell's accounts show payment of £5 'to the laird of Wedderburn when in Prison', and payments to other members of the extended Hume family. Writing to her brother Andrew on 15 December 1715, Grisell says 'We have heard nothing from Murray which I'm glad of. Our Merse folks & he with many others is over in Sutherick [Southwark] in the Marshalsie [Marshalsea Prison]. I intend to enquire after poor Wetherburn for I'm afraid he be in great straits. I hope their friends will inquire after them & not let them want necessisars [necessaries]. My heart bleeds for them.'

Away from the scenes of conflict and the political arena, life for Grisell and her daughters carried on as usual. Grisell's losses at cards in December 1715, amounting to a not inconsiderable £1:8s, give clues about her social circle in London. The losses were incurred while she was being entertained by 'Dutches Montrose' (Christian Carnegie, wife of James Graham 1st Duke of Montrose), 'Lady Lowden' (Margaret Dalrymple, daughter of the 1st Earl of Stair and wife of Hugh, 3rd Earl of Loudon), 'Lady Marr' (Frances Pierrepont, daughter of the Duke of Kingston, wife of John Erskine, Earl of Mar), and at 'Duplins', (the home of Abigail, daughter of Robert Harley Earl of Oxford and wife of George Hay, Viscount Dupplin).

While his wife played cards in London, the Earl of Mar, though still considering himself victorious at Sheriffmuir, had received news of the defeat of the Jacobites at Preston and saw his Highland army dwindling as the troops returned to their homes. He had had a successful career for many years as a Court politician, but when it appeared there would be no place for him in George I's new Whig administration in 1714, he had diverted his energies to the Jacobite cause, so being perceived as a turncoat and earning himself the nickname 'Bobbing John'. He had begun raising an army in the summer of 1715, though the Stuart court in exile in France had not asked him to do so. Just the previous summer Mar had re-married, choosing Lady Frances Pierrepont for his bride, who brought with her a huge marriage portion of £8,000. Lady Mar had borne her husband a daughter on 9 August 1715, and the very next day he left London for Scotland. Mar met with James III, the 'Old Pretender', on his arrival in Scotland in December, after Sheriffmuir, but it soon became apparent the cause was lost and by 4 February 1716 Mar was persuading James III to write a letter of farewell to the Scots. Both men fled into exile on the continent the next day and shortly afterwards Mar was attainted for treason, and his earldom forfeited.

The period November-February 1715-16 when the fate of the Jacobites was decided was a very cold one, with a frost fair being set up on the Thames on 24 November, remaining for three months. Grisell must have visited the fair at least once, buying bellows, a brush and 'a brun vernisht tee brood [brown varnished tea tray] on the yce on Tems'. Although London had been largely unaffected by the 1715 rising, expatriate Scots there no doubt felt some relief that the threat of unrest seemed finally to be removed, and that they could look forward to a period of political stability under George I. Scotland must have seemed half a world away, though estate business still had to be carried on by factors, and Grisell sent 300 lime trees and 90 fruit trees to Mellerstain to continue the garden improvements. Meanwhile, London social life went on, with Rachy seeing several plays and operas, and the spinet being tuned, presumably for Grisie's benefit. It was natural that at this time Grisie and Lady Mar should develop a firm friendship, as both were in the unusual situation of being married, but estranged from their husbands. Still quite young at 22 and 25 respectively, they could not attend social functions either as wives, widows or marriageable single women; in a letter to her brother Andrew, Grisell suggests that Grisie is suffering from public censure, having received a letter from Murray. 'I would not speak of it, for it can do no good except people should blame her for not owning him more at this time.' Murray is still imprisoned in the Marshalsea, and his fate uncertain. Grisell continues, 'If he come off [gets let off] at all it must be upon his madness'. Grisie and Lady Mar probably remained cloistered in the houses of their close friends and family, who included Lady Mar's sister, Lady Mary Wortley Montagu, but Lady Mary left England in April 1716 to accompany her husband Edward Wortley Montagu when he was appointed ambassador to the Turkish court, leaving Lady Mar and her baby daughter even more isolated.

Grisell's brother Alexander [Sandy] was appointed ambassador to Denmark in 1716. By this time he had a family of three sons and four daughters, and it seems that he did not think his wife, Margaret Campbell of Cessnock, capable of overseeing the education of his sons, entrusting that instead to Grisell, adding George, 12, and twins Hugh and Alexander aged 8 to her burden of responsibility. Lady Murray wrote: 'She had the whole management of his affairs all the time he [Alexander, Lord Polwarth] was at Copenhagen and Cambray; the care of the education of his children; his eldest son she sent abroad, and with trouble and difficulty procured Mr Maclaurin, who was then Professor of Mathematics at Aberdeen, to go along with him as his tutor; she brought the other two sons from Scotland, and placed them at a school in London; where she had, even to the smallest necessaries in clothes to provide for them, till it was fit to send them to Holland; she provided a tutor for them, answered their bills, and I will not say how much trouble and anxiety they cost her, since she did everything for her father's family, with the same zeal and affection she could do for her own.' Grisell mentions the eldest in a letter of April 1721 to her brother Andrew. 'I'm just going with Docter Arburthnet [Arbuthnot] to my nephew George he fell ill yesterday but say nother [nothing] to his mother [Margaret Campbell, Lady Polwarth]'. She appears also to be supervising the education of Andrew's own son Patrick at Eton. 'I have Pate [Patrick] still with me here because I thought so long as the cold rainie wather lasted Eiton being a moyst place it might put him in his ague he scarse ever pairts with me where I go he gos.'

While neither Grisie nor Lady Mar is in a position to seek a marriage partner, Rachy, now aged 20, is certainly marriageable, and even as early as 1711 when her sister Grisie had not become pregnant after eight months of marriage, George Baillie had said, 'It makes me a little anxious to have Rachy disposed of sooner than I would have thought of it'. Grisell is keen to put approved suitors in Rachy's way, though it seems she is allowed to have preferences, as Grisell writes in a letter in March 1717 to her brother Sandy: 'I forgote if I wrote you that Mr Elliot [possibly Gilbert Elliot] was come up again to renew his sute to Rachi pray let me know your opinion of the match tho I'm afraid she will not hear of it she seems to have a dislike of him I would fain have her well married, tell me how you would like John Muntgumery if such a thing should be proposed'. Having signed off the letter, she continues it again the following day, having in the interim had a conversation with Thomas, 6th Earl of Haddington, which has shocked her. 'I wish I could remember all he said it surprised me so that I lost the half of it'. It seems Lord Binning, Haddington's son, was in love with 'Mrs Earnly', whose father [possibly Sir Edward Ernle] was deemed unlikely to provide any cash for a marriage settlement, and Haddington is convinced that his son is 'twise as much taken up with Rachy as with her [Earnly] & keeps a close correspondance with her [Rachy]'. Haddington must have got wind of Grisell's desire to get Rachy married off soon and, says Grisell, 'beged of me for God sake not to be hasty in disposeing of her for that she wo'd keep'. Charles, Lord Binning, referred to in the letter as 'Binny', is 19, and a year younger than Rachy, 'but that is nothing', says Grisell, obviously keen to pursue this advantageous match. Lord Binning appears to be currently in Holland, as Grisell's accounts in January, just a few weeks before the interview with Haddington include 10 shillings 'For covers of Fans sent to Utright [Utrecht] to Lord Binning'. He is still in Holland in July as Grisell pays customs duty on 57 pounds of ham 'sent from Holland by my Lord Binning', but Binning writes, also in July to 'Dear Rachie' from Paris, excusing himself for not having replied sooner to her letter, 'but my excuse isn't proper to give one that people are in cerimony with. If anybody knows the effects of the Seine water they can tell you, in short I had the Reverse of a belly in perfect order.'

With sister Rachy embroiled in courtship, music continued to be Grisie's consuming passion, with January 1717 seeing 12 shillings spent on ruled [manuscript] paper and 2s 6d on 'a Desk to Grisies spinet'. As well as being a welcome distraction, the opera was also a place to be seen, and to meet people on neutral ground where no invitation was needed. The Queen's Theatre, Haymarket had opened in London in 1705, and the arrival of George Frederick Handel for the 1710-11 season sealed opera as London society's favourite entertainment. The Haymarket theatre had been patronised by Queen Anne, then after her death it was renamed the King's Theatre, and King George I frequently attended operas there, commanded performances and paid leading performers 20 guineas at their benefit nights. The opera company was to collapse in the Summer of 1717, but Grisell's accounts suggest personal connections with some of the performers. 'Mr Barnackie' [Antonio Bernacchi, a castrato singer] had sent his footman with a present, 'sinorina the Dog', for which the footman received a tip of five shillings. This gift was reciprocated in July by Grisell buying Bernacchi a gold watch and chain totalling almost 30 pounds, so he was obviously held in very high esteem. 'Mrs Robison' [Anastasia Robinson, a celebrated soprano] had to be reimbursed for some opera tickets she had supplied, and tickets were bought for 'Castruches Musick meeting', Pietro Castrucci being a virtuoso violinist and leader of Handel's opera orchestra. In May, four tickets for 'Mr Barnackies opera' and two tickets for 'Berenstats opera' are bought. Handel had had great success in 1711 with his opera *Rinaldo*, the first opera written in Italian for the London stage, and it was revived several times up to 1717 when the previously bass role was re-written to suit the voice of Gaetano Berenstadt, an alto castrato, so on this occasion, though Grisell doesn't name it, we can be confident that it was *Rinaldo* she went to see. As well as opera, King George also enjoyed 'water parties', when the royal barge would be accompanied on the Thames by another barge carrying an orchestra, and Grisell and her daughters perhaps attended such an event as a tip of 7s 6d is paid in April 'To the Kings watermen'. Handel's now familiar *Water Music* was first performed on 17 July 1717, but the accounts give no hint that Grisell or her daughters were present, perhaps with good reason, as plans were afoot for Rachy's marriage.

The Earl of Haddington's plea in March that Rachy should not be 'disposed of' until Lord Binning had been considered as a husband had paid off, and the wedding was fixed for August. Grisie's disastrous marriage was an ever-present shadow on the family in both emotional and practical terms, but George Baillie and Grisell would have been certain that a match between Lord Binning and Rachy held no similar dangers, as Lord Haddington was a long-standing friend and fellow member of the Squadrone, so Lord Binning had been known to the family all his life. It was natural that the marriage should take place in

Scotland; accordingly, £32:15s is laid out 'For a coach and six horses to carie us to Scotland in 9 days', with a further £14:13s9d 'For expenses of 5 in the coach on the road to Scotland till we came to Tiningham on the 14th Aug'. The fifth person in the coach is presumably May Menzies, who had already been given 10 pounds to buy a gown for the occasion. Once in Scotland, there were legal matters to be attended to, before the marriage ceremony took place in Edinburgh, though it is recorded in the registers of Earlston, it being the bride's parish. '24 Aug 1717 Charles Lord Binning and mrs Rachel Bayly younger daughter to the honbl the Laird of Jerreswood'. Grisell's clothing account shows the purchase of '25 yeards silver stuff for goun and coat' for Rachy's wedding outfit, as well as the usual favours, bride's garter and a garland to break over the bride's head, and £2:10s is spent 'For a Cotten Satine Night goun to Lord Binning'. Guests were regaled with 'Confections Plumcaks and Bisket from Mrs Fenton at my Rachys mariage' costing £15:3s. The *Weekly Journal or Saturday's Post* of 14 September 1717 reported, 'Last Sunday the Duke of Montrose came here [Edinburgh] from the West to be present at the Wedding betwixt the L. Binning, eldest Son to the Earl of Haddington, and Mrs Bailie, Daughter to one of the Lords of the Treasury, which was celebrated last Night with an Entertainment and Ball, and a great deal of the best Company in this Kingdom.'*

In among the expenses occasioned by Rachy's marriage is a total of £52 'To Mr Aickman in pairt for picturs' and 'In full payd for the picturs at 5 guinys sitting and 5£ coppys'. Although Grisell does not name the sitter or sitters in the portraits it is likely that she needed to translate her pride at Rachy's marriage to a future earl into something tangible and permanent by commissioning from William Aikman the portrait of Rachy which still hangs close to a portrait of Lord Binning (Plate 14) at Mellerstain. The convention of showing women in portraits at this time wearing a simply styled very low-cut gown and no jewellery probably belies the way they normally dressed. Grisell buys rings and makes presents of earrings and necklaces, and there are many purchases of aprons, not seen in portraits at this date, and gloves bought by the dozen, suggesting that gloves were worn at all times and all seasons when people were out of their own domestic setting. Grisell's 'Account of my own Cloathes' for 1719 includes 51 pairs of gloves. George Baillie's clothing account for that year includes one new suit, very many shirts, 20 pairs of gloves and the surprising item of two shillings spent on 'a Leek on St Davids day'. (The 'sundries' accounts on several occasions mark Scotland's national saint's day with the purchase of 'St Andrews crosses', though it is uncertain what form these took).

Having made the expensive and difficult journey to Scotland for Rachy's marriage, Grisell took the opportunity to remain in Edinburgh for some time, to travel around and visit friends and relations in Scotland, paying out £29:10s in tips to other people's servants, in addition to the £15 she had given in 'drinkmoney' at Tyninghame 'when My Rachy went home'. Mellerstain and Jerviswood business for 1715, 1716 and 1717 has to be settled, it seeming not to matter if payments were three years late, and bills for the continued improvements of Mellerstain parkland to be paid, together with the cost of the inevitable repairs to Mellerstain Tower. George Baillie had not lingered long in Scotland after Rachy's marriage, having important Government business to attend to, though writing to Sir Patrick in October 1717 he says, 'I had been so ill that I had no heart to write but where it was absolutely necessary', and imparts the news that 'I have this minute a letter from Hanover acquainting me that…a peace between Sweden and Denmark is agreed much to the honour of my Ld Polwarth'. (Grisell's brother Sandy had been appointed envoy-extraordinary to the court of Copenhagen in

1716). In November, again writing to his father-in-law, George
Baillie gives a first-hand account of the extraordinary story of
the disagreement between King George and his son the Prince
of Wales about who should stand Godparents to the Prince's son,
which culminated in the Prince calling the Duke of Newcastle
a rascal and apparently offering to fight him. Baillie says that
the King has given 'orders to the prince to keep his apartment
till his fathers pleasure' and ends, 'I pray God this affare may
have a happy issue'. Life at court was apparently never dull on
account of this animosity between the King and the Prince of
Wales, who effectively had two separate courts, more or less
frequented by two separate sets of courtiers. George Baillie had
to make a hasty trip back to Scotland in December when his
younger brother died at the age of 42. Grisell noted £11:16s6d
'For charges of my brother John Baillies Funarals'. Grisell and
four others she does not name set off in the stage coach on 11
January 1718, probably from Berwick, reaching London again
on the 25th.

Grisell had become accustomed in her childhood to
separation from parents or siblings and, since her marriage, to
being parted from her husband. Grisie and Alexander Murray
had lived for the most part under George Baillie's roof during
their short periods of cohabitation, so there had been no lengthy
time of being apart from her elder daughter, but it must have
been a wrench to travel back to London, leaving Rachy behind
at Tyninghame. Grisie too, had always had the companionship
of her sister, companionship especially valuable since Grisie's
legal separation had led to her undefined place in society. In
1718 Lord Binning had been appointed to the rather nebulous
post of Knight Marischal of Scotland, which brought with it the
useful salary of £400, providing Rachy and her husband with an
independent source of income, and means to support a family.
After a few months came the news from Tyninghame that

Rachy was expecting a child, so Grisell then had a new focus in her life, preparing all that was needed for her first grandchild. Under the heading 'My Rachys childs clothes', noted in August 1718 are various items such as 'litle wastcoats' and '4 p. litle threed Mittons', as well as 'For child Bed Linins and every thing she wanted £74:4s3d'.

Grisell travelled north again in March 1719, paying half the cost of a coach, to support her daughter during the birth of her child. Rachy was safely delivered of a daughter on 6 April. Taking no chances, the child was christened at Tyninghame the following day and named Grisell after her grandmother. Witnesses to the christening were 'Mr Thomas Lindesay sone to the Earl of Crawford and Colonell Hope Brother german to Sr Thomas Hope of C[r]aigehall', the witnesses' lineage appearing to the minister to be as important as that of the child. A month later, Rachy is recovered, and ready to travel to Polwarth to introduce her daughter to her great-grandfather Sir Patrick and other Hume relatives but, as Grisell writes to her father, there is a transport problem. 'If your Lop: [Lordship] could spair the coach and horses to bring us to the Merss & to make two or three visits here about it would be very convenient for us for Hadintoun is alwise using his, & Rachy being to go along with us the chariot will not serve us'. On the back of Grisell's letter, Sir Patrick wrote a short poem in Latin, which he seems to have expected to be read by posterity, as he helpfully supplies a translation, and a note on the parentage of the child.

> *Long may my Dear child ever as happy live*
> *As she of whom the happy name you give*
> *of virtue Patterne, and a Patroness*
> *til god her take to endless happyness*
> *Votum, my prayer to god, for Grisel Hamilton*

my great grandchild, Daughter of
Charls Lord Binny, & Rachel Baillie
his spouse & my grandchild by Grisell
Hume my eldest Daughter

(Sir Patrick's hopes for his first great-grandchild were fulfilled as she lived to the age of 92.)

Chapter 7

ϑℚℓ

TURBULENT YEARS

_1719–1724_

After visiting Polwarth and Mellerstain following the birth of her granddaughter, Grisell returned to London in July, this time paying the entire cost of the coach, £30. She needed to be on hand to supervise the household's removal from Broad Street to Marlborough Street, then being developed with fashionable new houses and already home to a number of earls. In 1717 George Baillie had become a Lord of the Treasury, so proximity to the Naval Pay Office in Broad Street was no longer necessary.

Grisell decided to immortalise her husband and elder daughter, (Plate 15) paying the artist Jonathan Richardson 12 guineas each for two portraits, and George Baillie is also painted by Sir Godfrey Kneller, who is dearer than Richardson at 15 guineas. Grisie, now aged 27, has her aliment, but is nevertheless reliant to a large extent on her parents. Music remains her chief occupation, and she is still receiving keyboard lessons, as Grisell pays 'St Dony [Pietro Guiseppe Sandoni] Grisies Playing Master' for four months' tuition, and buys 'The French spinits' for 11 guineas. She also buys Italian books for Grisie, possibly to help her to sing Italian arias more beautifully, or perhaps to understand the operas. There had been no operas performed in Italian in London since the collapse of the company in 1717, but in 1719 George I had pledged £1,000 a year to 'The Royal Academy of Musick' which had been formed with the intention of performing Italian operas, so Grisie has something to look forward to. The connection with Anastasia Robinson had been maintained, as Grisell buys 'A Fan to Mrs Robison the singer'. Musical expenses in 1720 include more lessons from Sandoni, more tuning of harpsichords and 'Binding Pastorfida', [*Il Pastor Fido*], a Handel opera first produced in 1712. Grisie is keeping company with her friend Lady Mary Howard, (Plate 16) unmarried daughter of the Earl of Carlisle, as the accounts record 'Lost a wager with Lady Mary Howard 10s 6d'. The writer John Gay wrote a poem in celebration of his friend Alexander Pope having finished his translation of Homer's *Iliad* where, along with mentions of her friends Lady Mary Wortley Montagu, Molly Lepell and Lady Mary Howard, Grisie is described as 'The sweet-tongued Murray' in reference to her beautiful singing.

Grisell, ever the careful housekeeper and family accountant who kept tabs on every last halfpenny of household expenditure, proved less cautious when it came to speculating in stocks and shares. In 1719 the South Sea Company was authorised by parliament to take on a larger portion of the national debt, having already assumed some of it in 1711, which was converted into South Sea Company shares. In January 1720, when the stock stood at £128, company directors began spreading rumours of great riches being made by South Sea trade, so that a month later the stock had risen to £175. The company applied in March, in opposition to a bid by the Bank of England, to take over yet more of the national debt to be converted into South Sea Company shares, and was successful. The Government's endorsement of the South Sea Company gave investors confidence and by the end of March the share price hit around £330. In the wake of this 'success', other equally nebulous investment opportunities had arisen until the whole of London was gripped by the infectious investment frenzy. The Bubble Act, legislation probably introduced by members of the South Sea Company jealous of the competition, was passed by parliament on 11 June, forbidding joint stock companies to trade without a royal charter. The South Sea Company received its charter, and its stock, already trading in May at £550, leapt to £1050 by the end of June.

The temptation of making some easy money for her family was too much for Grisell, even though she knew George Baillie disapproved. Writing to her brother Andrew on 19 June 1720, she says 'To this hour he [George Baillie] never was on chaing allay [Change Alley, where coffee houses functioned as a stock exchange] nor indeed is it fitt for on[e] in his post to be runing about after these things'. Bowing to Grisell's pressure, Baillie has applied for a subscription, though she admits, 'If Jerriswood gets any thing its not by his own management but in a manner against his will, for he never had a good opinion of the stocks, & had I not tiesd [teased] him to death he had not had a sixpence in them'. Even after the death of her sister Annie, Grisell kept up a lifelong correspondence with Annie's husband Sir James Hall, as he managed various business affairs for the family, and in a letter of 29 July 1720 she is scolding him roundly, as she is anxious to keep part of her South Sea dealings secret from George Baillie, so had told James Hall to address his letters to Grisie or to her niece Rachel Dundas, which he has failed to do. 'Your last post derected one to Mr Baillie, good luck he had the tooth ack and I gote the letter to read'. Even more deceit is involved, as she then has to claim the letter has been torn up. 'Next morning he cald for the letter but it was tore, tho it be just now lying befor me you see what you have put me to, to ly and cheat'. Grisell was attempting to get subscriptions for her brothers and brother-in-law Lord Torphichen; it is not known whether she succeeded, but shortly after this letter was written, the shares plunged to £800 in August, and by the end of September were only £175, causing financial distress to many people, especially those who had borrowed money in order to buy the shares. In addition to detailing the depressing fall in South Sea stock, the newspapers in September carried alarming news from France, as the city of Marseille was being ravaged by plague, with up to 800 people dying on one particular day, and dead bodies littering the streets. Grisell had been born in the year of the Great Plague in London, and the memory of its horrors still gripped her father's generation, as well as stories of the devastating plague of Edinburgh in 1645. Plague in the Middle East was often reported in the newspapers, but France was a little too close for comfort. James Hall has asked about Grisell's preparations for the plague, but she replies, 'As for providing for the plague I can tell you nothing about it for we make non I hope we shall have no ocasion for it, a good dyet is the best preparation I know & a good life in case we be carried off by it.'

Brighter news came in October 1720, with the birth on the 23rd of a son and heir for Rachy and Lord Binning, Grisell noting a payment to 'Mrs Muntgumery midwife when Tamie was born'. 'Tam' or 'Tamie' was more formally named at his christening on 29 October, recorded in the registers of Whitekirk and Tyninghame parish: 'Thomas S.L. [son lawful] To Charles Lord Binning and Dam[e] Rachael Baillie; Witnesses The Duke of Montrose, Sr Andrew Home of Kimmerghame'. Lord Binning had decided around this time to try for election as an MP, which he could only do in England as his father was a peer in Scotland, so it made sense for Rachy and her family to join her parents' household in London. Even though the house is rented (from a 'Mrs Magget' [Meggott]), £350 is spent 'For the building ane adition to the House in Marlburg Streat' with an extra £15 to 'Mr Gibb for his pains', as the architect of the extension was none other than James Gibbs, who had just won a commission to build a new church at St. Martin in the Fields. The Meggott family owned three houses, original numbers 17, 18 and 19 Great Marlborough Street. When George Baillie and Grisell came there in 1719, the Westminster Rate Books show that number 15 Great Marlborough Street was occupied by Henry Howard, Lord Morpeth, brother of Grisie's friend Lady Mary Howard, and another friend of Grisie's, Molly Lepell (later Lady Hervey) was across the street at number 29, so there was plenty of close acquaintance among the neighbours. The rent for the house in Great Marlborough Street is £120 for the year 1721, in addition to which taxes had to be paid for highways, watchmen, 'scaffingers' [dustmen], water and window tax and £4:13s4d tax for the poor of the parish.

In 1721 Grisell has her extended family about her in Great Marlborough Street, with both her daughters, her son-in-law Lord Binning, a little granddaughter and a baby grandson, all happily together under George Baillie's roof. Rachy's husband, unlike her sister's, proved to be the perfect son-in-law, and was treated as if he were Grisell's own son. Lady Murray says, 'Her particular affection to him was equal, if it did not surpass, that to her own children.' A not insubstantial part of the household expenditure was that for coach and horses, so that the family could travel around in style and comfort, so what more suitable toy for her granddaughter than 'a little coach Grisie Hamilton 10s'. Her baby brother may have been the recipient of 'toys 10s' and 'more [toys]' 6s, but it is clear Grisell was enjoying indulging her grandchildren, noting a further purchase of 'toys for Tamie and Grisie £1:12s'. However, this idyllic family peace was to be shattered utterly in the early hours of Sunday, 15 October when Lord Binning's footman, a man called Arthur Gray, arrived home at 4 a.m. after a night's drinking with friends and burst into Grisie's room armed with a sword and pistol obviously with the intention of raping her. She kept him talking for a while until she saw an opportunity to disarm him and raise the alarm. Gray ran from the room and escaped from the house but was discovered in a farrier's house nearby and detained while a Justice of the Peace was sent for, and Gray was conveyed to Newgate Prison to await trial.

The occurrence soon became the talk of the neighbourhood, and first made the newspapers on the following day, with the *Daily Journal* of 16 October erroneously saying that Gray was 'a Footman of the Lord Bellingham's'.* The same mistake is made in *Applebee's Original Weekly Journal* for 21 October, but which carried a much fuller account, presumably communicated by a servant as it is inconceivable that a member of the family should have spoken to the newspapers. The account says 'That at Midnight he went to all the Doors and finding everything fast, and the Family asleep, he went to the Young Lady's Chamber and forc'd the Door open Armed with a Case of Pistols, and a drawn Sword; one of the Pistols he left at the Door, and approach'd the Bedside with the other in one Hand, and the Sword in the other. The Lady being awak'd or disturb'd by the Noise, sat up in her Bed, and ask'd him what he wanted that he came in such a Manner? He told her he must Lye with her, and made some advances towards it, but she reason'd with him and told him the Danger and Mischief of it, and kept him near half an Hour in parley; assuring him that if he would retire and desist from so horrid a Purpose, she would forgive him and keep it a Secret: But this would not satisfy him, for having laid the Sword down, he went to lay his Hand on her; upon which, finding her

Opportunity, she laid hold of that Hand which held the Pistol, and strugling with him threw him backward, got the Pistol from him, cry'd out, rung a bell and alarm'd the Family'.* Such detail can only have come from within the household, but the story was printed on the same day in *The Weekly Journal or Saturday's Post*, which described Gray more correctly as 'a Scotchman, Valet de Chambre to the Lord Binny, eldest son to Lord Haddington', and this time the victim was named as 'Mrs Murray, his Lady's sister'. The writing of this piece was sensationalist, even 'quoting' what was said both by Grisie and Gray, who is supposed to have declared, 'I know you to be a Lady of so much prudence, that you won't expose your Character to an ill-judging World, in prosecuting me'.*

For Grisie, the shock of the attack must have been difficult enough, but then to find herself named in all the newspapers would have been unbearable. The distress of the affair affected the whole family. Grisell, in a letter to Sir James Hall on 2 November 1721 is worried about the effects of the attack on both her daughters, blaming it for Rachy suffering a miscarriage: 'Poor Rachy never recoverd the fright till she miscarried which grived me nother Gris nor she is well'. There were eight long weeks between Gray's apprehension and his trial at the Old Bailey, when Grisie knew she must give evidence against him, but there were further embarrassments to be endured even before then. In a letter of 10 November, again to Sir James Hall, we learn that Gray has written what Grisell describes as a 'scurrelous letter' and that George Baillie, while undoubtedly concerned for his elder daughter, is also worried about the family's reputation as he has forbidden his wife to make any copies of Gray's letter 'for he [George Baillie] said he found the world so wicked that many that did not know us would believe it & he did not think it prudent to spred such scandal of our selves'. Far worse than the letter from 'that villain' Gray is a crudely humorous broadside ballad being sold in the streets, entitled 'Virtue in Danger', purportedly anonymous but, Grisell says, 'We are informed that Lady Mary Wortley has made the scurrelous bawdy verses that is handed about upon Grisie's storie which makes Lady Mary the worst of wretches for really she had no such stive [staunch] friends in London'. An attempted rape by a household servant might have seemed betrayal enough, but to have her distress increased by someone of her own class whom she had thought of as a close friend was devastating to Grisie.

After Lady Mary Wortley Montagu's betrayal Grisie has no wish to go out in society but, writes Grisell, 'Her friends would have her go to the opera to night, I did not incline to it and nother did she, but they all condem'd us for it yea even Lady Hadinton. Lady Stairs came for her. I wish the footmen do not some rude thing I live in continual fear & believe will do so all my life'. We are indebted to Rachy for a detailed though unpunctuated account of the trial on 7 December, to which Grisie was accompanied by Lady Haddington, Lady Stairs, Lady Letchmere, Mrs Hervey, Mrs West, the Duke of Montrose, the Duke of Roxburghe, Lord Haddington, and Lord Polwarth, to name but half of the friends that turned out in support. Rachy reports that when Grisie was first asked to speak 'she spoke with a faint voice being a little dashed which was no wonder for besids the folks that went with us there was a vast many people of qualittie that went there for their curiositie and a vast mobe and all their eys was upon her'. When Gray was invited to speak, he scandalised the entire court by asking Grisie if Mr. Burnet [Gilbert Burnet, Grisie's cousin, chaplain to King George I] was not often in the house after Mr. Baillie had gone to bed, was he not often in the room alone with her. Even after a reproof from the judge that the questions had nothing to do with the case, Gray continued by asking if Mr. Burnet was not often in bed with her, which last Grisie denied, as did her maid when

Gray asked her 'if Mr Burnet was not very often in the room when her Lady was undresing & naked'. A number of other servants were called to give evidence, and Gray asked them all the same questions, with all of them denying any impropriety, until the judge lost patience and reprimanded Gray again for asking impertinent questions. The Justice of the Peace who had apprehended Gray, and to whom he had confessed when arrested, testified next, and letters were produced that Gray had written to several family members asking for forgiveness, which he now denied having written. Gray was then invited to give his account of what had happened on that October night, and afterwards Chief Justice King summed up the evidence for the jury 'which he put in as fair a light for him as he could which we was very glad of for he cant nor anybody els say he was hardly delt with'. After they had retired to deliberate, 'the forman pronounsed him giltie of the Burglerie & felloni'. Rachy says that Gray's impudence 'raised indignation in the whole audence the whole mobe was his anymy [enemy] which they are very seldom to a criminal of ther own rank but they met him as he went out & told him they were glad he was to be hangd for his impedence'. (Curiously to modern thinking, the verdict seemed to hinge not on whether he had intended rape, or threatened Grisie with weapons, but on whether or not the door had been latched when he entered the room).

While no doubt pleased to have her reputation cleared of any suggestion that she had encouraged Gray, and embarrassed at Gilbert Burnet's name having been dragged through the mud, the 'Guilty' verdict imposed a huge burden on Grisie and her parents, as it carried a sentence of death for Arthur Gray. If Gray were to be hanged, people would say that the Baillies were heartless and cruel in having brought the case against him, and if reprieved, that the verdict was wrong and that Gray had spoken the truth regarding Gilbert Burnet. Despite possible damage to

Grisie's reputation, and that of the whole family, George Baillie and Grisell decide to try to reprieve Gray from the noose at Tyburn. On 14 December '11 at night', George Baillie writes to a duke, probably the Duke of Montrose. 'My Lord, Im sorry to give your G[race] any trouble but I depend so much on your friendship as to presume to beg youll lay befor his Majesty my most humble & earnest request that he woud be graciously pleas'd to transport that miserable wrech Arthur Gray. If his Majesty had think fit to grant this it will make me easie & tho I doubt not malicious people will reflect reproach upon me for interceeding for him, Im willing to bear it rather than be thought cruel, whatever your G: thinks fit to do in this must be done airly [early] since for to morrow is the day of execution.'

We also have Rachy's account of what transpired the following morning, 15 December. 'The fridie sevennight after arther was condemned Papa got up pritie arely & sent for Grisie befor nine a cloke to put on his wig as she used to do but they told him she was gon out of fut in a riding hood it struk papa when ever he heard it coud not imagen where she was gon at that time of day he came up & asked me if I knew so I told him I suposed she was gon to Mr Mitchells or to some place els to make a visit tho I thought it lookd od that she had gon allon at that time o day Papa went out about busines & stayd about an hour & came in again just after him came in my Lord Polwarth telling us he had got a letter from Grisie telling him she had suferd so much upon the ackcedent that had hapend her & did sufer so much every day by people that talked of it that she was quit distracted some told her if he was not hangd she was ruend in her reputation for ever others told her if he was hangd she was ruened so that whatever way it went she thought it best for her to go out of the way & live in some place in the world where no body knew her & that she was resolved to go in to a convent in france if there was one that woud receve protestants'.

Lord Polwarth was not the only one to receive a letter that morning, as Grisie had also written to her father, her mother and her sister. Rachy says, 'mama went perfitly mad and papa was so shoct that I was afraid he woud have taken some sudden fit & died Lord Biny was in the utmost grief'. Grisie had asked Lord Polwarth to reply to her, under an assumed name, at a nearby coffee shop, so he was able to discover where she was. He found her sitting weeping with her Bible open in front of her and, having told her what a dreadful state her parents were in, persuaded her to come back with him which, says Rachy, was a good thing as her absence could never have been concealed from the servants if she had been missing overnight. As soon as he had read Grisie's letter, George Baillie had written a reply to be delivered by Lord Polwarth. 'Dearest Child it is impossible for me to express my surprize at the fatall resolution you have taken, my grief is so great that my tears interupt what I would say'. He wonders if he has seemed harsh to Grisie. 'If I have done or said anything that you might judge harsh it was from kindnes to you not that I in the least suspect your innocence'. At the bottom of the page is a single sentence in Grisell's handwriting. 'If you do not return you breck the heart of a poor mother who loved nothing more than you.'

Grisie had also written a note to her friend the Duchess of Montrose, and another to Gilbert Burnet. 'To Mr Burnet You cannot now think me in the wrong for not telling you last night what I meant, when I had then determind to go away wc [which] I knew you woud prevent, I beg you may make your self easie about it & don't imagin its in the least owing to you, I coud have lived on wt you all my life in the way I did without ever dreaming it had the apearance of a crime, I own I had a great pleasure in conversing wt [with] my friends of wc number I always believed you to be, & shall ever remember wt gratitude I think Im in the right but adieu God help me Im affrayd my head is turnd.'

Thankfully the newspapers had not got wind of Grisie's intention to go into a convent though the *Daily Journal* reported the following day, 16 December: 'Great Intercession is making to save the Lives of Arthur Gray, the Footman, and Christopher Samuel Graff, the High German Doctor'.* Writing to Sir James Hall on the 19th, Grisell is still unaware of the outcome of their plea for clemency. 'Whichever way it gos we are at a lose, but I bliss God go as it will we may be easie in our own minds'. The suspense was over by 22 December, as the *Weekly Journal or Saturday's Post* reported, 'Yesterday Arthur Gray, the Footman, was reprieved, the rest before mentioned in the Dead Warrant were executed at Tyburn'.* In another letter from Grisell to Sir James Hall on 26 December it becomes clear that, although George Baillie had written the letter to the Duke asking for the King's mercy for Gray, he had written it at Grisell's insistence, and possibly unwillingly. She says, 'I made a bold play to save that wrech Gray when not one Mortall was on my side & have born much since in being told I have confirmed the world of the wicked reproaches was cast upon our famely…I'll never repent it. If I was to buy the reputation of our famely at the price of blood I would rather bear the outmost malice could be invented.'

On 18 January 1722 *The Post Boy* carried the news that 'Arthur Gray, the Footman, by the Indulgence of the Family he had offended will have Liberty to enter or engage himself in any Foreign Service, without being sold, provided he doth not return into Great Britain or Ireland'.* For Gray, the outcome was better than he could have expected, having retained not only his life but his freedom; although George Baillie and Grisell's consciences are clear of sending a man to his death, in the eyes of many people the family's reputation was tarnished. A less wealthy family could not have afforded to pursue the case against Gray, as among the 'sundry' accounts for December 1721 is the large sum of £43:2s6d, 'The expence of my Doughter

Grisell's Plea'. (Arthur Gray would be last heard of in the *London Journal* of 22 June 1723 when it was reported, 'Arthur Gray the Footman, who was lately Transported for attempting a Rape on his Lady near Piccadilly is now in the service of General Hart, Governour and Commander in Chief of the British Leeward Islands in America').*

One thing that Grisie may have found cheering after these months of turmoil was the première on 22 February 1722 of a new opera by Italian composer Giovanni Bononcini entitled *Griselda*. The libretto, a revision by Paolo Rolli of an earlier one by Zeno, based on a tale from Boccaccio's *Decameron*, told how Gualtiero, King of Sicily had married Griselda, a shepherdess, but the nobility were in revolt as they did not think someone of her rank was fit to be queen. Gualtiero, in order to prove the nobility wrong, set up a series of ordeals from which Griselda emerged as the epitome of feminine patience, virtue and faithfulness. To have someone bearing a name of which her own was a variant held up as a shining example of virtuous womanhood can only have revived Grisie's spirits. The title role was sung by Anastasia Robinson, and Gualtiero by Senesino (stage name of Francesco Bernardi, an alto castrato). Opera-goers could purchase, for one shilling, a little booklet of the libretto, with the Italian text on each right-hand page and an English translation on the left, and Grisie's copy of *Griselda*, with other libretti, remains at Mellerstain, as does the copy of Allan Ramsay's *Collected Poems* published in 1721, for which Grisell subscribed two guineas.

Grisie's mental state was very precarious, so in the spring she is sent to stay with her friend Lady Mary Howard in the seclusion of Castle Howard in Yorkshire, away from the disapproving eyes of London society. In a letter of 14 July 1722, Grisell writes to her daughter that she has sent a present of a straw hat for Lady Mary 'from your papa' and reveals that 'it is dearer than any ever we bought 23sh[illings]…do not tell her the price of it'. Though it might have been kinder to leave Grisie immune from London gossip, Grisell, still angry at Lady Mary Wortley Montagu for increasing Grisie's distress by writing the bawdy ballad, cannot resist relaying one or two occurrences which show Lady Mary in a bad light and says 'I shall never come in her company if I can shun it'. The item immediately above the expensive 'stra hatt' in the accounts is 'a Nightgoun Scots Plade Gibie Burnet £2:2s', perhaps a gift by way of apology for inadvertently causing Gilbert Burnet's name to be mentioned scandalously in court. On the same page is a payment for 'handkerchiefs Mitchels & Mrs West', Mary Mitchell and Elizabeth West being Gilbert Burnet's twin sisters. Grisie must have left Castle Howard in August, as there is expenditure 'For my Grisies coach hire from York etc £5:14s6d' and £5:15s6d 'Drinkmoney Castle Howard'. One rather enigmatic entry is 15 shillings for 'mending heads [head-dresses] eat by hogs at Castle Howard'. Dogs would seem to be more likely culprits, but Grisell's writing is perfectly clear.

With the additions to the house in Great Marlborough Street to accommodate the extended family had come the expense of more furnishings, and we have descriptions of rooms as 'the green damask' and 'the yellow damask', presumably referring to the wallcoverings. '6 Dininroom chairs from Mr Moor' cost £8:18s and 'a large walnut tree bookcase' is £25, with '2 gilt Tabels' at £12 for the pair. Two more large mirrors are bought, and there is a sign that women's fashions are changing as '3 hoop peticoat chairs £1:10s' and '2 hoop peticoat chairs for green damask £6' are seen to be necessary for the ladies to sit comfortably now that skirts were supported in a fashionable shape by under-petticoats with stiff oval hoops of cane or baleen ['whalebone']. Most of the family's acquaintance have a country house in addition to their London town house. The most fashionable place within the last decade is Twickenham, or 'Twittenham' as Grisell usually spells it. George Baillie's uncle, Secretary Johnston, has built an impressive mansion there (known at a later date as Orleans House), visits to which probably occasioned the 'drinkmoney Twittenham' in the expenses. Lord Binning and Rachy, together with Grisell and George Baillie, take a country house in less fashionable East Barnet, some eight miles north of London and still at that date surrounded by open countryside. Grisell notes rent paid 'For house & fields' to the owner, variously named as Mr. Pickard, Piccarin or Pickert. The fact that Gilbert Burnet had been instituted to the rectory of East Barnet in 1719 may have influenced the choice of location. Although central London offered many amenities and entertainments, the pure air of the country, unpolluted by London's thousands of coal fires, was considered healthier, and it may be that Lord Binning's health was beginning to give cause for concern. The accounts have sums 'For cariing furniture to Barnet' and 'cariing servants to Barnet'. An unknown writer, possibly Gilbert Burnet, writes to Grisie from East Barnet on 19 August 1722, painting a picture of the hectic life in a household which includes two infants, and saying what a doting grandfather George Baillie is. 'He is so fond of the Boy [Thomas or 'Tamie'] I never saw any thing like it. I believe he counts every minute he stays in town [away] from him. He plagues Lady B's [Rachy's] life with him, fancying she does not mind [look after] him enough. Your friend Tamie is grown a Fury, & encouraged by his Grand Papa in it: & Grissie is the most governable child grown I ever saw.' Little Tamie's mischief is also recorded by his grandmother Grisell in 1725 when she notes the loss of a half crown coin, 'To little Tamie he put down a holl in the Floor at Barnet'.

In 1722 the Princess of Wales, Princess Caroline, caused a furore by having her daughters Amelia and Caroline inoculated against smallpox by the process of variolation, as advocated by Lady Mary Wortley Montagu who had seen the technique widely used when she was in Turkey. Inoculation produced a mild form of the disease from which the patient soon recovered, and gave lifelong immunity. Though there was a general deep suspicion of this new practice, Lord Binning and Rachy must have decided in its favour, and we learn from Grisell in a letter of 20 May 1723, 'The poor bairens [little Grisie and Tamie, aged 4 and 2] is to get the smallpox on wednesday which you may beleive puts us all in no small anxiaty'. Lord Binning, writing 10 days later to Grisell's brother Andrew, Lord Kimmerghame, says, 'I hope my children are in a good way, the small pox are come out & they are both as well as can be expected, poor Grisy has been much sicker for some days than her brother but they think she'll have fewer of them'. Happily, little Grisie and Tamie recovered in time for the infection to have vanished before their baby brother George was born the next month on 24 June 1723. Grisell, writing to her brother Andrew a week later, reveals how much in demand she is in the household, conjuring up an image of a queue of seven people clamouring for her attention: 'I was in such a hurry when I put up your last letter the whole House caling upon me at a time, Mr Baillie to scold me for being so late tho it was not eight, Rachy to help her to rise, the nurs to dress the bairen, Grisie to come and intertaine some body she did not like, & James Park wateing for 2 guinys to keep Mr Halls man Purves out of Prison, David the Butler wants a word with my Ladiship this is really as it was with the adition of May Menzies's plaugeing [plaguing] me to know who shall site up with the nurs & the two bairens for her own is here yet'. The nurse is rewarded with a pair of shoes costing 6s6d 'for Georges first tooth', having successfully brought him through the first months of infancy. The busy household also includes at least one dog who got lost and had to be advertised for: 'crying a Doge 2s', and was presumably found as the next item is the cost of bringing him back: 'carr[y]ing Spy 5s'.

Soon afterwards, there is a trip to Scotland for Grisell. Lady Murray tells us, 'She went to Scotland every second year to see her father; and when he wanted assistance in his old age, and could not take the trouble of looking after his own affairs, she took in and settled his steward's accounts...When in London, she never failed writing to her father, or her sister Julian, who then lived with him, and took affectionate care of him, every other post; sent him the newspapers, and any new book or pamphlet she thought would divert him'. Some years previously, Sir Patrick had left Redbraes for a town house in Berwick-upon-Tweed, closer to amenities than his isolated, rambling ancestral home at Polwarth. Grisell's visit in 1723 was followed by another in April 1724, which would be the last time Grisell saw her father, as he died on 2 August 1724, aged 83. Lady Murray says, 'None of our family were in Scotland but Lord Binning, who came to see him the first notice from Lady Julian of his illness, and attended him to the last...My mother's concern for his loss was great, though his age could make it no surprise to her.' The world Sir Patrick inhabited at the end of his long life was so very different from that of his youth. In the blank pages of an almanac, he had meticulously noted the birth dates of all 33 of his grandchildren, and there were now several great-grandchildren as well to inherit the world he had hoped to make better by suffering for his beliefs.

The death of Sir Patrick was the end of an era, and 1724 also marked the end of George Baillie's career in the Government. He was to remain an MP until 1734, though increasing deafness made it difficult to continue. 'Mr Baillie is now so deaf that he is quite heartles [disheartened].' Wishing to record for posterity his position as a Lord of the Treasury before he relinquished the post, in 1724 he commissioned a new bookplate for his library, engraved by 'A. Johnston'. In August 1725, Grisell recorded 'for a coper plate for Books £1:1s' and '400 prints 5s 0d'. More must have been subsequently printed, as 400 prints would have not have sufficed for the number of books that George Baillie had amassed by 1724 and had sent to the bookbinder's to be beautifully bound, many bearing his emblem of the golden fleece in gold tooling on the spine. A handwritten catalogue of his books dated 1725 lists 762 volumes in English, French and Latin whose subjects are religion and theology, history, geography, Classics, law, politics, a little English literature and poetry and one solitary book on *Husbandry and Gardening*, though Mellerstain's library shelves still hold numerous books on the subject published before 1725. Perhaps these were not listed, along with books on cookery and housewifery, as they belonged more to Grisell's domestic sphere. Grandson George Baillie continued to use the same bookplate, as can be seen in volumes from the 1770s in the Mellerstain Library. George Baillie was now 60, and ready to live a quieter life devoted to his family, his books and his prayers.

Chapter 8

~∂Ωe~

A NEW HOUSE FOR MELLERSTAIN

1724–1731

When the marriage of Rachy and Lord Binning had been planned in 1717, there must have been discussion about where the young couple would make their home. It was quite usual for a newly married pair to live under the roof of one or other set of parents, at least for a time, and we have seen that Rachy's first two children were christened at Tyninghame, before the couple moved to share the Baillies' house at Great Marlborough Street in London. However, the 20-year-old Lord Binning had his sights set on a seat of his own once he was married. At the time of the marriage, Lord Binning's father Thomas, 6th Earl of Haddington was aged only 37, so might be expected to occupy the family seat at Tyninghame for many years to come. In the weeks after the wedding, George Baillie had returned to London and Grisell had embarked on a round of visiting friends and relations in Scotland, but at the end of September Rachy fell ill of a dangerous fever at Tyninghame, which her parents learned of in letters from Lord Haddington, so it looked for a time as if her married life might be a very short one indeed, but happily she slowly recovered, and she and her husband were able to make a trip to Mellerstain, where Lord Binning had never been before. In a letter to George Baillie on 22 October 1717, Grisell wrote, 'We came to Mellerstaine on saterdays night went to church on Sunday I think the whole parish gathered about the coach to gase on us as we came out'. Apparently there had been some previous talk of Mellerstain as a suitable seat for Rachy and Lord Binning, as Grisell continues, 'Bining was exceedingly surprised with Mellerstaine he thought it so much better than he expected he walked about the whole fields as soon as ever he could & has pitcht upon one of the finest seats ever he saw except Marlly [a small château built by Louis XIV]… it is doun below the tower upon the brea [brae] head where he has carved out [in his imagination] the finest terrases sloping banks the finest waterworks and ponds in short the pleasantest things that can be about a house with the half less expence that any such things could be made any where ever he saw…so you see what a fine place Mellerstaine is.'

The day after Grisell, Rachy and Lord Binning's attendance at church, they were joined at Mellerstain by Grisell's brother Andrew, by Lord Haddington and Mr. James Smith, a renowned architect and engineer, Overseer of the Royal Works in Scotland, who had been tasked with assessing the safety of Mellerstain Tower. All had different opinions about where a new house should be situated, but it is Lord Binning's vision which most corresponds to Mellerstain today, with the house at the brae head [top of the slope], a vista to the top of the hill on the north side and down to 'the pritiest pond' on the south, Whiteside brae in the west and Sneep brae in the east being planted with trees; Grisell gloomily observes 'in our days we can never be tolerably sheltered', as the trees will not have grown up enough in her lifetime. She is now not even sure a new house is necessary: 'It's a doubt indeed if we ever build the House for

I'm exceedingly pleasd with this same [Mellerstain Tower] since Mr Smith asurs [assures] me the tour is in no hazard of falling.' A new house must have been under discussion even as early as May 1717 when Grisell's brother Alexander writes to Grisie, 'If Mama be for Scotland she may lay the foundation of her house for I have the draught of it ready. Its a pretty little thing and will be very cheap I promise her but I'd rather have her build it in East Lothian. Melisten [Mellerstain] is a wild place'. Despite Alexander apparently having drawn up plans (how detailed is not known), and despite Lord Binning's enthusiasm for Mellerstain as the perfect site for a new house, with the focus of George Baillie and Lord Binning's political lives being in London, the old Mellerstain Tower and its outbuildings remained undisturbed until 1724, although Grisell's 'sundries' accounts for 1723 give a hint of things to come: 'To Mr Adam for takeing a Plan etc of Mellerstane £15:17s6d'.

With George Baillie about to give up his post at the Treasury, a new kind of life beckoned. A document declares, on behalf of King George I:

> 'In consideration of the good, true, faithfull and acceptable Service to us heretofore done and performed by Our Trusty and Wellbeloved George Baillie Esquire as of the Steady and Zealous Affection for us and Our Family and for other just Causes and Considerations...Do give and grant unto the said George Baillie One Annuity or yearly Sume of One thousand six hundred pounds of Lawfull money of Great Britain... The first payment thereupon to commence from the Twenty seventh day of May in the eleventh year of our reign [1725]...to be made quarterly at the four most usual feasts'.

The annuity is a substantial sum, equal to George Baillie's salary at the Treasury, although he had more than most reason to drink to the King's continuing good health as he writes in May 1725, 'what I am to get being only a grant of £1600 during the King's life and mine I mean when either of us dye the grant is at an end'. By June 1725 George Baillie was probably relieved to be out of the Government when riots broke out in a number of Scottish cities, most seriously in Glasgow, in protest against the imposition of a tax on malt, making beer more expensive.

The extended family of Grisell and George Baillie, Grisie, Rachy and Lord Binning and their children little Grisie, Tamie and George continued to live in the manor house at East Barnet, where another daughter, named Helen after Lord Binning's mother Helen Hope, was christened on 23 October 1724. On her return from Scotland the previous year, Grisell had commissioned portraits of herself and her husband, 'For my dears Picture by Ritchison in full £12:12s', and other portraits followed thick and fast, with a portrait of Grisie for her friend Lady Hervey costing 16 guineas, 'Patr Hume my Nephews Picture' at 10 guineas, all in 1724, and 'Grisies pictor copied by Mrs Varels [Maria Verelst] (14 guineas), 'My nephew Patie Humes pictor to his mother' (three guineas), 'My pictor by Mrs Varels' (16 guineas) in 1725. Maria Verelst, in common with other artists, must have had ready-painted backgrounds and figures lacking only the head for clients to choose from, as Grisell's portrait showing her in low-cut velvet gown, red drapery on the right and a building and foliage on the left, is almost identical to portraits of three other ladies, one of them Sarah, Duchess of Marlborough. Rachy was also painted by Maria Verelst in 1725 (Plate 17). In 1726 'the first [sitting of] Lady Mars pictor' cost four guineas, and in 1727 'My doughter Grisies pictor for Mr Mitchell' was 12 guineas. Also in 1727, 'My Grandchild Georges pictor on the frame with his grand father' (Plate 18) cost 15 guineas, with an extra five shillings as a tip to 'Mr Aikman the painters servant'. This charming double portrait of George Baillie and his four-year-old namesake has his little grandson resplendent in a blue silk dress as small boys and girls were dressed alike, largely for practical purposes of toilet training, until the beginning of the twentieth century. In 1724 Grisell notes the purchase of 'Duble clouts [double cloths or nappies] to Hellen 2 dozen £1:6s'. On 30 January 1725, George Baillie writes, 'My youngest Grandchild has been taken so ill that we have been looking for her death all day'. Helen survived on this occasion, as in July Grisell writes, 'You never saw so fine a child as Hellen Mr Baillie is now as fond of her as George and she can speak and cry Papa even Gibie [Gilbert Burnet] is fond of her.'

Grisell had paid a visit to Scotland at the beginning of 1724, staying at first in Edinburgh but was at Mellerstain by April. She hated being separated from her husband and family. Writing to Grisie on 7 April 1724 she says, 'Well as I like this place [Mellerstain] I have no pleasure in it without your Papa I write him every step of my business & he will have a guess when I can begin my journey every day is a year to me.' In letters to her daughters in the preceding weeks, Grisell dispenses lots of motherly advice, urging them to keep warm in order to stay well, but not to drink warm ale. Now aged 60, Grisell's eyesight is obviously not good, and strained with her copious letter-writing, though the first mention of spectacles in the accounts occurs 10 years previously in 1714 when one shilling is paid for a 'spectickle eye'. Thereafter spectacles are a regular purchase, though she rarely says for whom they are bought, so it is difficult to say whether there are several recipients in the household, whether people are very careless with them or whether spectacles at the time, which were still just two lenses linked by a bridge, without sides, were particularly flimsy and apt to break. Grisell, in a letter to Grisie, says, 'I'm quite blind wt [with] writing to Papa'. Grisie herself is named as a recipient of spectacles, and a writer in East Barnet apologises for troubling her with having to read an answer to a letter, 'since you tell me your eyes are weak'.

If eighteenth century optometry was beginning to make progress, dentistry remained primitive. Grisell often notes payment to a 'tooth-drawer', rarely saying who benefited from his services, and there are purchases of tooth powder (applied with a cloth as the toothbrush was yet to be invented), tooth picks and 'teeth water', and remedial action could be taken in the hopes of avoiding the tooth-drawer, as in 1717 when five shillings was paid 'For stoping Rachy's tooth with Leed [lead]'. In 1718 Grisie, writing to Rachy, thinks she has found a panacea for problems with teeth. 'I begin now to chaw tobaco, that is to say I rub my teeth every morning wt a leaf of it, you can't imagin what good it dose them, pray try it, your teeth will never come out nor you'll never have the tooth ache'. Rachy followed her sister's advice, which displeased Grisell. 'My Dearest Rachy you cha tobaco most intolarably in the afternoon was what I could never have thought of Ld B: will certainly hate you for it'. Grisie's hopes for the miraculous cure offered by tobacco must have been dashed, as we learn from Grisell writing to her in 1724. 'My Dear Heart nothing of a long time has given me more vexation than the account you give of your teeth I fear that fellow has ruined them I sent up a recept [recipe] that is exalent for them Lady Hall had a fortooth [front tooth] just droping out & aploying a piece of a gall that Ink is made of repered it again'. No connection had yet been made with wealthier people's increasing consumption of sugar and dental ill health.

William Adam had been in correspondence with Grisell's brother Alexander in 1724 regarding possible work at Redbraes, which came to nothing. Alexander had been appointed ambassador to the congress at Cambrai in January 1722 and, writes Margaret Warrender, 'By the curious irony of Fate, the day in March on which, with the utmost pomp and magnificence, he made his public entry into the city of Cambray, was the very day [16 March] his wife died in Edinburgh.' Margaret Campbell seems not to have been particularly lamented, but her passing probably left Grisell with the task of making arrangements for Alexander's four daughters in her brother's absence. The youngest daughter, Margaret, died aged 11 just a year after her mother in March 1723. Alexander continued in Cambrai until 1724, which proved a dreadful year for him as, in addition to losing his father, his daughter Grisell aged 23, and his son George aged 20, also died. Small wonder after five bereavements in such a short space that Alexander didn't pursue his building ambitions, but he may also have been put off by Grisell writing in July 1725, 'What are you to make of Adams it will be dear work I'm afraid if you medle with him'. William Adam had worked in 1721 at nearby Floors Castle in Kelso, and was engaged in alterations by 1725 for Lord Binning's uncle Charles Hope at Hopetoun House, and despite Grisell having reservations about the expense, he was commissioned as architect for a new house at Mellerstain, and paid 10 guineas for plans.

Grisell's 'Account of Expences of building a House at Mellerstaine founded by Lord Binning the [blank] of September 1725' (Plate 19) includes '50 days at the Foundation of the Pavilion befor Mr Adams was agreed with to build it £1:3s4d'. This suggests that not only was the house to be built to William Adam's plans, but that he was subsequently engaged as contractor as well. Even before the first stone of the new house was laid, landscaping had begun according to the vision seen so clearly by Lord Binning in 1717, with many trees being planted, and work being started on Binning's 'pritiest pond', (Plate 20a) which Grisell refers to in the accounts as 'the cannall'. 'Pond' implies something quite small, but impressive dimensions are revealed on 'The Plane of the Canal at Mellerstown 1200 foot Long 400 foot broad 12 foot deep at the Cleansing or Draining Box'. Work on this must have been at least begun by 23 May 1724 when Grisell records £7:10s spent 'for oak to the sluice', as the 'canal' was being formed by damming the Eden Water. Grisell is not impressed with the progress of the 'canal', as she thinks William Adam does not properly understand the sluice mechanism, and is unhappy with the cost. 'I wish it were ended it has cost a good sum already above duble what Adams estimat is but I hope he understands Building better'. Beyond the 'canal', once the ground rises up again to the south, stood the remains of an ancient peel tower, the stones of which were to be re-used to form an eye-catching folly on the mid horizon, leading the eye to the Cheviot Hills beyond. Demolition of this tower also began before construction of the new house, with 'fivepenny men' being paid £3:16s8d for 184 days' work 'pulling down the old Tower' as well as stonemason Will Gray supervising the demolition (£2:12s) along with wright [joiner] Will Hardy (11s 8d). The first mention of the folly (Plate 20b), whose name has been corrupted over time to 'Hundy Mundy', is in 1725 'For 16 days at Hunymundas 6s 8d'. Perhaps to help with the positioning and proportions of these landscape features, in 1724 Grisell had purchased a theodolite, an expensive instrument at £6:8s6d. A hand-written volume of poetry all composed by Lord Binning reveals that in writing gallant poems to his wife Rachy he assumed the persona of 'the knight Bellamir' and she was 'the princess Hunimonda'. It is clear from Lord Binning's inscription composed for the foundation stone of the eye-catching folly that it was built in honour of his wife:

> *To Hunimonda's charms I raise*
> *A lasting monument of praise*
> *This stone shall gain immortal fame*
> *By wearing Hunimonda's name.*

(The stone, if ever inscribed, is no longer legible).

Grisell's brother Alexander's two surviving daughters had apparently been 'farmed out' to other households after their mother's death, and Grisell's brother Andrew is obviously thinking of taking over the care of the youngest, Jean, aged 14. (Andrew's own son Patrick, named as 'Patie' in Grisell's accounts, had added to the catalogue of family bereavements in 1724, dying at the age of 18). In a letter of 2 April 1725, Grisell cautions against it. 'As for our Ni[e]ce Jean, she gives me more vexation than Anne [Jean's sister] did because I re[al]ly never expected good of her because she has no sence. I am altogether against your takeing of Jean... She is very well where she is as long as she is not troublesome to them, but with her sister she shall never be again.' She repeats this injunction in a letter of 29 May, when she is also scolding Andrew, and trying to keep the peace between him and Alexander, who is complaining that Andrew never writes to him. Still reeling from his multiple bereavements, Alexander 'eats nothing but a rost Chicken & chicken broth & a little soup... he has eat nothing els this twelvemonth he drinks no wine & has been vastly worss than ever I aprehended'. Lady Murray says Grisell 'had no notion of those depressions that most people labour under', clearly demonstrated here by her lack of empathy with her brother's mental state.

In a letter of 8 May 1725 William Adam, writing to Lord Binning, apologises for being tardy in submitting his estimate, which is obviously for the central, main block of the proposed house, and confirms that the plans have been modified according to Lord Binning's wishes. 'This Estimate Cutts of[f] the 4th or Attick Storie and gives Lodgeing in the rooff in place thereof, as I proposed to yor Lop [Lordship] in My Last; and I'm still of the oppinion yt [that] it is the best Method wheir rich ornaments or at least a handsome Cornish [cornice] & parapet with vases etc are not alow'd; but if yo'r Lop is positive to have the platform

& parapett then Ile upon first notice from yo'r Lop add to this Estimate.' The East and West Pavilions, at least at this early stage, do not appear to be William Adam's design, and Adam is rather dismissive of Lord Binning's ideas. 'The 2 pavillions yo'r Lop mentions are not containd here, but their expence can not be great of the dimentions yor Lop proposes, tho I'd wish them Something Larger.' Adam's estimate also does not include any internal ornamental plasterwork. 'Now their remains the finishing within which I have left to yor Lop because of the Stucco which yor Lop seems to like and to use it much.' Lord Binning's knowledge of architecture is well respected by Grisell's brother Alexander at Redbraes, as William Adam also says, 'I Understand the E[arl] of Marchmonth has delay'd his house of Redbraes until yor Lop considers the Plan.'

William Adam had submitted several preliminary sketches for the main house at Mellerstain, with different arrangement and styles of windows, and differing decoration, all designs being seven bays wide and most with a central pediment at roof level. This central block, 110 feet wide, was to be linked to the squat, square pavilions on either side by a curved, single-storey covered corridor (Plate 21a). Internally, William Adam's plans show that on the 'Principall Floor' (Plate 21b), there was to be a grand entrance hall, 40 feet wide by 20 feet high and with parlours either side, leading to an inner hall (a 20-foot cube) with staircases going off to left and right. From the inner hall the visitor could progress straight through to the grand south-facing 'Sallon', 38 by 25 feet, which was 22 feet in height, with the drawing room, principal [guest] bedchamber and its dressing room on the east side, all still an impressive 20 feet high. On the west side, 'Mr Baillie's Dressing Room' and closet, connecting with a Family Bed Chamber and dressing room were all at a reduced height of 12 feet, permitting of a mezzanine storey containing a charter room, two nurseries and a closet or 'My Lady's Gentlewoman's room', this being destined for May Menzies' occupation. Curiously, nothing is described as 'My Lady's bed chamber' or 'My Lady's dressing room', so it appears that Grisell will occupy the 'Family Bed Chamber' with George Baillie and claim the adjacent dressing room.

On the 'Lodgeing storie or Second Floor', 'Lady Binnie's closet' and bedchamber (22 feet by 20) lead off a central antechamber, as does 'Lord Binnie's dressing room' (shown with a bed in it) and closet, but the two suites do not interconnect. There are four unassigned bed chambers, two with closets and two provided with smaller, triangular 'stool rooms' for the all-important chamber pot or close stool. The largest room on this floor is the 38 feet by 25 feet 'Librarie', 25 feet high, which is ensuite with a library closet leading to a bedchamber with closet, bed alcove and stool room. The 'Attick storie', described by William Adam as having been removed in the latest plan, houses 10 small bedchambers and a 30 feet by 20 feet billiard room. Downstairs, the 'cellar storie' is the province of servants, with William Adam showing a Porter Lodge, cheese room, milk house, ladner [larder], Room for Plate, Pantry, Poudring Room [for dressing wigs], Butler's Room (with bed), Little bedroom (one bed), Woman House (with three beds), Housekeeper's room (with bed), second table room and closet, servants' hall and closet, and Mr Baillie's servant's room, together with store rooms and cellars. There are no 'back stairs' for servants' use, the two spiral staircases running through all floors of the house from bottom to top.

Writing to her brother Andrew in October 1725, a month after the foundation stone of the East Pavilion was laid, Grisell is having doubts about the financial viability of the Mellerstain building project. 'You know I have a growing famely & some of them has not overmuch to defray their present expence & ye may believe without us could not do it, I'm vext that Bin: has begune that House altho I will not say so to vex him, Mr Baillie said too much of it to him which freted him'. Grisell admits she is concealing debts from her husband 'but it is impossible to manage everything with that exactness that he imagens'. She also thinks that her brother Andrew is living beyond his means, and compares her debt to his own. 'What gri[e]ves me most is that this is but a mite to what you owe ten times the sum will not pay your Debt...if you do not retrench in everything you are ruined.' A year later, in December 1726, Andrew's financial problems must have caused him to sink into a depression, which prompts a lecture from Grisell. 'For God sake Dear Brother keep up your heart remember my father saying never to fret at what we cannot help nor at what we can help, all we can gete by doing otherwise is to make ourselves useless, besids I realy think it below a man of any spirit.'

Meanwhile, the family continued to live in London, at Marlborough Street, and in the country at East Barnet, where the christening of Charles Hamilton is recorded on 26 October 1725. That summer, a young poet called James Thomson had come to be tutor to Tamie, now approaching his fifth birthday, and in between teaching him to read and write, Thomson composed an extended poem entitled *Winter* which was published in April 1726 to great acclaim, before Thomson left the household in May. Another boy, John, was born on 22 October 1726 and christened at East Barnet on 24 November. Family friend Gilbert Burnet no doubt officiated at the christening of Charles the previous year, but not that of John, as Burnet had died in June 1726. Lady Mary Wortley Montagu, ever obsessed with society's intrigues and scandals, says in a letter to her sister Lady Mar, who is living with her exiled Jacobite husband in Paris, 'I don't hear much of Mrs Murray's dispair on the death of poor Gebby [Gilbert Burnet], and I saw her dance at a ball where I was, 2 days before his death'. Relations with Lady Mary continued to be strained, especially as she and Grisie moved in a fairly small social circle and were bound to meet each other occasionally. Grisie had also, from time to time, found herself in the same room as her estranged husband at social events, such as at a 'music meeting' in November 1717, when Grisell is so apprehensive of Alexander Murray's unpredictable behaviour towards her daughter that she seeks out the Duke of Montrose and the Earl of Haddington 'to take care of Grisie'. Murray, after intercessions from the Duchess of Marlborough and promises of loyalty to George I, had been released from the Marshalsea Prison in 1716, though he did visit the Pretender's court in Italy in 1718. The danger of meeting Alexander Murray socially lessened in the mid-1720s after his father Sir David Murray sold land in Peebleshire and bought land in the Ardnamurchan peninsula in Argyll in the hopes of reviving the ailing Murray family fortunes by exploiting the mineral deposits there. A bookseller's bill for 1723 shows that Grisie's husband bought, among other volumes, *Opera Mineralia Explicata* and *The Project of the Mine Adventure* and the Baillie family were no doubt pleased that this new obsession with mining removed Murray physically and mentally to a greater distance from them. In March 1725, Grisell's accounts show payments to 'George Robinson writter for my doughters affairs...for Lifting her Aliment for three years'.

1725 was also the year that Grisell became a published, if unacknowledged, authoress. Her only complete song, *Were na my Hearts light I wad die*, a tale of love and loss in pastoral vein, was published in that year by William Thomson in *Orpheus Caledonius*, a collection of Scots songs to which a second volume was added in 1733. Thomson did not attribute any of the songs to particular composers, so Grisell's name does not appear in the volume. Thomson was born in Edinburgh in 1683, but went to live in London in the early years of the eighteenth century.

His father, Daniel, was the King's trumpeter in Scotland when Grisell and George Baillie were living in Edinburgh in the 1690s, so the talented boy singer and his family were likely to have been known to them at that time, but Thomson was also a favourite at court in the 1720s, often giving recitals of Scots songs, so there may have been a personal connection with the family there. Grisell's own name does not appear in the list of 276 subscribers to the first edition of *Orpheus Caledonius*, many of them nobility, but her brother Alexander, Earl of Marchmont, and her daughter Lady Murray both subscribed to a copy, with Grisell noting the expense in the accounts for 1725 of 'Thomson's book of Scots songs first payments £1:1s'. Thomson's volume had appeared just two years later than the first volume of Allan Ramsay's *Tea-table Miscellany*, also a collection of Scots songs, and in fact included many lifted straight from Ramsay's collection without his permission. Ramsay relied on his readers knowing the melodies he named for the songs, but Thomson left nothing to chance, printing the musical notation for the melodies, together with a bass line, suitable for a low-pitched instrument or for harmonising at the keyboard. Quite a number of melodies additionally appear in a more suitable key for the 'German flute' as the transverse flute, just beginning to be popular, was called to distinguish it from the recorder which had hitherto been the most popular wind instrument and was usually called 'flute'. In 1726 a small pocket-book of tunes suitable for Ramsay's collection was published, within which were six sections, each dedicated to a lady, and the third section is 'Inscrib'd to the Honourable Lady Murray of Stanhope'. The 'song writers' of the late seventeenth and early eighteenth centuries ought more properly to be described as lyricists, as the majority wrote only the words of songs, simply naming a pre-existing tune to which the words were to be sung. Most of these tunes had originally been composed for instrumental performance, particularly for violin, and often had a wide range of an octave and a half making them difficult to sing. Grisell's song was not among those appropriated from Ramsay's *Tea-table Miscellany* as it does not appear until Volume IV of that work. Grisie no doubt sang her mother's song in her beautiful soprano voice and, because of its inclusion in Thomson's volume, *Were na my hearts light* became popular, and was known to have been quoted by Robert Burns toward the end of his life. Grisell's incomplete song, *The ewe-buchtin's bonnie* was first published as a broadsheet in the early nineteenth century by Charles Kirkpatrick Sharpe, set to a tune he said was composed by his father at the age of seven. There is a somewhat incoherent version of six stanzas in Grisell's handwriting, of which Sharpe appears to have selected the first and third, to which Kelso poet Thomas Pringle added eight further verses at a later date, and Lady John Scott added two verses to those selected by Sharpe. 'Ewe-buchtin' refers to the rounding up of sheep for milking at morning and evening, which would have been a familiar sight in Polwarth to Grisell in her youth. Her housekeeping accounts show purchases of 'sheap buter'.

It is now clear that the building of the new house at Mellerstain was a joint venture between the two generations of the family, George Baillie and Grisell, their daughter Rachy and her husband Lord Binning. Grisell says, in a later letter to her factor William Hume, 'I desire you'll let me know the sum of Lord Binning's money that you have laid out for Mr Baillies use. either his, or ours are to go for his or our use as it is cal[le]d for without destinction of whose money it is'. While Lord Binning was the chief mover as far as the siting and design of the new building was concerned, the task of dealing with the workmen and keeping the accounts fell to Grisell, never an easy task and made even more difficult by the fact that for much of the time Grisell was in London, some 350 miles from the building site. The family must have decided to start building the pavilions first as, being smaller and plainer than the proposed main house, they would be more quickly habitable. Grisell's accounts for 1725 deal with timber, ironmongery and quarry tools, with oxen and carthorses for hauling stone from quarries in Fans (part of Mellerstain estate) and Coldstream, and feeding for the beasts. The principal source of stone in 1726 is Catmoss quarry near Greenlaw, on Grisell's brother's Marchmont estate, and William Adam has now subcontracted to builder James Runciman, invariably spelled 'Runchiman' by Grisell, revealing a difference from the modern pronunciation of the name. Plasterers are at work by November 1726, and other internal work such as flooring continues in 1727. However, despite the pooled financial resources of the two families, sustaining two households in London as well as a major building project in Scotland was proving difficult, despite William Adam's assertion that the pavilions would be very inexpensive. Grisell's brother-in-law Sir James Hall continued to assist with the business dealings of George Baillie's estates, and in a letter to Sir James on 2 March 1727, Grisell exhorts him to chase up various tenants for their rents as 'that House of ours… has gone so very farr above the reckoning that I must at present keep it a secret from Mr Baillie…you'll not guess what that silly building has cost'. Grisell's reason for keeping the difficulties from her husband is not from a motive of deceit, but 'I alwise keep things from him that can only serve to fret him and do no good… a ston[e] more shall ne'er be built till I have the money in my hand I would not be at the trouble again for the best house in the world'. The original intention must have been that once the pavilions were built, a start would be made on the main house, but at present Grisell's only ambition is to see the stables, on the west side, finished. 'I want to have the stables up, and there it shall stand, and even these shall not be done till I see r[e]ady money'. Matters may have worsened some months later with the death in June 1727 of George I, presumably bringing an end to George Baillie's annuity of £1,600 which was only payable during the King's lifetime. The grandson Charles born in October of 1725 must not have survived long, as another child named Charles James is christened at East Barnet in October 1727. In the same month, Grisell pays out two shillings towards 'Ringing Bels at Coronation', as George II was crowned on 11 October, when Westminster Abbey resounded with a new coronation anthem by Handel, *Zadok the Priest*.

Grisell starts to buy furniture, and furnishings for the new house in 1727, and the 'Account of Household Furniture 1727 for Mellerstane' begins with the remarkable purchase of a pair of silver 'his and hers' chamber pots, the larger weighing over 37 ounces, the smaller 22 ounces, at a total cost of £18:15s1d including 'puting on the Crest and burnishing them'. According to the custom of the day, it is likely that these impressive chamber pots were not destined for use by Grisell and George Baillie in their bedchamber, but by their guests in the dining room. Although a seemingly extravagant purchase, and one which seems incongruous with Grisell's claims of lack of cash, silverware was never a wasted investment, as the metal held its value and could always be re-used or even pawned or sold in times of difficulty. The price of the chamber pots pales into insignificance compared with the cost of a large amount of silver tableware which had been bought in January 1725, before the new house was started, with an astronomical total of £231:6s2d, perhaps a safe way of investing part of George Baillie's newly awarded pension. The list of furnishings for Mellerstain continues into 1728 with many items of tableware, kitchenware and linen. Wooden furniture in the earlier years of Grisell's accounts, even up to 1725, was often of 'walnut tree', but the items for the new house are almost exclusively of the newly fashionable mahogany, including '18 mahogany hall chairs', a good investment at £1:3s each as they are all still in regular use today, almost 300 years later.

In 1728 funds must have been sufficient to continue the interior finishing of the East Pavilion, as [James] 'Norrie Painter' appears in the accounts and 'Shells' [James Shiells], a local blacksmith, is paid £13:10s for the 'Iron Rail to Stair', no ordinary banister but a beautifully executed 'birdcage' newel (Plate 22). In the grounds, the eyecatcher folly is still not complete as £5:6s5d is spent on 'Hunimundas Tower'. Various tradesmen are tasked with overseeing the work of the day-labouring 'fivepenny men', and James Runciman is paid half a crown a day for overseeing the whole works. Grisell's long-suffering factor William Hume is required in turn to keep an eye on James Runciman, as well as collecting rents, overseeing the planting and enclosing of the estate, paying schoolmasters' and ministers' stipends and giving charity on Grisell's behalf to any poor people in need on the estate and in 'Mellerstain toun', (a relatively small huddle of cottages, not equating to a 'town'). Hume, brother-in-law to Polwarth minister George Holiwell, had been overseeing events at Mellerstain for some time, having succeeded a Captain Turnbull, but a deed of March 1729 officially appoints him as 'baron baillie' [factor] to George Baillie and, as the east wing of the new buildings is now habitable by the family, the vacant tower house becomes the factor's house (which it remained until 1780). Hume received his instructions from Grisell in lengthy letters at least once a week, some of which, to Grisell's great frustration, failed to reach their destination, as did some of Hume's answers. George Baillie is worried that Grisell is exhausting herself with overseeing the house-building and furnishing, saying in a letter to Grisie, 'I always feared the toyl in fitting up the house would bring some mischief on her if it be so it had been well it had never been built.' A letter from

Grisie's friend Elizabeth, Lady Lechmere in March 1728 tells us that it is George Baillie's own health which is giving cause for concern. Lady Lechmere is aware that the family is about to set off for Bath and says, 'I know Mr Baillie has given you a full and Mellancholly employment a great while', and she hopes the waters at Bath will cure him. Lady Lechmere's concern for the Baillie family was also expressed in practical terms as she lent Grisell, jointly with her daughter Grisie, the large sum of £2,000 sterling in June 1728.

Before leaving for Bath, Grisell gave a dinner on 30 March for some of their closest friends, listing the guests as 'Ld Carlyl' [Charles, 3rd Earl of Carlisle] and his daughters – 'Lady Lechmoor, Lady Mary [Howard], Lds Stairs [John, 2nd Earl of Stair], Hadinton [Lord Binning's father], Marchmont' [Grisell's brother Alexander]. She notes that there were 12 at table, and including herself, George Baillie, Grisie, Rachy and Lord Binning brings the total to 11, with one mystery diner, so probably May Menzies was considered sufficiently part of the family to dine with them. The menu consisted of:

'1st. 4 dish: Soup, Lamb sid[e]s, 4 boyld chickens and a pudin; 2 relefes, crimp hard and forsadle of mutton.

2nd. 5 dish: 2 Duclins, date py, Kidny beans and sheaps tougs rosted; sids, a crab and Asparagras.

Deseart: Jellys and Sillibubs, curds and cream, pears and aples, pistaches and scorcht almonds, Bisket round the milk.'

Eleven dishes, including the two intermediate 'reliefs' was a generous but not hugely extravagant dinner by the standards of the time. Anything not consumed by the invited diners would be passed to the 'second table', the higher-ranking members of the servant establishment, including the housekeeper, cook, and butler. The menu above would have been prepared by the cook John Mills, who was cook from 1723 to 1729, Grisell noting in her accounts that from Whitsunday 1727 his wages were to be

£14 a year. When dining at other people's houses, Grisell often notes not just what was eaten and how many were at table, but also how the dishes and even candles were arranged, obviously keen to keep up with the latest fashions for presenting a meal. The Mellerstain library contains around a dozen cookery books ranging in date from 1685 to 1741, and those of 1685, 1703 and 1727 have fold-out illustrations of table-settings and of fashionable shapes for pies.

In addition to running the households in Great Marlborough Street and East Barnet, caring for a growing brood of grandchildren, managing her daughters', her husband's and her brothers' financial affairs and overseeing the building and furnishing of a house in Scotland, Grisell found a strange circumstance demanding her attention in the summer of 1728. Lord Mar, in hopes of a pardon, had abandoned the Jacobite court in Rome and had been living in Paris, where he had been joined by his wife, but when it became apparent no pardon would be forthcoming and that Lord Mar would remain in exile, his brother Lord Grange was granted permission by King George I in 1724 to take over the forfeited Mar estates, provided he paid an annual rent of £1,000 to Lady Mar, and that he promised Lady Mar's daughter Lady Frances Erskine a dowry of £10,000. Despite financial security, Lady Mar was very depressed by her circumstances, and wrote to her sister Lady Mary Wortley Montagu, 'Lazyness, Stupidity and ill humour have taken such hold on me that I write to nobody nor have Spirrits to go any where.' Lady Mar's mental health continued to worsen, and in March 1728 she returned with her daughter to London, where she still owned the lease of an apartment in the private garden at Whitehall. A battle ensued for the custody of mentally fragile Lady Mar and her £1,000 a year, between her sister Lady Mary and her brother-in-law Lord Grange, who was supported by her stepson, Lord Erskine. Without consulting

Lady Mary, Grange decided Lady Mar should be moved to Alloa House, her husband's former seat in Scotland, and as the Baillie and Hamilton families were about to travel to Scotland to take up residence in the new East Pavilion at Mellerstain, it was arranged that Lady Mar should travel with them. She had been conveyed from her London lodgings and spent the night at East Barnet with the family on 20 June. The party had only gone about 25 miles to Stevenage the next day when Lady Mary and an officer rode up with a warrant from the Chief Justice ordering that Lady Mar should be returned to London. Lady Mary did not take her sister to her own lodgings but to the Wortley Montagu residence in Covent Garden. Lord Grange, presumably having been alerted by the Baillie family who had also travelled back to London, took possession of Lady Mar and returned her to Marlborough Street, where Grisell, Grisie and Rachy were sitting with her, along with Lord Grange, when Lady Mary burst in, subjecting her sister and Lord Grange to a violent outburst. Lord Grange had signed an affidavit affirming that in her lucid moments Lady Mar had expressed a wish to go to Scotland, but Lady Mary Wortley Montagu, having been granted guardianship of Lady Mar on 24 June petitioned for a Commission of Lunacy. The *London Evening Post* of 27-29 June, which always documented the comings and goings of the nobility, simply reported that, 'The Countess of Mar, who was at Barnet on her Way to Scotland, is come back to Town and is under the Care of the Lady Mary Wortley-Montague'.* The Commission of Lunacy sat on 12 July 1728 and judged that Lady Mar was insane, and soon afterwards the Court of Chancery granted the custody of Lady Mar to her sister Lady Mary. Grisell notes 'the Expences of our Journey Home begune 25th June', so it seems Grisell and her family did not wait for a decision from the Commission of Lunacy before leaving for Scotland. They broke the journey with a short stay at Castle

Howard, where Grisell lost £2:12s to Lord Carlisle playing the newly fashionable card game quadrille, then continued to Tyninghame via Berwick.

When the family were all together at Mellerstain, there was no need for letters between them, nor to William Hume, the factor. However, letters written by others in December 1728 hint at some catastrophic illness which has befallen George Baillie. An unknown correspondent (probably David Mitchell) writing to Grisie from Grosvenor Street, speaks of his 'verry great concern at the late Accounts from Mellerstain' and that his thoughts are 'so continualy fixd on Mr Baillie and the dismal situation you are all in...Lady Grisel I pity from my heart'. Lord Binning's younger brother John Hamilton was about to get married, and the seriousness of George Baillie's condition prompted Lord Haddington to consider postponing the wedding, but he must have been thought to be out of danger by 8 December, when the marriage took place. Rachy is eight months pregnant at this time, and any impending birth was a cause for anxiety, but Rachy was safely delivered of a daughter on 3 January 1729. The child, who was to be Grisell's last grandchild, was named Rachel. Despite George Baillie having survived his bout of unspecified illness, Lady Hervey writing to Grisie in February 1729, says 'I'm truly concerned for the sad situation you are all in. Mr Bailly's illness would alone touch me very sencibly but the fear I'm in least your concern on that account & continual nursing shou'd impair yr own health'. However, in her next (undated) letter, Lady Hervey writes, 'I heartily rejoyce at Mr Bailly's amendment...I wish Bath and Bristol success in their operations upon your two invalids'. This is the first hint of the great concern for the health of Lord Binning, now aged 32. Grisell wrote in her account book, 'March 22nd 1729 we left Mellerstain'. On 17 April, Easter Sunday, Grisell writes to her factor from Bath, 'We came safe here on Saterday last there never was such bad Roads as betwixt this & Nottingham…Mr Baillie held better out than I expected & seems to agree with the waters. Lord Binning is much the better of the journey'. The rest of the letter is taken up with directions concerning the continuing building work at Mellerstain, and the family having now occupied the East Pavilion for some months, defects have become apparent. 'I find Lord Bin is against takeing in the scullery chimny in to the Kitchen if it be possible to help the smokeing of it another way'.

The family remained in Bath until June. Grisell, writing to her factor on the 7th, is frustrated that she has had no answer to her request that Mr. Runciman should give a precise account how far the work is advanced on the 'back offices' and the stables in the West Pavilion at Mellerstain, and directing that other than making things wind- and water-tight, no more building should take place 'for we have great use for all our money'. She tells Mr. Hume to send his reply to Lord Binning, 'for Mr Baillie would be out of all patience to see so many adrents and accounts owing'. The family left Bath for Bristol, also famed for the beneficial properties of its waters and where the Jacobs Well Theatre was newly built in 1729 as Bristol sought to rival Bath for entertainment. Grisell is able to give a cheerful report on the two invalids from the 'hott wells' of Bristol on 11 June. 'Mr Baillie is much recoverd and Ld Bin almost as well as ever he was & I hope shall get his flesh again in some time they are to continue at the waters here until the midle of August & then to Bath again'. The family did not in fact quit Bristol until September, when letters to William Hume are still flowing thick and fast from Grisell's pen concerning, among other topics, the harvest, the tenants, the rats and the building work at Mellerstain, no detail escaping her even at great distance. 'When the painter comes which I think there is no occasion for until the spring I'll have the whole of the East Pavilion gone over again (if it be free of smoke which you must make the strictest tryal of this winter). Have the outer door made a Chocalet Colour'. In October a whole page of Grisell's letter to Hume is occupied by the problem of the smoking chimneys, and with regrets that the new house had been started at all. 'It gives me a great dale of uneasiness. I wish many time[s] never a ston[e] had been laid', though Grisell can happily report, 'both Ld Bin & Mr Baillie are dayly better & better'. A petition from George Baillie to King George II around this time, reminding the king of his exemplary public service, presumably resulted in the granting of a new pension to replace the one which had ceased with the death of King George I.

The purchase of '15yd Popline for mourning for brother Kimmergham' bears witness to a sad event recorded in the *London Evening Post* of 21 March 1730, the death of Grisell's brother Andrew. 'Edinburgh, March 17. Yesterday dy'd the Right Hon. Sir Andrew Hume of Kimerghame, one of the Lords of the Session and is to be interr'd tomorrow in Cannongate Church-yard.'* Andrew was succeeded as Laird of Kimmerghame by his 19-year-old son John, known in the family as 'Jackie'.

Poor health keeps the family in Bath in 1730. While Grisie is staying with 'Lady S' in Great Tew, Grisell has a bout of illness where she 'was seised with her paines as bad as ever', reports Rachy, who admits to having been very frightened. On the advice of 'Dr Carlenton' she has administered two of the universal remedies of the day, some laudanum and an emetic, and Grisell has recovered. Writing to her brother Alexander in October 1730, Grisell says, 'Mr Baillie has had his fitts very severly this month'. Apart from illness, Grisell is under strain from overseeing and financing the Mellerstain building project, and writes, 'Drudge I must for those that is to come after me'. At some time during the autumn of 1727, the household had been augmented by two black slaves, a youth named Cyrus and

Judy, a young girl whose image survives in the 1728 portrait by William Aikman of Grisell's grandsons Thomas and John (Plate 23). Expenditure for clothing, bedding, shoes and stockings for Cyrus and Judy are noted in Grisell's account book, though it seems she was not the purchaser of the slaves. The first item noted in connection with Judy is a bill for stockings and shoes in September 1727, at a time when many poorer women and girls went barefoot. Cyrus acted as footman or postilion, and 'Spurrs to Cyrus' tell us he was taught, or already able, to ride a horse. Fifteen shillings is among regular amounts spent on 'learning him to read and write', and James Massy, the Mellerstain schoolmaster receives a couple of shillings for teaching Judy, who also had a 'reading mistress'. Despite medicines costing a substantial £2:5s being spent for him with 'Foord Apoticary', and the services of a nurse being paid for, Cyrus died while the family were in Bath, and was buried there in St Michael's church, where the register simply records, '7th May 1730 a Black boy was Buried in the Church yard'. Cyrus was accorded the dignity of a decent burial, with the funeral bill listing amounts paid for the church, the minister, the clerk, the certificate, a coffin, a shroud, digging the grave and ringing the bell. The family were still in Bath in January 1731, remaining until April, plenty of time for George Baillie to sit for a bust by an unnamed sculptor, Grisell paying six guineas 'For my Dears Busto', together with four shillings for a box for it.

The damp British climate was thought to be injurious to people suffering from tuberculosis and so, whether at some physician's recommendation, or at Grisell's own insistence, it was decided that Lord Binning should travel to benefit from the sunshine of Naples. George Baillie, being unwell himself, according to Lady Murray 'pressed Lord Binning extremely to go with some friend to take care of him; but he absolutely refusing unless we went altogether, he yielded to what was both disagreeable and inconvenient to himself.' The party of travellers set out for Holland in the yacht *Mary*, the same vessel which had carried the future Queen Mary and her retinue, including Grisell and her mother, to Britain in 1689. We know exactly who was in the party, as Grisell notes in her account book, 'London 20 May 1731. This Day went aboard the Mary yaught for Holland, Lord Binning Mr Baillie his two Doughtes his grandchild Grisie & myself 3 manservants. John Culbertson, Will Bower, & James Harly 2 maids [blank] Mushet and Janet Gibson.' Lord Binning's two eldest boys Tamie and George were sent to school in London, and Charles James and Rachel, aged 3 and 2, were left in the care of May Menzies at Tyninghame. 'Litle Johnie' born in October 1726 features in Grisell's accounts in 1730 as a recipient of various toys and a cap, but must have died before May 1731, aged 4, the third of Grisell's grandchildren to die, having been predeceased by his siblings Helen and Charles.

Chapter 9

⁓ɔᴆɛ⁓

JOURNEY TO NAPLES

1731–1733

The journey to Naples took just over six months, a difficult journey for anyone, made more difficult, no doubt, by the fact that one member of the party had advanced tuberculosis and another was very frail and at 67 elderly by the standards of the day, as was Grisell herself. Grisell's notebook contains the expenses for every stage of the journey through modern-day Netherlands, Belgium, Luxembourg and France, then over the Alps into Italy, and she shows incredible facility at getting to grips with the many different currencies encountered along the way. 'We came to Rome the 23 Novemr at one a clock of the day 1731, here a sequin is still 20 Julios or Pols in some payments (half) poul more, a sequin is 2 Phillips, there is half phillips and quarter phillips which is 2 and a half Poul. A Powl is 10 bycocks, there is half and quarter pouls and 5 quotrins for a bycock.'

Having safely crossed the North Sea in the yacht *Mary*, the family landed at Rotterdam, and visited, among other places, Delft, Leiden, Haarlem, Antwerp, Amsterdam and, of course,

Utrecht, so fondly remembered by Grisell as the place of safety where her parents and siblings had lived in exile, and where her relationship with George Baillie blossomed during their secret engagement. Grisell's powers of persuasion in her native tongue seldom failed, but she suffered a great disappointment there, as Lady Murray recounted: 'When she came to Utrecht, the place of her former abode, she had the greatest of pleasure in showing us every corner of the town, which seemed fresh in her memory; particularly the house she had lived in, which she had a great desire to see; but when she came there, they would not let her in, by no arguments either of words or money, for no reason but for fear of dirtying it. She offered to put off her shoes, but nothing could prevail, and she came away much mortified at her disappointment.' The family travelled via Maastricht to Aachen [Aix-la Chapelle] and Spa, the two latter towns both being famed for the curative powers of their waters. Having reached Spa at the beginning of July, they remained there for about 10 weeks. Like Bath, Spa was a very fashionable place to be, and must have been frequented by many British visitors. The family apparently gave a ball, and supper to 70 persons, costing 196 livres [11 pounds sterling], before proceeding to Liège, Namur and Luxembourg and then towards Burgundy. On 3 October Grisell makes the first mention of customs officials searching their considerable baggage. 'Din[e]d at Dampier [Dampierre] lay at Champain [Champagne-sur-Vingeanne] in the Dutche of Burgundy was serched here overly and gote a pass', and on the 6th October, 'was stopd at Shalong [Chalon-sur-Saône] 3 days by the impertinance of the Bourro [Bureau]'. 'Serchers' were also paid when they reached Lyon, where they stayed for six days, gathering their forces for the difficult next stage of the journey.

Grisell names various forms of wheeled transport employed by the family, including coach, post wagon, berlin, diligence and chaise, but the section of the route from Lyon to Turin presented special difficulties for travellers as a high mountain pass in the Alps had to be crossed which was impassable to wheeled vehicles, so on 23 October Grisell notes 'For car[ry]ing 6 chairs over the Alps called Munt Sines [Col du Mont Cénis] to men to drink 12:0:0 [livres]'. (Traveller John Wilkes, writing some 30 years later says of the 'chairs', 'The chair in which I was carried was not a sedan chair but a small wicker chair with two long poles; there is no covering of any kind to it'). Once over the pass into Italy, more customs officers had to be paid. 'Serchers the Duan at Novalies [Novalesa] 2:0:0.' Five nights were spent at Turin 'Seeing Palices and other places', and making use of opera tickets, and where it was thought prudent to buy '6 geografical maps'. Further towns visited were Milan, Parma, Reggio, Modena, Bologna, Loreto and Terni before Rome was reached on 23 November, and Naples five days later. Churches and palaces were viewed at every place along the route, with tombs, libraries, hospitals, treasures, relics, amphitheatres, and mosaic work for variety – a punishing itinerary even supposing all the party had been in perfect health.

Along the way, most of the purchases not directly related to travel, sightseeing, food and lodging costs had been for items of clothing, and for laundering them. In Lyon, long established as a silk weaving centre, silk is bought for a gown for Grisie, and another for Grisell, with Grisie's 'floord silk' costing twice as much as her mother's, and also about twice the cost of 'silk for a sute cloaths' presumably destined for George Baillie. Once in Naples, a house is rented, apparently furnished except for table linen and tableware, some kitchen items and chamber pots. An Italian maid and footman and a French cook are hired to add to the five servants who have travelled with the family. May Menzies, writing at Tyninghame on 20 January 1732 reports that, 'My Lord [Haddington] had a letter from Lord Bining from Naples…his Lord'p was pretty well then was wearyed with the journey… they had got lodgings my Lord writes with twelve rooms of a floor two of them only had chimneys and one of them smoked.' Grisell had noted a payment in October for 'Sundry things layd out by Bower [a manservant] for Gibson [the maidservant Janet Gibson] when sick', and May Menzies reveals the cause of her illness in a letter: 'Mrs Gibson…was taken very ill upon the road with eating green fruit'. Servant problems were exacerbated by the fact that the newly-hired ones were not English-speaking. Lady Murray writes: 'At Naples she [Grisell] showed what would have been a singular quickness of capacity and apprehension at any age, much more of hers. She knew not one word of Italian, and had servants of the country that as little understood one word she said; so that at first she was forced to call me to interpret betwixt them; but in a very little while, with only the help of a grammar and dictionary, she did the whole business of her family with her Italian servants, went to shops, bought everything she had occasion for, and did it so well, that our acquaintances who had lived many years there, begged the favour of her to buy for them when she provided herself.'

The Mellerstain factor William Hume has received news from Lord Binning at the beginning of February 1732 of the family's safe arrival in Naples which pleases him, 'but am very sory to hear that Mr Baillie had had a Return of his Ilnes and that your Lop [Lordship] continows still tender'. He expresses surprise that the family are 'even att Naples troubled with Smokie Chimnays', and goes on to tell of several pleasant walks now established at Mellerstain, and the progress of various instructions about the planting given by Lord Binning. George Baillie's unspecified illness prompts various correspondents to send good wishes, including Lady Mary Howard at Castle Howard and Lord Haddington in Tyninghame, who writes once a week and will continue to do so as long as George Baillie is happy to receive his letters, although 'I am old, Weak and have very bad health'. (Lord Binning's father is now 52 years of age). In May the family moves from Naples just a few miles south to the port of Portici. We learn from Grisell, writing on 22 May to William Hume from 'Portiche at the foot of Mount Vesuvious' that 'my Lord Binning is much mended and so is my Doughter. [Lady Mary Howard had mentioned that Rachy was ill]. Mr Baillie has lately had a return of his fitts but in the main is much better in his health but what troubles him most is his Deafness which rather grows wors and is a great discuragment to him. We are made believe that this air may perfite all their cures. I pray God it may.' Lord Binning continued to write verse to amuse his family and friends, and one example gives us a snapshot of the household in Portici. His daughter Grisie, now 13, like her brother George has inherited her grandfather George Baillie's fondness for household pets and at this time these include a cat which has caused little Grisie great distress by killing her guinea pig. The pigeons, turkey, geese and chickens in her care may have been destined for the table, but she can't forgive the gratuitous murder of the guinea pig, 'the Dearest of all my Dear Dears'. In another poem, Lord Binning jokingly complains of being neglected by his wife Rachy who is too engrossed in her needlework, and in a verse letter writes a sketch of the occupations of each member of the household: George Baillie smoking his pipe and lamenting the loss of his senses, Grisell dashing upstairs and down at the behest of the family, always leaving her spectacles behind, and Grisie making the tea and giving instructions to the cook in Italian. Rachy has set herself up as the household physician and dietician, forbidding others certain foods but consuming the same herself, and little Grisie, 'Like Grand mama is ever busy/ Has Birds & Rabbits, Cats & Messons [lapdogs]/ And masters three to give her lessons.'

Lord Binning also includes a description of himself: 'Binning is always full of flights/ of Buildings or some strange Delights/ He eats his meat but where it goes/ 'Tis only He that made him knows/ For such a lean unthriving Creature/ I never yet beheld in nature.' A marble bust of Lord Binning probably created during his stay in Naples or Portici and now in the library at Mellerstain does indeed show a very emaciated figure.

We learn from Lord Haddington, writing on 22 August, that Grisell's touching faith in the health-giving powers of the air at Portici is unfounded, as he writes, 'I had not a letter from Portici for a Fortnight which made me Long very much for one and to see the vanity of our Hopes and wishes in this World, when I got the Letter it hurt me Exceedingly for I find Lady Grisel and you [George Baillie] much cast Down, Lord Binning much out of order and Lady Binning at great pains to keep up his illness from me'. He goes on to say that he would rather not be shielded from bad news, and it seems as if true accounts of his son's health had reached Tyninghame at the beginning of October, when May Menzies reports to George Baillie, 'My Lord & my Lady [Haddington] & the children [Charles and Rachel] are all in good health but in great affliction for the ill accounts they get of my Lord Bining...my Lords two sons at London [Tamie and George] are very well.' As well as running the ailing household in Italy, Grisell is still attempting to supervise Mellerstain, with the distance and the precarious state of the post creating extra difficulties. When writing to her factor, she numbers her letters as well as dating them, so that he will know whether any are missing but, writing on 26 December, she admits to confusion. 'I have no account of what I have wrote but shall begin my numbers again, indeed considering the state I have been in by Lord Binnings constant illness its no wonder I forgot it. He has keep'd his bed neer six moneth & has often been dispaird of but I still hope that

God will spair him'. Despite his frailty, Lord Binning remains anxious to give directions regarding the continuing landscaping at Mellerstain: 'he bids me tell you…The diaginall walk on snep brea [Sneep Brae] must be caried on as far as it can go 40 foot broad planted with firrs and other trees'. (Landscaping had been a lifelong passion for Lord Binning who when he was aged just 10 had designed some of the walks in Binning Wood at Tyninghame being newly planted by his father in 1707). Other messages from Lord Binning are included in the letter, as well as Grisell's own instructions about paying servants' wages and her complaints about the excessive amounts demanded by the painter and plumber, and her regrets that she had not dismissed Will Bower, Lord Binning's servant, sooner than she did as 'he was taken up with nothing but Mistresses where ever he came'.

The whole family had a novel and unwelcome experience on 29 November, when the region was struck by an earthquake. Grisell wrote: 'Sur[e]ly youll have an account in Print of the terrable earthquack here which had very near destroyd us all it is to[o] frightfull to describe its a great mercy there was so few kild here but many hunder is kild, 40, 30 & 20 miles round & when all here run out of their houses and lay abroad all next night, the best in tents & coaches & the rest in the open fields, poor Lord Binning was in so weak a state as not to be moved & we all stayd to take our fait with him'. The decision that the family should remain indoors with Lord Binning during the aftershocks proved to have been a wise one in other respects as a correspondent in the *London Evening Post* of 21 December reported, 'The British Consul and his family and other English Gentlemen lay on board Ships of their Nation in our bay, and others slept in Coaches in the broad Streets. The Viceroy's Palace, and most of the Churches and publick Buildings, were much crack'd and scarce a House in the City escaped without damage. Those which had kept in their Houses fared best, for some few were kill'd and many hurt in the Streets by the falling of Stones from the Tops of the Houses.'*

Throughout 1732 Grisell's accounts show that despite family illness, life went on much as usual. The personal expenses of granddaughter Grisie, Rachy and Lord Binning are not recorded by Grisell, but daughter Grisie is still provided for by her parents with many items of clothing, and her love of music is still clearly the most important thing in her life, as Grisell funds lessons from 'S[ignor] Carmany Playing Master' and pays for music to be copied and bound and a hired spinet to be frequently tuned. Once the family has moved from Naples to Portici, an additional expense is the hire of chaises to transport the music master and an Italian master to give their lessons in Portici. During the time in Naples and Portici, a couple of suits, a waistcoat, a nightgown and two pairs of shoes are purchased for George Baillie, but there is a far longer list of items of female clothing and accessories for Grisie and Grisell, including jumps, [corsets], hoops [hooped petticoats], stockings, garters, petticoats, gowns, robes, wrappers, sacks [sack-back dresses or jackets], waistcoats, cloaks and aprons as the basic items to be accessorised with shoes, hats, tippets, mittens, gloves, ribbons, wigs, handkerchiefs and fans. (In 1729, one surprising item in Grisell's 'Account of my cloaths' had been 5s10d for 'Dyaper for 3 pr drawers', as drawers were not worn as female underwear for another half century, but possibly they were to ensure modesty when bathing at Bath.) Both Grisie and Grisell evidently take snuff as Grisell provides her daughter with three snuff handkerchiefs and herself with four. Other than clothing, by far the largest item of expenditure is for '2 Marbel Tables Fiore de persico' and many others, including wooden cases and 'Shiping in the *Barcelona* and custom house officers', amounting in all to 3,299 ducats, estimated at 660 pounds sterling. By 'tables' it is probable that Grisell means marble slabs rather than complete pieces of furniture, some destined to be used in various ways to adorn the house at Mellerstain, and others purchased as commissions for friends in Britain.

At the end of the year, any remaining hopes Grisell might have had that the family's lengthy pilgrimage could save Lord Binning were extinguished with his death on 27 December. [This was 27 December Old Style, according to the Julian calendar prevailing in Britain, though by the European New Style Gregorian calendar it was 7 January]. News of his death does not reach Tyninghame until 28 January, when May Menzies, relaying the news to William Hume in Mellerstain, writes: 'he gave all the marks of a happy change, an unexpressable loss to two families I may well say a nationall loss many good qualitys had he and none of his bad was ever known, what a loss his poor bairns has of a good pattern his corpse is shipped to come over to England and from that to be brought down to Tiningham a sorrowful meeting will that be its not known yet what course the distressed familie takes his poor Lady has had vast toyl & is very thin'. Grisell had noted, 'His heart, etc., was buried at St Corrolas Church Yeard and his corps sent home to Tiningham'.

Three days after Lord Binning's death, Grisell wrote a letter to Queen Caroline, reminding her that Lord Binning had at a very young age become Knight Marischal of Scotland and hoping that his son might be similarly favoured in the future. (Tamie is still only 12 years old). She further requests help for the education of Lord Binning's numerous family for which there will be 'a lasting fund of gratitude in me for this smal remainder of a sorrowfull life'. On 8 March 1733, May Menzies reports that 'they [Lord and Lady Haddington] heard from Naples today my Lady Bin: is in a very bad state of health, they are to travel as soon as she is able'. She also says, 'there's no word yet of that ship that brought away the corpse from Naples'. All the household goods, books and souvenirs of no further use on the journey, including the large quantity of marble, are despatched to London on the ship *Union*, whose captain John Burton signed a receipt for 148 cases of goods, stating that he did not know the contents of the cases. Later in March Rachy's health must have improved, and the family's sights are set on returning home. Grisell buys macaroni, hams and 165 pounds of Parmesan cheese to be sent home by sea, and a number of purchases seem likely to be intended as presents to take back, including six snuff boxes, 11 sword belts, 26 more expensive fans and 18 cheaper ones, six tortoiseshell combs and '2 caps to the boys', presumably Tamie and George. By the end of March they have reached Rome, and several weeks are spent in Florence, when spirits have sufficiently recovered for 'seeing Churches Palices and villas' and 'the great Duk[e]s Gallarie', precursor of the Uffizi, still at this period renowned more as a 'cabinet of curiosities' than as a collection of works of art. Also when in Florence, Grisell pays 36 crowns 'For 3 Pictor of Mr Baillie, my Daughter Grisie, and my grandchild Gris by Mr Martine' [Charles Martin]. The first two of these pictures still hang at Mellerstain, and are pastels in a much more informal style than the previous oil portraits of either sitter. George Baillie has not shrunk from realism, apparently happy to be depicted in casual dress, and using his ear trumpet. Other souvenirs added to the family's baggage in Florence include '2 volums of the gallery of the great Duke' and '10 vol. Italian books', as well as '2 alabaster figures' and '2 Lyons of Marbel' (Plate 24b).

Mid May sees the family in Bologna, where the most considerable expense was 'For the box in the opera house', which then required a 'cushen in the box' and a 'cloath to ly over the box' as well as '18 Tickets to the opera' and '2 opera book'. By accident or design, Grisell and her family had arrived in Bologna just in time to hear the castrato singer Farinelli, the superstar of his day, sing the title role in the première of Hasse's *Siroe*. The

Earl of Essex, British ambassador to the court of Turin, was also there and reported that there 'was a vast deal of Company there thirty-two English besides other Strangers'. It seems probable that the Baillie family were included in the 'English', and also likely that they met people they were acquainted with in many of the principal towns along their route. By 11 June they have reached Venice where a 'Gundala' is hired for eight days at a costly £8 a day, presumably including the services of a gondolier to convey them to the various places they visited, including a glass works and the Doge's palace. Some of Canaletto's paintings of Venice date from around 1733, so we can have a very clear idea of the 'Gundala', and the sights that met the eyes of Grisell and her family.

In addition to Grisell's accounts of the expenses incurred along the way, she must have made careful and copious notes of what was to be seen, where they stayed and where they ate as this was later neatly written down and the resulting 'travelogue' given to her grandsons Tamie and George to advise them when they are about to set out on their grand tour in March 1740. In addition to seeing palaces in Venice and fine paintings (Titian, Tintoretto, Veronese and Bassano being mentioned), Grisell directs that they must eat ice cream at the 'house near St Marks famous for making every thing in Ice the best of any place it is like a Coffie house'. After seeing the sights of Venice, the towns of Padua, Vicenza, Verona and Trento are the remaining places visited in Italy. Grisell warns that near Peri there is 'A difficult passage where they take out the horses and dragg the chaises up by men about 200 yards'. Despite her own youth and that of her husband being entirely shaped by adherence to Protestantism, Grisell does not seem uncomfortable surrounded by all the trappings of Catholicism she meets with on her travels. There are payments to priests, churches and convents, purchases of 'Saints Pictors', '2 wax pop[e]s' and '2 Corinthen brass pop[e]s', and

17   Rachy, Lady Binning 1725 by Maria Verelst

18 George Baillie with grandson George 1727 by William Aikman

163

Account of the Expences of Building a House
At Mellerstaine founded by Lord Binning the
of September 1725

For a large Punch for the quarie 4 ft at 4ᵈ pr ft	1	14			
a lesser punch 3 ft 4 pound		15	4		
6 Picks 55 ft at 5ᵈ pr ft	1	11	3		
2 Pick howes 1 stone 5 ft	0	1½			
18 wedges 6 ft 5 ft at 4ᵈ & 4ᵈ more	1	10	4		
a Mell & Sledge 1 st 9½ ft all by Dᵛ James Hall		11	3	6	10	3½

September 6

To Mr Adams for his Slaves	10	10		
cariages Lime 1ᵈ & sometimes 2 a horse		7	2	
50 days at Foundation of the Pavilion before Mr Adams was agreed with to build it	1	3	4	
184 days 5 men pulling down the old Tower	3	16	8	
753 days at Fans quarie	13	13	9	
quariers at 10ᵈ pr day at Fans quarie	5	16		
296 days 5 men Leading stons	6	3	4	
67 days digging stone 178 & 9 mens harvest 2ᵗ	3	8	4	
145 Loads Lime 5ᵈ pr Load Col & score 8ᵈ	3	18	8	
15 days &c at Leading Coldstream stons		11	3	
will Hardys account wright pulling down tower		11	8	
7 oz. Laces 1 9ᵈ		1	9	
will Gray Mason for pulling down Tower	2	12		
Lead for Crooks 2 s 6ᵈ Cement for stons 6ᵈ		3		
1 Coge to four Lime 5ᵈ a tub for quarie 10ᵈ		1	6	
timber pr David Chisholl recet 3 £ expences 6ᵈ	3	6		
Buttocks of timber one of 10 tree & rails		5		
200 plancher nails 200 floor nails		10	4	
eleven oxen bought 37 £ 15 s 3 oxen got og £ 10ᵗ	28	5	6	
65 pecks Merchfield oats to cart horses	3	15		
a pair wain wheels 4 £ 8 s 4ᵈ a pair 3 £ 5ᵗ	7	18	7	
shoing 12 oxen 4 s grease 2ᵈ 6ᵈ 5ᵈ		6	6	
quick silver & Ment salve for an oxe		1		
Drink by Ld Binings Order		10		
2000 Divets for covering walls new built		2	97	12	4

To Mr Adams to account of his work given this winter	34	2	5½	
143 days payd his borrowmen	2	19	5	
54 dayt souring Lime	1	2	6	
payd Robert Maine		10	4	38	14	8⅚

£ 142 17 4

19   Page from Grisell's account book 1725

20a   View to the 'canal' and 'Hunimonda's Tower'

20b   Hundy Mundy tower built 1725

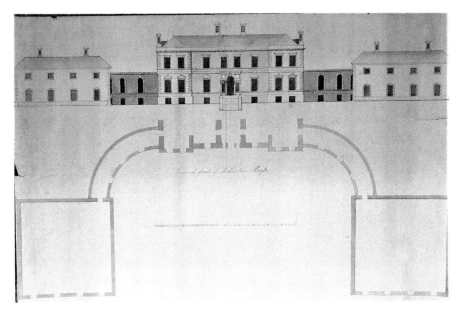

21a   William Adam plan 1725

21b   Adam's plan of the 'principall floor'

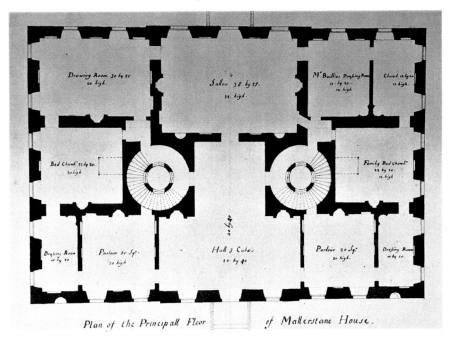

Plan of the Principall Floor   of Mallerstane House.

22   Stairhead newel 1728 by James Shiells

23 Thomas and John Hamilton with Judy by William Aikman 1728

24a   Silverware

24b   'Marbel Lyon' purchased in Florence 1733

25a The 'Monument' 1738

25b Stone hall, east pavilion with Norie landscape c1742

26   Dutch tiles purchased in 1742

27a East Pavilion begun 11th September 1725

27b Sketch map of Mellerstain as it was by 1740

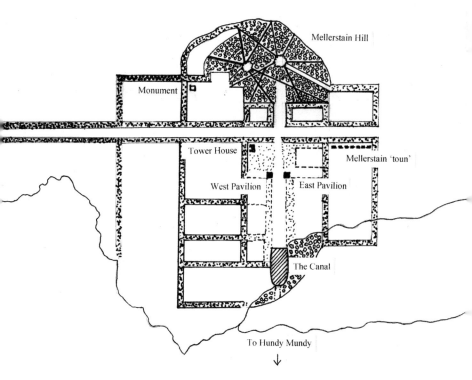

28   Grisell, Lady Stanhope by Allan Ramsay 1740

29 George Baillie by Allan Ramsay 1747

30 Grisell by Allan Ramsay c1745

31 Rachel and Charles Hamilton 1740 by Allan Ramsay

32   Bust of Grisell by Louis-François Roubiliac 1746/7

Grisell shows a surprising enthusiasm for organ music. Since the Reformation, Protestant churches in Scotland had not used the organ in worship, and pre-existing instruments had been ripped out and destroyed, so it is unlikely that she had heard organ music while growing up. James VII and II had installed an organ in the Chapel at Holyrood Palace in 1687, but, said John Macky in his *Journey through Scotland*, 'the Mob at the Revolution pull'd it all to pieces, thinking it smelt too rank of Popery'. In Trent[o], Grisell advises, 'See the church where the Counsell was held in which is a very fine organ, hear it play' and at other places on her travels, 'Hear the fine organ in the great church' at Amsterdam and 'remember to hear the organ in the great church at Alckmaer [Alkmaar], the finest in the world'.

After Trento, the slow journey northwards continued via Innsbruck, Munich, Augsburg, and Frankfurt to Cologne. In Grisell's own words, 'We went by water doun the Rhine in two days and a half. We hierd two boats, one for ourselves close coverd like a Pleasur Barge upon the Tames, in which we lay all night upon good straw and Pillows for our heads, and never went on shore. An open boat for the servants and chaises. We payd 75 Florins for all, Taxes included, of which there are many at every toun you pass by. It was in the sumer and no danger of catching cold. We caryd our provitions, had tea water boyld and every thing dresst [cooked] in the Boat with the servants which was tyd to ours. The water men or servants went on shore at any toun we came to and got us what ever we wanted.' Aix la Chapelle [Aachen], Spa, Liège and Brussels are the next towns along the route, with many places trying to make money from tourists, but Grisell finds a little bribery is the cheapest option. 'At every Bureau, which is the same as our Custome house officers, they inquire if you have any old money [currency from previous places visited], which is prohibited. If you have any you must take care to hide it well, for some times they serch very narowly, and if they find it you loose it, but a little money given in time generaly prevents it.'

Even before reaching Brussels, a large purchase of lace has been made in Liège, as well as 19 pairs of gloves for Lady Hervey [Grisie's friend Molly Lepell], and three days in Brussels is long enough for a surgeon to be consulted for some reason about Grisie's arm and 'For bringing the Brass Trumpets for Deafnes from Ipers [Ypres]' for George Baillie's use. Having reached Brussels it might be expected that the family would continue towards the Channel coast, now only some 70 miles away, but instead they turn south-west towards Paris, crossing into France at Valenciennes where again the party's passage at the customs is smoothed by 'giving a little money and without hesitation telling them at the same time we gave the money that they might serch if they pleasd for we had nothing counterband nor any Merchandise which is the question they ask'. En route for Paris, one of the highlights is at Chantilly where they view 'the house and Gardens, the finest thing to be seen in France'.

As a stay of several weeks in Paris is projected, an apartment is rented in fashionable St. Germain. 'Here we had privet lodgeings at the Hotel d'Ambour, Rue de Four, Fauxbourg St. Germain, payd 300 livers a munth for all the first floor, containing 6 handsome well furnished rooms, 3 rooms on the floor over it, a Hall for servants and other conveniences'. The list of places visited is extensive, featuring many of the houses possessed by the King [Louis XV] including Marly, which had been said by Lord Binning to be the only house whose situation was equal to the house he envisaged at Mellerstain when he first went there in 1717. Marly was famed for having water features supplied by a massive feat of hydraulic engineering. Grisell says, 'There is no water but what is supplied by a vast machine half a league below the house, which may be said to throw the river Sein up a vast hill, which is there received in reservoirs to throw it back again into the Garden, where water abounds in all shapes'.

Having become accustomed to the sunny climate in Naples, and enjoying summer weather on the journey northwards, adjustments are needed to the family's wardrobe in chilly October in Paris. Several pairs of stockings are bought, variously described as 'worsit' [woollen], 'baver' [beaver skin] and 'thick travelling stockings', and also 'Baver skin gloves', all necessary to keep their wearers warm while travelling around to see the sights, but Paris, then as now, was the foremost city of fashion, and numerous items are purchased so the family can appear suitably dressed in Parisian society. George Baillie needs two new wigs, 'a ty one and a bob', and head coverings and hairdressing seem to take on a new importance for Grisell who buys four hoods, two dozen combs, wires [for headdresses], 14 ells of black lace, a gass [gauze] head [headdress] and quilted caps. New French clothing-related words enter her vocabulary, with mention of an '*Antoylage* head', entoilage being the fabric that lace was mounted on, '6 bread[th]s white satin with a deep floord border for a *Jupon* [petticoat], and 'Muslins for *fashus*' [fichus] to fill in the neckline of low-cut dresses. Either Grisell herself or Grisie was the proud wearer of a gown and coat made from '13 ell floord [flowered] silk' costing 338 livres, estimated at almost 15 pounds sterling, and to complete the elegant outfits six pairs of footwear including '4 pr Imbroidered shoes'. As well as the endless round of sightseeing, tickets to the opera are bought, and the family must have been entertained in private houses, to judge by tips of three livres each paid to 'Mr Knights coachman' and 'Mrs Horners coachman' as well as to Lewis, a servant of Horatio Mann. Mann, writing to Horace Walpole almost half a century later, recounts a curious incident about Grisell: 'I remember that when I was young and in company with old Lady Grizle Balie at Paris, I told her that I had dreamt that a large tooth had fallen out of my head. She immediately said that I should certainly hear of the death of an old and near relation and lo! the next post brought me news of the death of my grandfather. This confirmed her reputation of a prophetess.'

Before leaving Paris more presents are bought including 14 ells of silk for Mally Mitchell and '2 pr rufles for my boys T[amie] and G[eorge].' Perhaps it was calculated that even allowing for the rest of the journey on French soil, there was going to be French currency left over, or maybe Grisell was just anxious to add some Parisian style to her dinner table, but she notes the purchase of 'Ane Eparn [Epergne, table centrepiece] french silver' at 205 livres, together with three pairs of candlesticks, salts, snuffers, snuff pans and fruit plates. Someone in the party unfortunately needed the services of 'Caparan teeth drawer', very expensive at 96 livres [4 guineas sterling]. At the end of October the final stages of the journey home were begun, with Grisell declaring that Clermont, Abbéville and Boulogne were all 'a good place to ly [sleep] at' on the road to Calais where 'we hierd a little shipe, on[e] of Mr. Minets'. The 'Master of the Sloup from Calice to Dover' was paid 96 livres, exactly the same fee as the tooth-drawer. Having left London in May 1731, the family are back there in November 1733 after 30 months, older, sadder and wiser. They have seen the chief glories of the art and architecture of much of Europe, but have lost Lord Binning, a beloved son-in-law, brother-in-law, husband and father.

Chapter 10

RETURN TO MELLERSTAIN

1734–1736

Despite the many distractions of life abroad, letters had continued to flow from Grisell's pen to Mellerstain, though it is not known what proportion reached their destination, nor how reliably she could receive any replies. Writing from London to William Hume her factor on 23 November 1733, Grisell expresses doubt about whether it is the postal system or William Hume's memory which is unreliable. 'Im vext to find you have not gote a long letter of mine from Naples or has forgot what I wrote about the Gardin I gave very particular directions about everything was to be planted and told you that Mr Baillie eat litle els than what was out of a Gardin'. She directs that 'all hands are to be sett to work in the Gardin & every place be filled with hearbs and roots of all kinds'. The next letter to Hume six days later indicates that the family has left London for Popes, the manor house near Hatfield in Hertfordshire, home of family friends David Mitchell (né Cooke) and his wife Mary, (known as Mally), a Burnet cousin of George Baillie. Grisell is again anxious for a good supply of vegetables for her husband. 'I beg you make the Gardner diligent in labouring the kitchen ground', perhaps forgetting the difficulties planting presents in the middle of a Scottish winter. May Menzies is directed, via Mr. Hume, to check on things like basins, chamber pots and servants' sheets which may be lacking at Mellerstain and need to be in place before the family's return.

Before the family had left for Naples, Tamie and George had been placed in the care of a tutor, Frenchman (or possibly Swiss) Gabriel de Saussure, and attended Dr. Newcombe's school in Hackney, an establishment much favoured by Whig politicians for their sons' education. They did not board there but were in lodgings nearby, as we can see from the meticulous, beautifully written account book kept by Monsieur de Saussure from May 1731 to May 1734. M. de Saussure sought doctors and medicines when the boys were ill, with George being particularly susceptible to coughs and colds; he paid for them to entertain their friends, had clothes repaired and bought new ones, doled out their pocket money of one shilling a week and bribed them with more money to speak French. M. de Saussure doesn't say how the damage was caused, but no less than three times he had to pay for the repair of broken windows at their lodgings, as well as a broken bed. In January 1733 their tutor buys toys to console George and Tamie 'after they had learned of the loss of their Papa', and Tamie, previously referred to in the accounts as 'M. Hamilton' is now 'Milord', having become Lord Binning, the courtesy title used by the heir to the Earl of Haddington, on the death of his father.

The Mitchells at Hatfield appear to have been keeping an eye on George and Tamie while the family are abroad, as both boys write letters from Popes on 21 May 1733. George, aged 10, writes to his grandfather George Baillie thanking him for the offer of a present, telling him they have been at Popes a fortnight and go fishing when the weather is good. (Either George or Tamie's fishing skills are in need of improvement as M. de Saussure had previously had to pay for a surgeon to remove a fish hook from Tamie's lip). George also says 'I made yesterday an end to my Task and shall not be affraid when I come to school again to appear before Mr Tikletail', meaning that he has done his homework, so has no need to fear being beaten with the schoolmaster's rod. Tamie, aged 12, is writing to his mother Rachy for the first time since the death of his father five months previously and begins, 'I did not write to you sooner about my Dear Papa's Death for fear of renewing your grief. My heart was most sore when I heard of it so I am sensible that it is an irriparable Loss. I whish I may one Day be like him'. At the end of the letter he signs himself, 'Your most Dutyfull Son Binning'.

Although the family had occupied part of the East Pavilion at Mellerstain in 1728, much apparently still remained to be done, as we learn from Grisell writing to Hume on 8 February 1734. 'If there is not Chimny pieces [fireplaces] and the window lind [shutters] of the room over against mine, the room under that & the low rooft yellow room… & washing [skirting] boards round them make a good Joyner fall about them immediately.… what is the closet of the Chince [chintz] room floord with. I should be glad to have as litle trouble wt [with] workmen after I come there as possible, sett 3 of the best closs [box] beds in that room, the weemen servants room I mean, & the rest over in the West Pavilion for our own comon men servants'. In subsequent letters Hume notes that a number of locks and snecks will be needed, which might be got cheaper in London, and Grisell replies with her intention to bring a number of fine locks from their London house for use in the East Pavilion, and stresses that whenever their goods reach Mellerstain, the long thin boxes which contain marble must be treated as if they contain glass, and that the boxes containing books must be guarded from damp at all costs.

Finally, we learn from Grisie writing to Hume on behalf of her mother on 16 May 1734 that Captain Stewart is to sail that night in the ship bringing all their possessions from London to Berwick. Grisell's instructions are, as ever, very precise, in that Captain Stewart is not to unload but to let Hume know as soon as he arrives in Berwick. Hume is to go there the moment he hears, along with James Harley and some of the workmen to help unload. 'You had best hier a wayn [cart] or two to get them the sooner home take great care how they are loaded that things may not be brock, that the havie [heavy] things are put undermost'. It is not just inanimate books, marble and furniture that Hume is given responsibility for, as Grisie adds, 'there are 6 dogs and a cat which must be taken great care of & imediatly got home for fear of they're being lost, they are all great favourits and fine of their kind'. Grisell herself writes several days later, repeating the content of her daughter's letter, adding that she now has Captain Stewart's receipt for the 152 parcels, 6 dogs and a cat, and increasing the numbers of wains likely to be needed to 'three or four or more'.

Having had to pay good money to Captain Stewart, and to numerous other shipmasters for carrying her goods in the past perhaps put Grisell in mind to invest in shipping herself, as on 28 February 1735 she purchases for £32:16s3d a one-sixteenth share of 'the Good Ship called *Helen* of Berwick about Eighty Tuns burden or thereby' from shipmaster Job Buck of Berwick, who promises in the sale document that she shall receive one sixteenth of the profits, the document also stating that the ship is currently in the harbour at Leith.

Letters are fewer once the family have followed their goods and chattels and household pets to Mellerstain. Mr. Hume had continued to supervise building both at the house and in

Mellerstain 'toun', where tenants' houses were repaired and Will Gray the stonemason was paid 3s2d for 'the Crose of Mellerstaine', presumably a stone cross to be the focal point for markets and fairs in the little village, the fairs being a mixture of business and entertainment. A new form of entertainment was to be had eight miles away in Kelso when in 1734 the first horse races were held at Caverton Edge, and Grisell's sundry accounts for 1735 include three shillings spent 'For [sedan] Chairs at Kelso races', which must have been a welcome diversion from all her hard work, though it must have been a relief to Grisell to be able now to personally oversee the elements of the building work and landscaping remaining to be finished. She purchases '20,000 Alldes [alders]' from Holland, and pays out £ 25:10s 'to 5 pence men at the Cannall' (which amounts to 1,224 days' work). She buys many fruit trees for the orchard and 'Glases for hotbeds' in the kitchen garden, whose produce Grisell deemed so essential to George Baillie's health. The whole of the journey from Naples to London seems to have been achieved without recourse to doctors, perhaps arising from potential language difficulties, though when they had been settled in Naples Lord Binning's diet had been supervised by a Doctor Cerilo, whose written instructions still exist. Once returned to Britain, George Baillie again has access to physicians, including the foremost among them, Dr. George Cheyne, a distant Burnet cousin. Cheyne had set up a medical practice in London and in Bath during the season, assuring himself of a wealthy and ailing clientele. By the mid-1720s he was morbidly obese at 32 stones, and had restored his own health by a diet of milk, white meat and vegetables, which he urged his patients to follow while also lecturing them on moral and spiritual matters. Despite George Baillie not being at all overweight nor in need of spiritual guidance, he does not escape Dr. Cheyne's censure, especially as he has had the temerity to eat some salt fish. 'I believe your having been too free in your dyet to have had a great hand in the loss of your hearing…I gave you warning of this fatal accident long ago and told you how many had perished Miserably by returning at Your time of life to a free or Common dyet again I myself without running your lengths of salt fish and season things have over and again Sufferd in extremity and now with Gods assistance shall never depart from Milk light soft and cool vegetables or seeds without Butter or suggar.'

When the family are in Scotland, it is one of Grisell's distant cousins, Dr. Andrew StClair, who is the physician of choice, but his advice conflicts with Dr. Cheyne's, 'tho' I be aware that it is imprudent to dissent from one of greater authority. But I can't believe a Dyette of milk, cheese and vegetables only and a total abstinence from wine the fittest for Mr Baillie because young light animal food especially tame land fowl (pigeons excepted) are easier digested than cheese or several of the vegetable kind and a glass or two of wine daily will strengthen his stomack without heating his blood or oppressing his spirits'. Grisell must have been in a quandary about what was to appear on the table in front of her husband. George Baillie's deafness continues to cause him to be depressed, but Dr. StClair is brutally honest. 'It is now as needless to expect the recovery of hearing as to hope for the return of youth', though he does have hopes for improvement of Mr. Baillie's indigestion and 'shaking fitts'. At this time George and Tamie's tutor appears to have been Samuel Toriano, and Grisell's accounts include £2:0s3½d 'for 6 shirts to Tory gote by Mrs StClair'.

Dr. StClair recommended drinking goat whey, and the family had a number of stays of several weeks at Wooler Haughhead in Northumberland where Ralph Gray kept an inn and provided accommodation, with goat whey being supplied by George Davison at nearby Langleeford. While the family are away from Mellerstain, the estate is again left in the care of Grisell's factor, who received a letter from her written at Wooler on 19 June 1736 containing her usual breathless torrent of directions on every conceivable subject including among other things the heather on the hill (which she has enough of for thatching and that Mrs Kennedy may have some of, but no strangers in case they spoil the trees), the colt (sent home to be sold), Jessie the 'Drudge beast' (who must be taken care of in retirement), the coalhouse door (which must be made the cheapest way, without an arch), and Earlston church, currently being rebuilt at the Baillies' expense: 'Tell Mr Runchiman that Earleston Church must have a stipl [steeple] & he would found the wall so as it can be made & that he must make our reteering [retiring] room to the south & have great care to make the floor dry.' While the family were enjoying the bucolic delights of drinking goat whey in the beautiful Northumbrian countryside, there was unrest in not-too-distant Edinburgh when John Porteous, Captain of the City Guard, ordered his men to fire into a hostile crowd at a public execution in April, and six people were killed. Porteous was said also to have fired into the crowd, and was tried and found guilty of murder in July, with his execution date set for 8 September, but deferred pending an appeal. The mob were incensed at the possibility of Porteous being reprieved, overpowered the guards on 7 September at the Tolbooth where he was being held, and lynched him from a barber's pole. News of the breakdown of law and order in Edinburgh would have been worrying, particularly to George Baillie whose own uncle, James Baillie, had been Captain of the City Guard. In happier developments in Edinburgh in 1736, the small infirmary there received a charter to become the Royal Infirmary of Edinburgh, and Grisell subscribed £20 towards the building of a new 228-bed hospital designed by William Adam.

Chapter 11

_ഛല_

OXFORD STUDENT DAYS

_1736-1740_

Despite indifferent health, the years 1734-36 spent at
Mellerstain must have been happy for George Baillie,
surrounded by his family, his books and his beloved pets in the
peace of the Scottish countryside, but the education of his two
eldest grandsons Tamie, aged 16, and George aged 13 in the
summer of 1736, became a pressing concern, particularly since
the boys' other grandfather, Thomas, 6th Earl of Haddington
had died at the end of November 1735, aged 55. 'Tamie' is
now Thomas, 7th Earl of Haddington. The family were already
closely acquainted with Dr. William King, principal of St. Mary
Hall, Oxford (later united with Oriel College), despite his
being an avowed Jacobite; this friendship no doubt influenced
the decision that Tamie and George should study at Oxford.
Accordingly, October 1736 sees the entire household on the
move again. Grisell records, 'Mellerstain 14 October 1736
Mr Baillie set out for London with his whole famely which
consisted of my two Doughtes [daughters] five Grandchildren

with my Brother Lord Marchmont coach & our own with seven servants viz Lord Hadinton & his brothers their Governer 2 Maids 4 footmen besids Lord Marchmonts servants we had 6 Coach Mairs and 4 riding horses'. There must have been some family discussion, even before Lord Binning's death, that grandson George Hamilton, as the eventual inheritor of Mellerstain, should be known as George Baillie, and in her accounts of George's student expenses at Oxford, Grisell names him as 'my grandchild George Baillie'. It must also have been agreed that Tamie, Lord Haddington's expenses would be paid by his mother Rachy, but that George's education would be paid for by his maternal grandparents.

Oxford was, however, not the immediate destination as first there was the excitement of Grisie being received at court in London, after two decades of social limbo, still feeling society's censure for being separated from her husband and tainted, however unjustly, by the attempted rape by Arthur Gray the footman. Sir James Hall's daughter Katie [Katherine] had also been present at the court reception and had reported to Grisell that 'all that was said was designed exceeding kindly, & Grisie took it so, & thought it vastly more so than she could have expected', but someone, unnamed by Grisell, has spoiled the warm after-glow by contradicting Katie's favourable account of the event, angering Grisell. 'So much for that lying gentleman who deserves another name'. Grisie herself is upset by the suggestion that she had not been well received at court. 'I wish to God folks woud let us alon[e] at least when we're so far from them, I never met with more sevility [civility], but there's nothing some people cannot turn to a wrong.'

By November 1736 the family is to be found in Bath, though the beginning of the stay was not restful as three different lodgings were tried until one was deemed satisfactory to accommodate the entire party of seventeen. 'This is the third lodging we have been in & you'll believe it no small trouble to remove bag and bagadg of so many as we are no less than 17 of us to gete a House to hold us all was no small defeculty'. Although Bath offered plenty of public entertainment, Grisie's chief pleasure remains music, and before leaving London an Italian music master, Girolamo Polani had been hired, Grisell paying five shillings in October for 'writeing Pulany's agreement for teaching Musick' and a further £1:18s in November for his coach and subsistence on the journey to join the family in Bath. Grisie says, 'I have got several musical acquaintance & a harpsichord in the house that I am not so much in the publick rooms as at home, except ball nights for Grisie' (her niece, now aged 17, whose attendance at the balls would bring her to the attention of potential marriage partners). The elder Grisie is disapproving of most people's gambling at the card tables every night. 'Almost every body I know plays for more than they shoud, I some times preach to them I wish well to but in vain.' Perhaps she was influenced by George Baillie's anti-gambling stance, or perhaps by her close friend Elizabeth, Lady Lechmere's attempted suicide a decade earlier at Bath having lost £700 in one sitting at the tables.

As well as providing entertainment in congenial company, in Bath miraculous cures were always to be hoped for, though sadly on this occasion health concerns actually increased. Grandchildren Grisie and Tamie had been inoculated against smallpox when they were small, but Charles and Rachel, the youngest of the family now aged 9 and 7 respectively, appear not to have been protected, as letters towards the end of December reveal that both have been extremely ill with it, especially Charles, who is reported to be still blind. Granddaughter Grisie, now often referred to in letters as 'Miss' Hamilton, as was the usual way of naming the eldest daughter of a family, has some unspecified illness as well as her younger siblings and is 'very bad'. On the last day of the year Grisell, writing to her factor, says that both her daughters Grisie and Rachy also have been very ill with a fever, but are recovering. William Hume, in reply, asserts that 'its next to a miracle that Mr Charles is still alive' but gives the distressing news of the death of Will Gray, who has been the chief stonemason during the whole of the building of the pavilions at Mellerstain, whose workmanship was excellent, and who will be very difficult to replace. A further calamity follows, as Hume receives a letter written by Grisie on 12 February 1737 which begins, 'You'll know from Mrs Menzies the terrible situation we have been in & still are by my Mother's illness'.

Ten days later, Grisie sends a further report on Grisell's condition, after she has apparently had surgery. 'My Mother is in a better way than any had reason to expect not having had the least hopes of her for ten days she is now in the surgeons hands wt [with] her leg wc [which] is a very large and deep wound & will be long of curing, but it has saved her life; she is yet confind to her bed and very low and weak, nor can we expect other. Miss Hamilton is better but has for this week past been in the utmost danger by a fever wc she had little strength to bear, Rachel again has her ague wc now comes every day, she began the Bark today [cinchona bark, a favourite remedy of the time, yielding quinine], our distresses are like to have no end, tho we have reason to thank God we are yet all alive'.

By April, everyone's health must have been good enough for the move to Oxford to be finally undertaken, as Grisie writes to Hume on 1 May 1737, 'We came here on Thursday and are pritty well tho my Mother and Miss Hamilton much fatigued, the boys are enterd in their College & we are settled in a very bad inconvenient house but there is non to chuse upon.' At last, after an enforced silence of four months, Grisell is well enough by 24 May to pick up a pen and write to Hume herself, though daughter Grisie is now ill and exhausted having taken over her mother's role for so long. Hannah Daniel, the owner of the 'bad inconvenient' house signs a list of agreed improvements in August, Grisell apparently demanding 'shutters to ye windows', 'window curtains to Ly Binnings Room', 'a feather bed changed for a better, or a new cover', 'a sufficient stable and coach house, both to be water tight' and 'a drain to carry off ye water from ye wash house'. It seems odd that the boys were to be educated at Oxford together, despite George, not yet 14, being almost three years younger than Tamie, but Grisell is well pleased with their progress, and happy that they come home to their family every day after their studies are done, which prevents them getting into bad company. Oxford though, is just as expensive as London, but there is at least no need to keep up appearances as they live very quietly 'which is a hapiness, there being no body here we desire to be acquent with.' Although it is only George's expenses which feature in Grisell's accounts, she is prepared to spend on Tamie where necessary. 'Lord Hadinton is much better of his stut[t]ering but 100£ will not defray the charges of it…I shall think all our cost and pains well bestowd (which is not small) if our boys answer the hopes we & all here that knows them has of them they go extremly well on in their learning & all in their Colege mighty fond of them'. She adds, in a letter the following month, 'Indeed it will put nothing in our purs[e] but the prosperity and safetie of the boys will be ritches to me.' The letter continues, as do subsequent ones, with more directions about the building of Mellerstain and the church at Earlston, and other business matters.

The list of grandson George's university expenses is long, including a very splendid student gown requiring 8 yards of green damask, 10½ yards of gold galoun [braid], 10 dozen buttons and 5 dozen tassels, costing in all over 33 pounds. Grisell lays out further sums for tuition expenses, money paid to the university music and for ringing the bells, the cost of food including special dinners and hall fees, with a substantial 12 guineas for caution money in case student high jinks caused damage. George has the use of a horse in Oxford, as Grisell buys a whip, saddle, bridle and lace-trimmed saddle cloth and, more touchingly, reminding us that he is still just a boy of 14, she spends four shillings on 'Rabits to George & rabit house'.

William Hume tells Grisell in August 1737 of the latest developments in a dispute raised by the plumbers employed to bring water into the house at Mellerstain, which has necessitated the involvement of lawyers. 'You must pay Graham his account of 3£15s most extravegent it is, but we must expect to be imposd on in such a case where they see our necessity'. Grisell seems often to be in fear of being cheated or imposed upon by people from every walk of life, and has received more alarming news from Hume in September. Landowners were under an obligation to provide accommodation for soldiers, either on the march or for longer periods, when they fulfilled a kind of neighbourhood policing role, and Grisell learns that a detachment of dragoons [cavalry] has arrived to be billetted at Mellerstain, and for an extended stay. She is personally acquainted with their colonel, Sir Robert Rich, who she is sure will permit no misdemeanours, nevertheless, she lays down some rules. 'I'll allow non of the Dragouns to have any pairt of the House…They must not be allowd to go into the hill to shoot the Partrages… nor shoot the wild ducks in the Cannall… let them not fish in the Cannall youll wish to be quit of them before the seven moneth be out'. Grisell grudgingly allows them candles for the stables which are to be their accommodation, and permits two of her servants to make the soldiers' [straw] beds if they do not do it themselves 'but no servant of mine to have anything els to do with them'.

The lake [canal] at Mellerstain, though still only 10 years old, is already more than the beautiful and dramatic landscape feature envisaged by Lord Binning, and is now obviously stocked with fish and colonised by wildfowl. Grisell had paid '5£10s for a Boat to the Cannal bringing it home 19s' and for the finishing artistic touch attempts had been made to populate it with swans, but swans have minds and wings of their own: 'For bringing a Swan by water from fife 5s catching him on Tweed when he flew away but gote him not & cariage from Tininghame'.

As well as some 'offices' including a brewhouse, bakehouse, washing house and slaughter house in the courtyard behind the East Pavilion, Mr. Runciman has also been instructed to build what is now termed the mausoleum, in the fields a little distance from the house. Mr. Runciman has been calling it the 'burial place' and Grisell 'the Sepulcher', but now, in January 1738 as it is nearing completion, she decides it shall be called 'the Monument'. At a later date she says, 'I desire to know how that door of the Monomount is to be. I will not have it colourd black with tears as the common way is'. Grisell is keen to add at least part of the farm of Girrick to the Mellerstain estate as that is where the Hundy Mundy eyecatcher stands, and 'Dear Binning wishd alwise to have that piece ground'. She is suspicious of neighbouring owners of other lands owned by George Baillie, directing Hume 'to have our marches [boundaries] clear, that it may not be in their power to make any incroachments & therefore I would have you go east when the days grows long & ride round them all', an annual riding of the boundaries being the time-honoured way of defining ownership of land.

While physical ailments were still poorly understood, mental disorders fared even worse. Grisell writes several letters in February to her brother Alexander at his house in Ealing, London, with concerns about his youngest daughter Jean, now aged 19. 'She was doing every exterordinary thing to destroy herself, such as going half naked, & her windows open night &

day & eating next to nothing'. Doctors have recommended that Lady Jean be moved to Edinburgh to be treated, and Grisell tells her brother, 'If you do not allow her to go to toun she will go on in that destructive way & her death will be laid upon you'. Shortly afterwards, she tells Willie Hall, 'I think the fit[t] est place for her is Bedlam' [Bethlem Royal Hospital, England's first institution for mental disorders]. Grisell also fears for Alexander's own health. 'I think closs poring on books at your time a [of] day is the worst thing for health and spirits, see what Mr Baillie has gote by it, in spite of a strong constitution'. We learn from the same letter that 'Mr Baillie is sometimes not able & often very unwilling to signe Papers… if I should dy and he become stile weaker, our affairs would go very heavily on…what I think would be right, is for him to signe a factory [power of attorney] to Grisie, which he may seal up and give to me to be made use of if necessary'.

Perhaps Grisell had scolded George Baillie also for too much 'closs poring on books', but without effect. Her 'sundry' accounts while still at Mellerstain reveal that he intended his library in the new house to be not only extensive, but very fine. He had had a bookplate made in 1724, but saw the necessity in 1736 for another one for smaller books, so we see an entry 'for cuting a small copper plate wt the Armes 15 shillings'. The extent of the book collection is revealed by his ordering 3,000 of the larger bookplates and 2,000 of the smaller ones to be printed. Grisell notes the prices quoted by the bookbinder, Gavin Hamilton, for the different sizes and qualities of bindings, and 'the best binding is lin'd with marld [marbled] paper'. Bookplates, ribbons for bookmarks, binding, gilding and 'od volums to make up diffitiencys in the Liberarry' resulted in a total bill for £41:14s.

In March 1738, Grisell is able to give Mr. Hume a cheerful account of the family's health, 'all the rest of us here very well, Mr Baillie better health than he has had the two winters befor', though she soon relapses into gloom: 'but still we old folks [Grisell and George Baillie are now 72 and 73 respectively] must dayly fail'. She is equally pessimistic in May, giving Hume directions about the continuing landscaping at Mellerstain. 'As for the Canall, let it stand as it is till some of us see it, God knows whether we will all or not, for much may happen in a years time'. In a letter to her brother Alexander, Grisell shows herself to be uncharacteristically irritated by George Baillie's passion for household pets. 'Altho we have poudle, and young pudle, & a son of pudles, Dutches, & murchie, the last an ugly beast a present from Lady Letchmoor 5 of them, Mr Nisbet has brought a little thing just now in his pocket, cald Jewel, as a love token to Ms Rachel [Grisell's granddaughter, aged 10]. I wish you saw Mr Baillie & the rest of them walking over to St Johns [College] & the whole 6 dogs with them, & he & they will let non of them be put away, Im doun right angry with them & would fain poyson them all'. 'Dutches' [Duchess] had been bought in 1736 for grandson George, who was apparently as fond of animals as his grandfather. Duchess had cost ten shillings and sixpence, when the more usual price paid for a dog in Grisell's accounts is five shillings, with a dog collar costing a further three shillings. She was possibly a replacement for a dog named Friday who was lost, a newspaper advertisement in hopes of finding him having cost Grisell a shilling. Duchess' collar was probably of brass with her name and her owner's name engraved on it so recognition would be possible should she go astray.

Although apparently not as fond of dogs as were the men in her household, Grisell always insists that horses be treated kindly, fed well and not overworked. Writing to Mr. Hume from the Mitchells' house at Popes in June 1738, she explains that 'Mr [David] Mitchell came home last night after being 12 days out making a progres with our young Gentlemen [Tamie and George] throw the west of England...and never traveld less than 30 Mills a day and yesterday traveld 40 Miles & came not here till 11 at night, & the first thing I saw this morning, was those very horses in the yock [yoke] leeding in the hay, this is far from our way of doing & not so strongly fed as ours are.'

Letters received by Grisell and by George Baillie in June raise the ghost of Grisie's failed marriage yet again. Alexander Murray's debts are now so great that 'it was proposed and agreed to by his Creditors and their Doers that application should be made to the Court of Session for sequestratting all his means and Estate both reall and personall and that the factory to be granted by the Lords should be expressly burdened with the payment of the aliment due to my Lady Murray your Daughter to which as we are Informed you have now right'. The creditors also agreed to pay aliment which was in arrears, so Grisie will be unaffected financially by her husband's bankruptcy.

In July Sir William Baillie of Lamington in Lanarkshire had died, leaving his sister Henrietta to inherit his lands and, as told to brother Alexander by Grisell, George Baillie sees an opportunity to bring the ancestral lands back into his own branch of the Baillie family. 'Mr Baillie has taken it in his head that he will have George married to The Heiress of Lamington & have me write to Charles St Clair, to know her age…he will be Adam and she will be Eve'.

An unusually short letter from Grisell to William Hume on 2 August, when she is returned to Oxford from Popes, contains her usual list of directions for the internal arrangement of rooms at Mellerstain and, in reply to Hume's last letter, she says, 'I hope Mr Adams has caried all their crossnes with him what was the ocation of the poor mans flux I would be content to know', suggesting all has not gone smoothly with the building recently. She has written to gardener 'Deans' about the gravel walk below the kitchen garden, and tells Hume, 'By all meens gete all about the Canall planted' and as for the hay, 'ye must lay a great heep of dry branches below, in the botom of the stacks to keep it from roting'. She concludes her message with, 'We are all very well. Adieu'.

Two days later, on 4 August 1738, a Friday, George Baillie bought a book costing two guineas, a commentary on the New Testament by 'Whitby', but it was to be his last as he became ill that day, and he died on 6 August. In Lady Murray's account: 'His physician pressed him, but the week before he died, (when he appeared to be in as good health as he had been for some years), not to shut himself up so constantly in his room, but say his prayers driving about in his coach, or in his walks in his garden; he answered him, "You are a better physician than a divine, since you would only serve God with your own conveniency". He breathed his last, as he did the whole time of his illness, which was but forty-eight hours, in petitions to his God and Saviour for his salvation, and that of his whole family. With a calm serene countenance, and scarce a groan, he left us to mourn our own unspeakable loss.' On a separate scrap of paper, Grisie wrote 'he died at twelve at night as the clock struk'.

The news of George Baillie's unexpected death probably reached London fairly quickly from Oxford, less than 60 miles away, though many friends and acquaintances were likely to be absent as it was August and the season for paying visits to the country, but the servants and tenantry at Mellerstain would not hear until several days later. On 7 August, May Menzies writes to William Hume at Mellerstain with news of George Baillie's illness and death, and Grisell's instructions for the funeral meal. 'The great table in the hall is to be covered, the kitchen table and the latter meat table wt cold beef, mouton, lamb and fowels, white bread ale and brandie for the tenents a plumb cake such as used to come from Kelso to the familie with wine for the gentlemen'. Grisell's account book notes, 'For Expenses of a most

Mellancoly ocation to this Family £122:10s', to which Grisie added 'My dear fathers burrial from Oxford to Mellerstain'. We learn from a letter written to Hume by Grisie on 9 August that 'the body sets out to morrow & without accidents will be at Mellerstain on Saterday the 19th we have apointed them that are to come from Edin to atend the funeral on munday the 21st at twelve a clock...there will be in all about 20 gentlemen.' (It will be noted that the funeral was an all-male event). Grisell's brother Alexander has 'orderd a Buck from Redbreas... wch must be backt in pys, there is also two hams, turkeys, fowl, lamb, claret white wine and brandy... let the meat that's left be given to the poor & the people in the toun'.

Lady Murray says, 'He was buried, according to his own directions, with but a few friends and near relations, and all his own tenants, in a burying place he ordered, three years before he died, to be built in his own fields, to save the trouble of carrying him far; having all his life a dislike to pomp and show, and giving others trouble. He then little imagined he was ever to stir from home; but what was thought proper for the education of his grandsons, made him readily yield to anything.' Grisell's account book shows £228:5s10d 'For Building the Monument by James Runchiman' and on the same page, 'For Building the Kirk of Earlestoun' a total of £290:4s10d. George Baillie was buried in a more grandiose mausoleum than he had intended, as we learn from Lady Murray. 'He ordered only a spot of ground to be inclosed with four walls, and often walked to see it, and showed an impatience to have it finished, thinking his end was near. When he perceived there was an ornamented front making to it, he turned to me in anger, and said he would not suffer it... With difficulty we prevailed to have it built with some ornaments; but he never once walked towards it after that, nor saw it, nor asked a question but when it would be finished; and it was but finished the week before he had occasion for it.' There are further sums in the account books for gates to the Monument, painting it and having the inscriptions carved (Plate 25a).

George Baillie's coffin was accompanied on its journey to Mellerstain only by servants, and not by Grisell or her daughters. Writing to her uncle Alexander, Earl of Marchmont on 31 August, when the servants had returned, Grisie says, 'This morning the servants came from Scotland, where we find every thing was don wt the greatest decency, & nothing omitted that was fit, wch gives us great pleasur, every body that was writ to was there but dundass & Mcfarlin. Professor Gowdie the Sunday befor preacht a sermon [in Earlston] on the character & memory & the great loss they all had that moved the whole congregation to tears'.

News of George Baillie's death had reached Alexander Murray on 14 August, and five days later he wrote what purported to be a letter of condolence to Grisie, but complaining of the 'injuries' done to him by George Baillie who 'was really less to blame in several of the Injurys done me than my Lady [Grisell] & you'. George Baillie and Grisell had always had suspicions that Alexander Murray might attempt to take possession of Grisie's inheritance once George Baillie was dead, so in February 1725 George Baillie had had drawn up a document of substitution of heirs which expressly debarred Alexander Murray from inheriting any of his property. A further deed had been signed in April 1734 'ratifying his former provisions to his eldest daughter but debarring her husband from any jus mariti'. Rachy, writing to her uncle Alexander, reveals that Murray has now written some 'very od letters' and 'what we are most affrayd of is that Mr Murray may come here & do some redicules [ridiculous] thing & as a separation in Scotland by Law is nothing here he may go to the Chife justes [chief justice] & get a warrant to take his wife if he dose this we cant resiste him.' While George Baillie was alive, Grisie herself and her property were safe from

Murray, and Rachy fears what may happen if Grisell were also to die, saying, 'you cant imagen how she [Grisell] gives her selfe up to every thought that can make her miserable, this I hope will prevale on her to be more careful of her self when she sees what consequence her life is to my sister'. Grisie, writing to William Hume on 9 October 1738 tells him that her mother, in addition to being overcome with grief at the death of her husband, is suffering from an intermittent fever and fits. She reveals that the last of Murray's 'od letters' mentioned by her sister amounts to over 120 pages containing many insults to George Baillie, which Murray would never have dared to do while George Baillie was alive, and also a demand for £20,000 for defamation of character, erasure of the deed of separation and return of all his letters. 'Its plain his view & intention is to get possession of all we have wc he has not a shadow of pretence to as long as my mother lives'. A succession of male friends and relatives are staying in the house as virtual bodyguards, as Grisie says, 'since he possibly may try to get possession of my person'. Murray had been living in France for some time but had travelled to London immediately on hearing of George Baillie's death, so the threat of his sudden appearance in Oxford to carry off Grisie was very real.

Grisie keeps up a regular correspondence with her uncle Alexander, frequently asking his advice now that he is the senior male in the family since the death of George Baillie, and in her letter to him on 15 October 1738 we learn of another family tragedy involving one of Grisell's nephews. 'We were greatly struck wt the same acc[oun]t you would have had from L[or]d Po[lwarth] of poor Jackie Hume it's dreadfull to reflect on a poor unthinking lad being taken out of the world so suddenly it will be monstrous if those that murderd him are not taken & brought to justice, but I suppose unless you write to somebody about it, no body will trouble them selves about him'. (Lieutenant John

Hume of Colonel Campbell's Regiment of Foot, son of Grisell's deceased brother Andrew, had been brutally murdered by a number of men at the George Inn in Roscrea in Ireland). We learn also from Lady Murray's Memoirs that Grisell's nephews Hugh and Alexander, twin sons of her brother Alexander are a source of great grief to her. She says: 'A misunderstanding with some of his family, (which I can give no reason for, nor any account of could satisfy any body), was very heavy upon her'. Despite Grisell overseeing her nephews' education while her brother Alexander was abroad, and making arrangements for his daughters Jean and Anne after the death of their mother in 1722, spending much time, effort and considerable sums of her own money in the process, her nephews and nieces vilified her. Lady Murray continues, 'It was no less grievous to her brother, who was acquainted with the whole: they never had any reserve nor secrets from one another, and he was ever fully sensible of the obligation he and his whole family had to her.' A note in Grisell's handwriting, found by Lady Murray after her death, reads, 'O God, the righteous judge, I make appeal to thee, who knowest the very worst of me, and protest, that whatsoever my mistakes or sins have been, which cannot escape thy sight, I never did them any injury, nor ever gave them the least cause to persecute me by lies, – On calumny by my nephews and nieces of Polwarth, 1739. Gris Baillie'.

Alexander Murray had allowed one month for his impossible conditions to be met, but when that period had expired without his taking any action, Grisie's friend Elizabeth Howard, Lady Lechmere writing from Whitehall at the beginning of November dismisses Murray's threats as 'the Calculations of a disorded Brain', but nevertheless offers Grisie her own house as a sanctuary if it should become necessary. Lady Lechmere says, 'I am glad Lady Grissell is tolerably well I wish she wou'd go to Popes it wou'd be a change of scene that wou'd perhaps be some relief to her.' We can see by a letter Grisie wrote to Hume from Popes on 22 November that Lady Lechmere's advice had been acted upon. The journey from Oxford to Popes, near Hatfield would take less than two hours in the first half of the twenty-first century, but in the first half of the eighteenth century it was an uncomfortable coach journey of two days, not only uncomfortable but dangerous as, in addition to the threat of attack by armed robbers, which Grisell had suffered at least once, coaches quite frequently overturned on the bad roads. Grisie says, 'We were over turned by the way in a bogue [bog] out of wch we had great difficulty to get the coach my Mother's neck was straind, but no other hurt nor did she catch cold, though forst to stand above an hour in the fields while the coach was getting up in the coldest day we have had'. The family has been in Oxford now for a year and a half, but Grisie makes it plain that they do not find it congenial, and that they only remain there for the sake of Tamie and George's university education. 'We talk of returning to our dismal habitation next week, nothing but so strong a ty [tie] as we have coud draw us there again, but our pains I hope will be all well bestowd for nothing can be doing better than the boys do.' The cheering presence, for Grisie, of an 'in-house' music master had ceased in the spring when Signor Polani had been paid his agreed £42:13s in wages and his £10 clothing allowance for the 18 months he had resided near the family, with his washing and lodgings costing a further £15:5s.

On 25 January 1739, Grisell puts pen to paper to Hume for the first time since George Baillie's death almost six months previously. She writes, 'you may believe I can have no sort of pleasure in this world but in so far, as I can be usefull to the memory of him that is gone & I shall alwise expect that you will have some regard to that to[o]. at the same time nothing can give me so much pleasure, as it will sorrow, but in such a way as I hope will be no breach in submission to the will of God'. The rest of the letter is taken up with business, and the news that tender-hearted grandson George 'cryd a whole day' because he had accidentally injured his brother with a tennis ball. Grisell is anxiously waiting for news from Mellerstain, and from Tyninghame, having read newspaper reports of a hurricane affecting the south of Scotland, where it was reported in the *Newcastle Courant* that, 'The most dismal Account is from the Merse, where it has occasion'd a terrible Destruction; few Houses are left standing, several Churches are blown down, Numbers smother'd in the Ruins, and an universal Havock made among their Sheep and Cattle'.

Grisie, writing to Hume on 14 February expresses thankfulness that no great harm was done at Mellerstain by the hurricane, but that her mother has been laid low for nearly a month with kidney stones. 'She cannot ly down in her bed nor sleep but wt Lawdanum'. By 26 February, the task of writing to Hume has passed to granddaughter Grisie, who reports that her mother Rachy 'has been extreamly ill, so bad she has been given over several times…We hope the best, but fear the worst'. By 6 March, when young Grisie writes again, the doctors give some hope of Rachy's recovery, and Grisell herself is able to resume correspondence with Hume for the first time on 3 May. She sympathises with him, as he also is suffering from 'gravel' [kidney stones], and offers advice: 'I must recommend to you to take pills made of Castile sope wt as much syrop of marsh mallows as will form them, begin with 2 drops in the day & by degrees to half an ounce'. Presumably following her own advice and taking the Castile soap and marsh mallow pills, we learn from Grisie in May that her mother is also 'stile obliged to be taking the Mercury purges'. Granddaughter Grisie has been following Dr. Cheyne's vegetarian régime but now, says her aunt, 'gose out of her vegetable dish by Licence under Dr

Cheyne's own hand & she begins by eating the finest large Turbot I ever saw Sr E[dward] Turner sent us last night by the Coach from London'.

Grisie suffered a further blow when the newspapers reported the death, on 10 April in Bath, of her great friend Lady Lechmere, aged 44. On Lady Lechmere's monument in Westminster Abbey her second husband Sir Thomas Robinson describes her as 'an accomplished woman, a sincere friend and an agreeable companion', all of which Grisie would have concurred with, perhaps adding 'rock in times of adversity'. Grisell herself was indebted in the monetary sense to Lady Lechmere who had insisted on lending her a further £1,000 on their return from Italy and France following the death of Lord Binning. A bond was signed, which Lady Lechmere had vowed she would tear up if she thought she was about to die, releasing Grisell from the debt. Lady Lechmere's father Charles Howard, 3rd Earl of Carlisle had died the previous May, just three months before George Baillie, depriving Grisell and her husband of a longstanding friend.

The summer weather seems to have improved the family's health as Grisie, writing to her uncle the Earl of Marchmont in September 1739, has nothing worse to comment on than the flood of visitors they have had over the summer including, at the end of July, the poet Alexander Pope. 'Mr Pope has been here two days, he is now below, & our boys just going to cary him ten mil[e]s out of town in our Coach in his way home'. Grisie adds: 'Mama continues surprisingly well, the cold weather begins to make us all complain a little except her, if she can but weather the winter we shall rejoice in leaving this [Oxford] in the spring & getting home [to Mellerstain]'. The 'city of dreaming spires' has not risen in Grisie's estimation as the following month she tells her uncle, 'many are the consultations we want with you about the boys, whose time now draws near for leaving this [place], thank God we have but one weary winter more here'. At 19 and 16, Tamie and George's university education is considered complete, so plans must be made for their next step. Grisie also has news of their sister, young Grisie, now 20. 'Grisie is growen a big fat woman & never ails anything tho she is not yet arrived at drinking of wine'.

In 1735 work had begun on the courtyard of 'offices' at Mellerstain adjoining the East Pavilion that was the family's accommodation. Work had continued steadily until by 1739 an impressive array of 'mod cons' was completed including a bakehouse, brewhouse, slaughter house, storerooms and a wash house with piped water, with one of the buildings surmounted by a low tower with a large clock. Grisell would have wanted her estate servants and 'fivepenny men' day labourers to be punctual, and few, if any, would have had a time-piece of their own. In November 1734 the Burgh Council of Lauder minutes read: 'The Baillies and Council having taken into their consideration that the clock of the Burgh is in great disrepair and very insufficient (the same having been visited by John Kirkwood, Clock Smith at Hardgatehead), have resolved that a new clock shall be made by him with the greatest expedition and sett up in the Steeple of the Tolbooth of the sd Burgh'. It was this 'insufficient' clock that was repaired and refurbished by Mr. Kirkwood and set up at the gable end of the range of buildings in the east courtyard, with the date 1735 on its dial. Mr. Kirkwood supplied only the mechanism at £18, as there were additional payments to 'Thomson Painter at Kelso for Dyel to Cloke £1' and to Sandy Baverage, 'Clock Case £1:13s5d'. For sunny days when 'old technology' would work, Grisell has ordered a sundial. 'For a Dyel from London stands in the Court £7:17s6d' and 'Cuting the Pedestel of Dyel by Burns £4'. The wages of the 'fivepenny men' seem unvarying at all times of the year regardless of the number of hours of daylight, but skilled tradesmen appear to get different rates in summer and winter. Charles Dods gets

14 pence for 'long days' and 10 pence for 'short days', as does George Young; Will Darline gets 13 pence for 'long days', and John Thomson and David Robison get 12 pence for 'long days'. Although they are employed on a casual basis, Grisell pays out 6s6d at this time 'To 5 pence men when sick'.

Having left Mellerstain in 1736, Grisell would have been anxious to see with her own eyes the progress made in the living accommodation and offices, but alarming news comes from Scotland in October 1739. Grisie tells her uncle Alexander that they had had 'no letters latly from Scotland, except one three days ago from Mrs Scot of Galla wc brought us very bad news of our offices being burnt down at Mellerstain, & the house we lived in very narrowly escaping'. A more detailed account came shortly afterwards from Ann Miller, writing on behalf of Mrs Weir, housekeeper at Mellerstain. She said she believed the fire had started in the north garret landing before spreading to the roof, and describes how efforts were made to save as many goods from the store-rooms as possible, with the china being handed out of windows to people waiting on ladders, some of whom had arrived to help from the 'toun' of Mellerstain, having seen the blaze. Mr. Hume was also quickly on the scene and, realising that if the firewood stacks close to the dwelling house were to catch fire then that too might burn down, he ordered that all the coarse sheets and blankets in the house be soaked in water and draped over the firewood stacks.

William Hume's own account of the fire is lost but Grisell, replying to it on 31 October, is more concerned about Hume's evident distress than her own loss. 'You may believe the account of the fire did surprise me but I soon reflected that God over rules all & blist Him that it was not worse & I can assure you I was as much affected by the thoughts of the consternation you would be in as with anything els'. Hume had been factor at Mellerstain for 10 years now, at an annual salary of £20, plus 'perks' of the tower house to live in, garden ground to grow vegetables, grazing for two horses and two cows and the rights to claim carriages of coal and to dig peats, but the job did carry an enormous responsibility, which he obviously felt keenly after the disastrous fire. He seems to have hinted that the fire was largely caused by shoddy workmanship from John Hume, the mason employed in the building of the offices. Grisell says that James Runciman, who has overall charge of the works, must have known what John Hume was like, but blames herself as being ultimately responsible for employing him. She says that money will be in very short supply with the need to rebuild, but nevertheless orders William Hume to divide £5 among those people from Mellerstain 'toun' who came to assist with the fire. Grisie continues the letter, also stressing the financial difficulties rebuilding will cause: 'we never coud have don it in a worse time as we must necessarily have so great a call for money upon our leaving this [Oxford] & our young men going abroad'. In 1724, in London, Grisell had paid £2:12s 'To the London assurance for our Goods in Marlburge street' and 7s6d 'To Royal assurance for a Policy', when household insurance was in its infancy, but it would seem that no insurance was in place with regard to Mellerstain.

In January 1740 Grisell is preoccupied with rebuilding the most essential of the ruined buildings, namely the brewhouse, as the servants must have their daily ration of beer, and enquiring if there is a good baker in nearby Smailholm. Since Christmas there had been a frost, and she hopes Hume is taking advantage of the good, hard roads to transport materials for the rebuilding. However, that was the only advantage of the freezing weather. January and February 1740 had a severe and extended frost, causing much hardship. A Frost Fair was again held on the Thames, but all classes of people, particularly the poor, suffered. People who relied on coal for heating could not get any as coal barges were frozen up on the Tyne, and many died from cold or scarcity of food. Grisell says to Hume in January, 'I'm scarse able to write this my fingers are so cold…severals are found dead here with the cold, a poor woman comeing to toun [Oxford] on Wednesday last with her butter dyed of cold siting on her horse between her panyers'. She instructs Hume to 'give the whole years money now to our poor that I use to give in the year that non dy there of hunger or cold'.

Rachy has been severely ill, and is only able to get from her bed to a chair while the bed is remade, this news being relayed to Hume in February along with Grisell's instructions that the 'mangle room' and the 'woman house' are to be floored with flagstones as no outside mason work is currently possible on account of the frost, and she is anxious to hear about marble to be got for the Monument. She laments a consignment of holland [linen fabric] that has gone astray, and has written to Edinburgh to enquire about an under cook who understands baking and brewing, and also a laundry maid and house maid for Mellerstain, in case none are available locally. Amid the difficulties caused by the severe winter, the continuing rebuilding at Mellerstain and plans for moving back there, 27 February brought the death of Grisell's brother Alexander, mainstay and adviser of the family. Not omitting any of his assets as a servant to the wider community and nation, his death was reported in the *General Evening Post* of 28 February 1740: 'Yesterday Mo[r]ning died in Saville-Row the Right Hon. The Earl of Marchmont; he was one of the Ministers Plenipotentiaries of Great-Britain at the Congress of Cambray and Knight of the most ancient Order of the Thistle and was one of the sixteen Peers for Scotland in the last Parliament.'* Alexander's death must have been relatively sudden, as the last letter appearing in his published correspondence with political allies is dated 16 February, and Grisie had written to him on the 25th. Grisell and her family now have no adult male blood relative to look after their interests. She had communicated one last time with Alexander's eldest son Hugh as there is writing, endorsed by Grisell as 'Scrol [draft copy] of a letter to Lord Polwarth 1740' in which she says, 'my daughter & I often asked you what we had said or don to occation such treatment, all you was pleas'd to answer was that L[or]d Boolinbrook & Mr Pope had turned your head.' Henry St. John, 1st Viscount Bolingbroke and Alexander Pope were Hugh Hume's closest friends. As Pope had stayed with Grisell and her household in Oxford in the late summer of 1739, relations with him were apparently cordial.

As well as preparations to return to Mellerstain, final arrangements were being made for Tamie and George to set out on their 'grand tour'. On the family's trip to Naples in 1731 and their return journey in 1733, Grisell must have characteristically made careful notes of the best routes to travel and which inns were superior, what was worth seeing in any place, how much to expect to pay for various goods and services, and how to avoid being robbed or cheated. All this distilled wisdom is contained in a notebook of 120 pages, though not in Grisell's own handwriting, headed, 'Memorandums for Earl Hadinton and Mr Baillie in their Travelling. Oxford, March 10th, 1740'. They left Oxford for London at the end of March, and in London on 5 April Grisell notes various necessary purchases to equip George for his journey, including a black cloth full suit, waistcoats, stockings, gloves, a hat, a wig, 14 Holland shirts, a powdering gown, six night shirts 'r[e]ady made', shoes, combs, a sword belt, a purse and leather bag, a writing desk and a case for it, a Bible and a travelling trunk to put everything in. There is a final generous parting gift of a gold watch costing 19 guineas with a case costing a further 18 shillings. Tamie the Earl of Haddington was presumably similarly equipped for his travels at the expense of his mother Rachy, Lady Binning. Having done everything possible to make her grandsons' trip a safe and pleasant one,

Grisell took her leave of them, as Lady Murray says, 'with little expectation of their meeting again'. Hume writes on 10 April, 'I am Exceeding Glad Lady Binning is better. I pray God may take care of the Earl and Mr. George in their travels and return them safe to their Countrie again'. Young gentlemen setting out on the grand tour were accompanied by a 'bear leader', a man whose role encompassed tutor, guardian and chaperone, and Grisell had engaged a Mr. John Williamson for this post, disappointing philosopher David Hume who had also thought of applying for the position, but was too late. Williamson's salary was to be 50 pounds per annum, though just before leaving Oxford Grisell had also paid 35 guineas 'To Mr. John Williamson to help to pay his Debt'. Various financial and legal matters also had to be settled before bidding farewell to Oxford, including registering George Baillie's will and paying lawyers' fees confirming Rachy as her father's executor, and paying three years' house rent to Mrs. Daniel in St Giles' which amounted to £210. In order to have something of George Baillie with her wherever she goes, Grisell pays £1 for 'Setting my Dearests hair in a Ring'.

Once the necessity of staying in England had ceased with the departure of her beloved grandsons on their European tour, Grisell must have been desperate to head northwards to Mellerstain but, writing to Hume on 2 June, she speaks of a possible delay. The family had left hated Oxford for London then travelled to Popes, the Mitchells' house at Hatfield, but Rachy's continuing ill health is causing concern and, writes Grisell, 'the Docters had given their opinion that Lady Binning should go to Tunbridge wells the seasone of which is not till the midle of this moneth'. However, Rachy made great improvements, and the spa waters of Tunbridge Wells were deemed no longer necessary, so plans began in earnest for travel to Scotland. Accordingly, they left Popes again for London, but not before buying from David Mitchell a large quantity of lead statues and flower pots to beautify the garden at Mellerstain. 'For Leed Statues from Mr Mitchell of Pops at half a Crown the stone & floor Pots £33:11s6d'. Using old imperial measure, this seems to amount to over a ton and a half of statues and urns. Planks, nails and labour to make wooden boxes to transport the statues, plus carriage to London added a further £8:9s10d. Mark Antony was the only historical figure among Classical deities Juno, Venus, Fame, Faunus [Pan] and Mercury. The statues were to be sent by sea on the ship *Elizabeth*, the ship's receipt showing 'five boxes full of status and flour potts' and that she also 'Brings a fire Engin six lether buckets', as Grisell wanted to be prepared for any future catastrophic fire. This was an insurance policy at considerable expense as 'a fire Mashien from Richard Newsime [Newsham]' had cost £25:6s8d even without the cost of its carriage from London, but its carefully preserved instruction and maintenance leaflet reveals that it was unlikely to lie idle in a shed as it also functioned as a garden watering pump. A second attempt was made at this time to populate the canal with two swans brought from Fife to Tyninghame at a cost of 12s6d, with another three shillings to get them to Mellerstain.

Finally, Grisell was able to write in her account book, 'The half of the expence of our Journey from Pops to Mellerstain seting out the 7 July with 5 of ourselves, 5 servants and 8 horses & came home the 18 July £15'. The '5 of ourselves' must have comprised Grisell, Grisie, Rachy, Miss Hamilton (young Grisie) and young Rachel, now 11. Grandson Charles, 13, doesn't often feature in Grisell's accounts, but there is one payment to him about this time of 15s6d, for an unspecified reason. It is probable that he was remaining in London at school. The 'home' reached after the 11-day journey must mean Scotland rather than Mellerstain as a round of visiting various friends and relatives ensued, revealed by the payments of drink money at a number of houses and small cash gifts to various nieces and nephews.

Chapter 12

SCOTLAND ONCE MORE

1740-1742

Grisell's joy at reaching Mellerstain again must have been greatly diminished by comparison with the previous two periods of residence. In 1734-36 George Baillie had been there with her, frail of body and in a world of increasing silence, but content with the peacefulness of Mellerstain and organizing his extensive library. In 1728-30 Lord Binning had been there also, energetically directing the landscaping and planting of the estate. This was Grisell's first opportunity to visit George Baillie's grave in the Monument a short walk from the house. Lady Murray says: 'Every thing at home so continually renewed her grief, that scarce a day passed without her bursting out in tears; though she did her utmost to command herself, not to give us pain, yet it often overcame her. Every thing she saw, the improvements or amendments of any thing about the place, though she endeavoured to amuse herself by them, only served to heighten her sorrow, and could give her no satisfaction, when she considered how little enjoyment they had had of it, for whom it was all intended. One fine day, looking round, and admiring the beauties of the place, she checked herself, burst out in tears, and said, "What is all this to me, since your father does not see and enjoy it".' Grisell had kept very many of George Baillie's letters to her, and re-read them frequently, telling Grisie that 'she intended sealing them up in a bag and bid me see they were buried in the coffin with her. I begged to read some of them, which she allowed me; and I earnestly entreated they might not be buried, but preserved for the sake of his posterity; and they are now in my custody.'

Among the letters and documents in the archive at Mellerstain is a copy of a letter dated 20 January 1738 by Rachel Chiesly, Lady Grange. This lady, whose behaviour had been troublesome to her unfaithful, Jacobite-sympathising husband, had been kidnapped on his orders and incarcerated in various places in the Highlands and Islands of Scotland, notably with a long period spent on St Kilda, and her 15-page letter took almost three years to reach her lawyer in Edinburgh in December 1740. Lord Grange was the brother of the Earl of Mar and Grisie's close friendship with Lady Mar meant she, along with many people including Grisell and others in the first rank of Scottish society, probably knew of Lady Grange's plight long before 1740, but took no action to help her, effectively sanctioning Lord Grange's treatment of his wife. The last sentence of Lady Grange's letter reads, 'They who ever's hands this comes to – They first cause write it over In a fair hand And show it to all my Friends'. The copy letter is annotated on the back in Grisie's handwriting, 'Copy of Lady Granges Cass [case]'.

Grisell continued to oversee the rebuilding of the offices and the finishing of the East and West Pavilions, as well as the planting on the estate, all expenses still being meticulously noted in her own hand. Lady Murray tells us that money was in short supply, and that Grisell made sacrifices for the sake of her grandsons. 'She had at this time, by her grandsons being abroad, occasion to spare and manage to the best advantage; which when my sister and I were uneasy at, she said she did not grudge it at all, for she never was so easy and pleased as when her purse was empty, by paying either what she owed, or was necessary.' The account books show that George's expenses were indeed quite considerable. His education at Oxford had totalled £547:18s, but foreign travel was more expensive, with over £650 being racked up by December 1741.

With George soaking up much of the available cash, comparatively little is spent on clothes at this time as the ongoing building of the pavilions and offices and planting of the estate have priority. Grisell's carefully itemised account for wallpaper, 'Stampd paper hangins', in December 1741 gives us some idea of her taste in interior decoration, and also of the principal rooms in the East Pavilion. As with furniture and silverware, she seeks out one of the best makers in Robert Dunbar, who trades in Aldermanbury in London. At his death three years later, Dunbar would be described as 'the greatest Dealer in Paper Hangings in England that brought that Branch of Trade to the highest Perfection'. Most of the wallpapers are purchased by the 'piece', at that time usually measuring 12 yards by an average 22 inches, so more or less equivalent in coverage to a standard roll of modern wallpaper. The hall and dining room are to have the same geometric 'octogan' design using 10 and seven pieces respectively, the tent [bed] room 10 pieces of red and white sprig and shell design, and Rachy's room requires four and a half pieces of the same pattern in green and white. The 'Green room', whose purpose is unspecified, is to have eight and a half pieces of a 'green vernish'd feather' design, all the above papers costing fourpence a yard. The second table room, where the upper servants eat, has six pieces of 'blew & white Roket', cheaper at threepence a yard. More expensive papers are bought not by the piece but by the yard, probably to avoid wasting money on unused paper, so the parlour has 56 yards of 'Blew on yellow revlils[?]' at ninepence a yard, and the most expensive of all is the tenpence per yard paid for '50 yards yellow on yellow Mantua', a paper that would echo the designs of brocade such as fine robes, 'mantuas', were made of, and which may have been a flocked or embossed paper. This is destined for Grisie's room. The library does not appear in the list, probably because the walls, being lined with books, have no need of paper, and the 'Damask room' mentioned elsewhere in the accounts, does not feature either.

Grisell's wallpaper is long gone, but another decorative purchase, from 1742, is still evident at Mellerstain, namely '400 Dutch tiles' for which she paid just eight shillings per hundred, some of which were used in the fireplaces of the hall and library. (The remainder would be used in the part of the house grandson George would later commission from Robert Adam.) 'To Colburn for a Marbel chimny to Liberarry & slab tyles putting up in dit. & hall at 1d pr piece £10:6s'. The tiles in the hall are blue and white with octagonal medallions showing maritime scenes and those in the library are polychrome designs alternating many different birds and flowers (Plate 26). The tiles would have been a poignant reminder of when Grisell and George Baillie were young lovers in Holland over 50 years before, beautifying a library he was no longer there to enjoy. In 1742 Grisell also settles a very substantial bill for £54:14s2d from 'Mr Norie Painter Painting the 2 Pavilions'. In her account book Grisell records Mr. Norie's rates for the more mundane aspects of the painting, viz. 'Mahogany doors 10d pr y[ar]d, marbleing 10d, full painting 8d, once over above old at 4d, Monument statues & pedestels 8d & the Gates & rails 6d whittening 1d', but does not separately note the cost of two landscapes incorporated into the decorative scheme, each an Italianate grisaille capriccio with elements representing ruined Roxburgh Castle and the River Tweed near Kelso (Plate 25b). A more detailed bill originating from 'Mr Norie' himself is endorsed by Grisell 'Account of the yeards &c of Painting In each particular Room & place By George Norie May 1742', though there is still no mention of the landscapes. George was the middle one of James Norie's three sons, a year older at 26 than brother Robert, both now fully engaged in the family business. Their elder brother James junior, also engaged in the family business, had died in 1736, aged only 25.

Externally, the East and West Pavilions were relatively plain, (Plate 27) intended as they were to be the wings of a grand central house, but each pavilion was topped with a small cupola surmounted by a ball and weather vane, the only slightly extravagant element of the buildings. 'For Gilding the 2 thains [vanes] & Balls top Pavilions £2'. The land on the surrounding estate continues to be enclosed by stone walls, and planting and pruning are ongoing. With Grisell back in residence at Mellerstain in 1740, the head gardener must have petitioned for a renewal of equipment as 20 scythes and eight pairs of shears are purchased, together with stones and sand for sharpening, one cart at £1:12s6d and another 'cart & harness compleat' at £7:12s and two wheelbarrows which came all the way from 'Joks lodge' in Edinburgh. She has added up the amounts paid out by William Hume to the 'fivepenny men' since she left Mellerstain in October 1736 to the end of 1741 which came to a staggering £413:5s, translating into 19,836 days' work. The fivepenny men would be directed by the head gardener George Wilson, who is paid £4 a year in money and also gets a house, specified quantities of oats and barley and also grazing or fodder for his cow, amounting to £10 a year in value. He is assisted by his son who is paid £2 a year, and by various journeymen gardeners who are paid mostly in oatmeal. Carriage is paid on young alder trees coming from grandson Tamie, 7th Earl of Haddington's estate at Tyninghame, and flowering shrubs travel from Hopetoun and from Newliston, seat of John Dalrymple, 2nd Earl of Stair, family friend and former colleague of George Baillie.

While much of the outside work was done by casual labourers, the permanent domestic staff had to be paid, fed and clothed. Grisie collected together some of her mother's 'Memorandums and derections to Servants'. The post of butler was a prestigious one, but onerous in Grisell's household, with his list of directions running to 37 items – nothing escaped Grisell's watchful eye. A strict timetable was to be adhered to: 'two bells are to be rung for every meal; for break-fast half an hour after 8 and at 9; for diner half an hour after 1 and at 2; for super half an hour after 8 and at 9. At the first bell for super lay the bible and cushions for prayers'. We learn that the sideboard at dinner and supper is always to be prepared with certain drinks and condiments: 'Bread, Water, peper, vinegar, Ail, wines, mustard, shallot, small Beer, sugar, oyle and salad'. Grisell lays down rules about how the various courses of a meal should be served and instructs, 'As soon as the company leaves the dining room after diner and super come immediately and lock up what Liquors are left, clean your glasses and set everything in its place and in order'. The only flexibility in the day's consumption appears to be the time tea is served in the afternoon. 'Have tea, water and what may be usually cald for in the afternoon ready, that it may not be wait for' (Plate 24a). Many more instructions concern the cleaning of cutlery, silver plate and bottles, and, says Grisell, 'You must keep yourself very clean'. 'N.B. Bring up your Account books every Monday morning and lay them at my room door'. Henry de Pallie appears to have fulfilled the role of butler to Grisell's satisfaction for quite a number of years at this time. The butler was assisted by an under butler who 'puts on the gentlemen's fiers, cleans their boots and shoes, helps to clean every thing, and to get breakfast and to cover the table, etc.'

The post of housekeeper also carried great responsibility. While the butler was responsible for the wine cellar, the housekeeper was in charge of all other food and drink for the entire household, keeping everything under lock and key, and had jurisdiction over all the female servants. She was supplied with every commodity from foodstuffs to soap by weight, and had to give it out carefully weighed to ensure nothing was wasted. The laundry, the dairy and cleanliness of the entire house were all her province, as was the production of linen yarn from the flax grown on the estate. As with the lower servants, there were to be no idle moments for the housekeeper herself as she was to 'help to make the cheese and every now and then as often as you have time to be at the milking of the cows'. The house was heated partially by coal, carried by packhorse or cart from Etal or Duddo collieries in north Northumberland, and partially by wood and peat cut on the Mellerstain estate, and all fuels required the housekeeper's management. 'Let them fill all their places with coals at once, that the kie [key] be not left in the door...be sur it be always lockt at night, that the Turf stack be not tred down but burnt even forward'.

Grisell lays out the servants' diet according to days of the week and the quantities of bread and beer allowed to each. Sunday's menu is boiled beef and broth, Monday, broth and a herring, Tuesday, broth and beef, Wednesday broth and two eggs each, Thursday, broth and beef, Friday, broth and herring, only Saturday having a possible surprise element. 'Saterday broth without meat, and cheese, or a puden or blood pudens, or a hagish, or what is most convenient'. In the printed extracts from the *Household Book* in 1911, Scott-Moncrieff calculated that it cost Grisell about threepence a day to feed each servant, so they probably ate better than the 'fivepenny men', many of whom had a large family to feed on their daily fivepence, with oatmeal porridge cooked over the fire being their usual fare. As Grisell had the luxury of a bread oven the servants' staple of oatmeal was served to them as 'oat loaf' of which they could eat as much as they wanted, 'but no pocketing or waste alowd'. The above diet was for the 'common servants', no allowance being made in the quantities for the 'second table', 'they getting what comes from the first table' i.e. what the family had not consumed.

The ubiquitous broth was varied according to its basis, for which one day's allowance for the potful to serve all the servants might be a pound of 'barly or gro[a]ts, [crushed oats, wheat or rye] or half and half' or 'a pound peas'. Vegetables would be added according to season, and the gardener's order of seeds to be sent in 1736 from Rotterdam gives a clue to what was grown, and in what quantity, in Mellerstain's 'kitchen ground'. At the top of the list are two pounds each of onion, leek, carrot, parsnip, yellow turnip and early turnip, probably mostly destined for the broth and reliable in growth in the Berwickshire climate. A modern seedsman estimates that two pounds of leek seeds would average around 340,000 seeds, and allowing for a germination rate of 50 percent might result in 170,000 seedlings, so perhaps the seed order was calculated to be used over two or three years. Thirty-four pounds of peas of different varieties including 'Dutch Admiral' and 'Spanish Moroco' are bought, together with an additional barrel of un-named peas, probably to be grown for the broth. Peas when they appeared on Grisell's family table were not necessarily frugal, economical fare as this recipe for 'peas soup' in her own handwriting demonstrates: 'three pints of cream or good milk pulp your peas eneugh to make it a proper thicknes season with pepper & what other spice you pleas & salt stir in a ld [pound] of butter or so much as you like scolded spinage [scalded spinach] hertichok bottoms [artichoke hearts] boyl a sprig mint if you like it & fryd bread cut in pieces [croutons]'.

Seeds of more choice vegetables are bought by the ounce, except for red and 'White Spanish' radish, one pound of each, and two pounds of 'round spinage'. There are five varieties of lettuce, Indian and garden cress, red and white beet, cardoons, and curled endive as well as 'short prickly Cuccumber'. The brassica family includes 'Colly flower, Best Early Dutch Cabbage, Red Cabbage, Rupia cabbage, Savoy Cabbage and boorcoal [kale]'. Herbs are represented by chervil, basil, dill and sweet marjoram and there is also a true exotic on most Berwickshire tables, '1oz [ounce] Best Mellon'. Although the family would undoubtedly have eaten melons fresh when living in Italy, a recipe for 'Pickled melon' in the recipe book of George Baillie's niece Rachel Mowbray suggests a different use in Scotland. Asparagus features on several of the menus or 'bills of fare' written down by Grisell, and the 1736 seed order includes four pounds of 'Sparagrass Seed'. Estimated at over 60,000 seeds, the asparagus beds at Mellerstain must have been extensive and asparagus eaten fresh has a short season, but can be pickled to preserve it. Notable by their absence from the Rotterdam seed order are any kind of beans, perhaps more easily obtained locally.

The orchard at Mellerstain had been planned by Lord Binning before his death, and was situated to the north of the East Pavilion. Its nine-foot high walls were built, with lockable gates to deter anyone who might be tempted to plunder the precious fruit, and planting begun during Lord Binning's lifetime. A further 804 trees were purchased from William Boutcher in Edinburgh and planted in March 1733, shortly after Lord Binning's death, so should have been fruiting by Grisell's return to Mellerstain in 1740. There were peaches, nectarines, apricots, cherries, plums, pears and dwarf and espalier apples, dozens of different named varieties of fruit, with their position in the orchard carefully noted, some varieties betraying their

Midlothian origins, such as 'Smiths Newington peach' or 'Dalhousie pepine [pippin]'. The woodland and hedging trees planted a decade earlier in 1731 should now have been growing strongly. In just three weeks from 15 February to 9 March in that year 29,550 trees or cuttings had been planted, namely 19,977 alders, 2,858 ash, 150 elm, 210 oak, 2,635 hornbeam, 100 laburnum, 360 rowan [mountain ash], 3160 saugh [willow] cuttings and 100 bourtree [elder] cuttings and in the eight weeks from 10 March to 7 May, 146,497 'firr' trees were planted. That same autumn, George Wilson planted 13,086 feet of holly hedge, equating to two and a half miles. Several species not mentioned in 1731 were planted the following year, namely beech, maple, lime, walnut and filbert [hazelnut].

Grisell continued to develop all aspects of Mellerstain, to honour the memories of Lord Binning and George Baillie, and always with grandson George Baillie's eventual inheritance in view, as well as providing a comfortable home for herself and her daughters. She also sought to perpetuate her husband's memory by having an engraving made in 1742 of one of his portraits. 'For Ingraveing a Copper Plate for my Dears Pictor 8:8:0…For Casting of 100 Prints from Dit 1:1:0.' The print, by Alexander van Haecken, was taken from the Kneller portrait that had cost 15 guineas in 1719. Though a whole decade had elapsed since the trip to Naples 'Fraught of marbel tables from London and Lieth' cost £3:11s4d, and Grisell sends a gift to Naples of 'black stuff sent to Dona Lavinia Aquviva a nun Naples' costing £3:13s6d.

If Grisell's grandsons Tamie, Lord Haddington and George Baillie wrote to their grandmother at intervals during their foreign travels, which seems likely, these letters have not survived, so we have no account of their adventures, or knowledge of the length of their journeying. Benjamin Stillingfleet reports having made the acquaintance in Rome of 'Lord Haddington, a

Scottish Peer; his brother Mr Baillie [and] their eccentric tutor the amiable Mr Williamson'. The only place actually mentioned in the 1740 accounts is Paris and some months into 1741 George and Tamie have settled in Geneva, where George's expenses in 1741 amount to £618:17s6d and for 1742, £900. George and Tamie joined a group of other young British gentlemen calling their association 'The Common Room'. 'This intelligent and cultivated society consisted of William Windham of Felbrigg in Norfolk...his tutor Benjamin Stillingfleet the naturalist; Lord Haddington and his brother Mr Baillie; Mr Aldborough Neville..:Robert Price...; Mr Chetwynd and last of all [Dr Richard] Pococke'. The citizens of Geneva, still an independent city state at this date, had always been content to view Mont Blanc and its glaciers from afar, but the scientific curiosity of the 'Common Room' demanded a closer acquaintance so an expedition was proposed to 'Chamouni' [Chamonix], led by Windham, who would later write about it. The expedition took a week in all and consisted of the eight above-named gentlemen, taking their servants, horses, provisions and a tent. Mr. Williamson remained behind in Geneva on account of his health. It seems that the intrepid party were the first Alpine explorers as, having reached Chamonix, they continued up the north face of Mont Blanc, reaching a point where they could look down on the glacier, which they compared to a 'sea of ice', and which has been known as the 'Mer de Glace' ever since.

There is little written evidence of grandson George's exact date of return, other than, in 1743, five shillings spent 'for Blooding George', unless it was the five shillings laid out 'For the Dog Kersy', perhaps a 'welcome home' present for the young man just as fond of dogs as his grandfather had been. The grandson may have been indulged by his fond grandmother, but so were the dogs, as in 1743 one shilling and eightpence is spent on 'Dogs Cushens'. Tamie and George must have been returned before June of 1743, when Grisie writes what is largely a business letter to a relative, but includes a none too cheerful account of the household's health, which includes Tamie. 'I this moment received your letter wc Mama has red but desiers me to answer it, not being extremely well herself but better than she was having taken a vomit last night, there is another distemper come among us of sore throats, Ld Hadinton is just now to be blooded for a very bad one & several of the servants are ill, [little] Grisie also has it, but not yet bad.' The family's physician at this time is Dr. [John] Gibson in Kelso whose modest one guinea fee is immediately followed in the 'sundry' accounts by what he presumably prescribed for the household, 'Chamberlain's pills' at 2s6d, leeches at 6d and '4 ounces vomiting pouder' at 3s8d.

The household servants at this period are fairly constant, with the same names recurring in the wages account over several years though in 1743 the faithful and conscientious William Hume died, and at Whitsuntide 1744 Andrew Frame is engaged in Hume's place, and on exactly the same terms. The servant establishment comprises a housekeeper and under housekeeper, a cook, a kitchen maid, two housemaids, two laundry maids, a dairy maid and a lady's maid, the only male indoor servant being the butler, but with Tamie and George abroad, the household in 1742 is an all-female one, so no footman or valet appears in the wages list. Outdoors, there is a head gardener and several assistants, a grieve [farm manager], herd, carter, hedger, coachman, groom and postilion.

In May 1743 an event normally provoking great sadness may also have occasioned feelings of relief at Mellerstain when the death was announced of Sir Alexander Murray, Grisie's estranged husband. Almost five years earlier, when George Baillie had died, Grisie and Rachy had reminded their mother that it was her duty to take care of herself and stay alive to prevent Alexander Murray's attempting to seize Mellerstain, or

Grisie herself, but with Murray's death this ever-present threat was now removed, and Grisie, over 30 years after her marriage, was now a widow, and a free woman.

Refinements continue to be added in 1743 to the internal arrangements of Mellerstain as we can see from a payment of £3:10s 'For Hanging Bels by Palmer'. Previously, one servant at least had to be within earshot of a handbell in order to summon another, whichever was most suitable to the family's needs, but a relatively recent innovation in Scotland at this date was a system of wires and pulleys leading to a central bank of bells in the servants' quarters so an appropriate servant could be summoned at the tug of a rope. Though later concealed within walls, at this time the wires were probably visible on the surface. Grisell had had bells hung in the house in Marlborough Street in 1721 at a cost of over £12, and obviously found them to be a good thing. Perhaps Mr. Palmer had not yet perfected this fairly new-fangled art of bell-hanging as the following year there is an entry of ten shillings and sixpence, 'To Palmer for mending his own bells-imposition.' It is at this time that Grisell's handwriting in the account books begins to be replaced by that of her daughter Grisie, though she is just collating entries from her mother's various cash books, so the 'imposition' comment is almost certainly Grisell's, and had probably been relayed to Mr. Palmer himself in no uncertain terms.

Chapter 13

⁓ℓ⁓

ALBEMARLE STREET, LONDON

1744-1746

Grisell had been 75 years old when her grandsons had left on
their foreign tour, so had expected she might never see them
again but, says Lady Murray, 'When her grandsons came
home, her joy was as great as it could then be for any thing;
her indulgent goodness to them, with the freedom of a friend
and companion, made every thing easy to them; they had not a
wish to make, she could prevent, even by often doing what was
neither convenient nor agreeable to herself.' They had returned
to Mellerstain with its East and West Pavilions, stables and
offices, enhanced landscape, orchards, gardens and woodlands
all now brought into being just as their father Lord Binning
had planned. (Plate 27b, sketch map of Mellerstain as it was by
1740, compiled using a fragile estate map of c1720 and Roy's
Military Map of c1747). However, by September 1744 'it was
thought proper her grandsons should go to London', writes Lady
Murray. 'As they were but just entering into the world [Tamie is
24, George 21], her knowledge, experience and continual advice,

could not but be of great use to them; she therefore resolved we should all go together, though she owned, and it was most natural her desire was, to end her days here [at Mellerstain] in quiet.' 'Yet cheerfully did she set out, to hide from us her uneasiness at going from a place where she thought she was settled for the remains of her life, and as happy as anything then could make her. We had bad rainy weather, which made it a fatiguing, disagreeable journey, but she never complained, was up first, and ordered [organised] everything for the whole company, with an alertness and spirit beyond us all.'

The expense of the journey which began on September 12th, though in Grisie's handwriting, is noted as being 'Copyd from my dear Mothers books'. 'For our journey from Mellerstain to London in 13 days, I, my two daughters, 5 grandchildren 8 servents, 14 horses 6 servants & baggage by sea £101:12s of wich Lady Binning & Lord Hadinton pays the half my part of it is £50:16s'. Grisell obviously thought that life opportunities and marriage prospects for her grandchildren, all now of marriageable age, would be better among London society than in the rural backwater of Mellerstain or provincial Edinburgh. Once in London, a house in Albemarle Street was rented from 'Mr Mumbery', where Grisell enumerates the accommodation as '7 rooms 3 large closets 4 Garits 9 Beds', but very soon afterwards the family set off for Tunbridge Wells in Kent, another fashionable spa town. Grisell's granddaughters are both indulged with presents: earrings, a tippet [scarf or short cape], an account book, and a fan and dressing boxes of Tunbridge ware were bought for young Grisie, and an 'imbroyderd tipet' for young Rachel. Even at this early date, Tunbridge was famed for the making of small pictorial wooden objects, and Grisell spends a further £4:18s6d on '76 pieces of Tunbridgeware mostly to give away'. Gambling is one of the diversions on offer in Tunbridge Wells as Grisell notes £1:1s6d 'Lost at

Tunbridge at E.O.' [Evens/Odds, a game played with a ball and spinning wheel similar to a roulette wheel]. The state lottery was a respectable form of gambling, in effect a long-term loan to the Government which funded wars and building projects, with ticket-holders receiving a small annuity and the chance of winning a cash prize, and Grisell buys two lottery tickets costing £22:12s4d.

It might have been expected that Tamie at 24 and in full possession of his estates might have gone to Tyninghame when the family left Mellerstain, but it was presumably left in the care of servants. Grandson George had long understood that Mellerstain was to be his, though not until after the deaths of his grandmother and his aunt Grisie, but for youngest brother Charles, there was no estate waiting. The career choice for younger sons was often between the army or the church, and Charles opted for the army, probably causing his grandmother Grisell some anxiety about the dangers of war. Although Charles can have had few memories of his father as he was only five years old at the time he and his sister Rachel were left in the care of May Menzies at Tyninghame when the rest of the family set off for Italy, he would have probably heard enough stories of his father and grandfather Haddington fighting at the Battle of Sheriffmuir in 1715, and of grandfather George Baillie's time in the army of William of Orange in the 1680s, to make him set his sights on a military career. Just having passed his seventeenth birthday in the autumn of 1744, Charles joined the Dragoon Guards, and was given what was probably a parting gift from his grandmother Grisell of a watch costing £8.

A letter in January 1745 from Grisell's new factor at Mellerstain seems to show him to be a worthy successor to the efficient and hard-working William Hume. Writing on 3 January 1745, Andrew Frame relays gardener George Wilson's weekly report of how the tree-planting is progressing, what teinds he has paid and the many legal complexities involved, what rents have been paid by tenants, and of Grisell's kind offer to advance John Adamson 40 shillings being refused, 'He being provided with a cow'. Frame praises the work of thatcher Thomas Barber although a new barn roof thatched with heather and a covering of divots [turfs] on the top is letting in rain, but cites nearby Legerwood church which was roofed the same way and let in rain for the first couple of years but has been dry for the past twenty. 'Heather appears to be stiff and unplyable and to require some time before it will ly closs together'. Frame concludes his letter with 'I was sorry to hear of you L[adyshi]p's indisposition and that of my Lady Binning's. I hope ye are now both got better again'. Despite Grisell's note in her accounts saying that the thatching of the barn was 'very ill don', Thomas Barber is later paid £5:4s7d for 'thatching old Tower and offices there', the old tower house now sheltering Andrew Frame as it had done William Hume. May Menzies, a member of Grisell's household for 40 years since being engaged as governess for Grisie and Rachy in 1705, writes to Grisell on 18 July 1745 with a less than favourable opinion of Andrew Frame. 'The hay go[e]s bravely on, Hew [Lawrie, the grieve] is very diligent about it and of every thing else, in short he has all to do the gentleman at the Tower [Frame] takes not nottice of any thing about this place'. May Menzies laments the absence of Grisell and the family. 'Sory are we to see this pleasant place without its owner your improvements here makes me alwise grave to think how glad you would be to see every thing in such beauty.'

Far from peaceful Mellerstain and London, the War of the Austrian Succession was raging in Europe, with over 20,000 British troops commanded by the Duke of Cumberland committed to the fighting, including Grisell's grandson Charles, still just 17, who wrote home to his mother Rachy on 12 May 1745, the day after having been involved in the Battle of Fontenoy. 'We had a most bloody battle with the French yesterday, we begun at five in the morning & left off at two in the afternoon, all which time the French keept cannonading us, I was forst to be very civil and make a great many bows to the balls which were very near me, both my right and left hand men were shot, & all round me there were men and horses tumbling about…the foot [soldiers] were very badly cut to pieces for the French put grape shot into their Cannon & cut them down just as if they were spring corn… I had my horse shot under me just in the knee with a musket ball, & I am affrayd he will always be lame. I was forst to go off the field to get my other horse. I did not regard the small bullets after the Cannon balls in the least tho they came buzing about like beas.' Charles' jocular tone probably did little to ease his mother and grandmother's worries for his safety.

While his young brother Charles was dodging cannon balls on the battlefield, George Baillie was devoting himself to music, Grisell's accounts noting the purchase in 1744 of a French horn costing £2:10s and a silver mouthpiece at an extra 5s6d. George's appearance in London society demanded more refinement than if he had remained at Mellerstain, with Grisell paying for 'gold lace to a belt and covering it with velvet' and '15½ yd gold chain for a Hussar wastcoat'. Accounts for the European trip have continued to filter in, but £317:14s3d in cash is laid out 'in clearing all Forain bills'. In 1745 George was provided with a bay gelding at £22, but his brother Charles' horse must have been a more splendid beast befitting a dragoon at £47:6s, though he got a second horse at £22 and a 'bagage horse' at £14:3s6d. Charles' servant was provided with boots, spurs and a whip for 17s6d. Keen, as ever, to be a patron of poets, musicians and artists, in 1745 Grisell purchases for a total of £5, in two instalments as they became available, a set of six Hogarth's prints. This was the satirist's *Marriage à la Mode* painted in 1743, so Grisell bought the engravings 'hot off the press'.

Charles' and George's elder sister Grisie is now 25 and by the standards of the day in danger of becoming an 'old maid', but perhaps the move to London has given an opportunity for renewing acquaintance with the Stanhope family whose estate at Chevening in Kent was some 30 miles south of the capital. James, 1st Earl Stanhope, who had died in 1721, having bought Chevening in 1717, had been a very close friend and colleague of George Baillie, so it was natural that there should be a continuing connection between the families. James Stanhope's son Philip, five years older than Grisie, had had a childhood blighted by a succession of deaths in the family including the loss of both parents by the time he was seven. He had been on the Grand Tour, and young Grisie, then aged 12, had met Philip Stanhope several times in Italy when he had visited the family during her father's illness. A British minister resident in Italy had said of him, 'he has read a good deal of Divinity, Metaphysicks, and Mathematics. He is really pious, sober, chaste and honest', a description Grisell would surely have approved as it applied equally to George Baillie. Stanhope had been elected a Fellow of the Royal Society, and took his seat in the House of Lords as soon as possible after reaching his majority. Grisie must have come to his notice in the weeks of Christmas 1744 and New Year 1745 when his accounts show tips paid to Tamie, Lord Haddington's servants, and on 16 May Philip Stanhope writes to his younger brother, 'You are like to hear of a marriage soon between the eldest Miss Hamilton and myself', though not until the following day does he say, 'This morning I had my first tête-à-tête with the lady in question.' Grisie had written her letter of acceptance of his proposal on the 16th, declaring herself to be surprised, and unworthy, concluding, 'I hope you'll consider that I have no fortune'.

The *St. James's Evening Post* for 25-27 July reported, 'Last Wednesday Night, about Ten o'clock, the Rt Hon the Earl Stanhope was married, at the Lady Bayley's in Albemarle Street, to the Lady Grizel Hamilton, Sister to the present Earl of Haddington; a beautiful young Lady with a large fortune'.* Lord Stanhope's own accounts show that he paid 12 guineas for a special licence, and £21 'Paid to Mr Williamson for marrying me to Miss Hamilton'. A further £21 was paid in tips 'To the servants in Lady Grizel Baillie's house', and £105 'To my wife, in an endowing purse'. Lord Stanhope's substantial wedding present to his new wife was eclipsed by the gift of wedding clothes from her generous grandmother, with Grisell noting the cost as £353:13s5½d. On 3 August the newly married couple set off for Chevening. To judge by her portraits Lady Stanhope, as she was now described in Grisell's accounts, bore a strong physical resemblance to her grandmother, and once mistress of her own household at Chevening, began keeping meticulous accounts of all expenditure, following her grandmother's example (Plate 28).

While the family were celebrating young Grisie's marriage in London in July 1745, trouble was brewing in Scotland. Just a couple of days before the wedding, Prince Charles Edward Stuart, 'Bonnie Prince Charlie', had landed on the island of Eriskay and began gathering support for a rising against Hanoverian King George II. Charles and his supporters entered Edinburgh unopposed on 17 September, and proclaimed his father as James VIII King of Scotland, and Charles as Regent. A hastily convened army of untrained Government troops under Sir John Cope was almost instantly defeated by the Jacobites at Prestonpans on 21 September. In October the *Gentleman's Magazine* published the words and notation for a new song which had been sung 'in both theatres' [Drury Lane and Covent Garden], to boost morale and show support for defeated King

George. The song began, 'God Save great George our King, Long live our noble King'. After the Government defeat at Prestonpans, the Duke of Cumberland was immediately recalled from the war in Flanders, together with 12,000 troops, including Grisell's grandson Charles. The *London Gazette* of 5-8 October carried a proclamation from King George, in which he declared: 'Whereas an unnatural Rebellion is begun and is now carrying on in the North Part of this our Realm, in favour of a Popish Pretender: And whereas for the more effectual Suppression theoreof, We have occasion for a speedy Augmentation of our Forces'.* Men who enlisted before 25 December could be discharged after six months or 'as soon as the said Rebellion shall be extinguished'. A letter reproduced in *The Penny London Post or The Morning Advertiser* of 30 September-2 October written by 'a Gentleman in Dundee' enabled the newspaper's readership to form a detailed picture of 'the young Chevalier', King George's 'Popish Pretender'. 'He dresses in a Highland Garb of fine Silk Tartan, red Velvet Breeches and a blue Velvet Bonnet with a Gold Lace round it, and a large Jewel and St Andrew appended: He wears also a Green Ribbon, is above six Foot, walks well and streight, and speaks the English and broad Scots very well'.*

Grisell and her family in London must have daily waited anxiously for news as the Jacobite army crept ever closer to Mellerstain. The *London Evening Post* for 29-31 October stated: 'Other Letters mention that the Pretender's eldest Son had his Quarters at the Duke of Buccleugh's House [Dalkeith Palace]: that the Rebels were 8000 effective Men...and that they rob and destroy all round them'.* The Duke of Buccleuch was grandson of the Duke of Monmouth, Charles II's illegitimate son, and therefore a cousin of the Prince, but other members of the lowland nobility were also supporters of the Stuart cause. The Prince's army, in three separate detachments, continued its advance southwards, acquiring horses and foodstuffs and recruiting men along the way. However, for some of the highlanders, going south of Edinburgh was perhaps a step too far, as it was reported on 10 November that many of the 'Rebels' had deserted on their march from Edinburgh, particularly at Kelso.

The rebel army had arrived in Kelso on 4 November, with the Prince reputedly staying at Sunlaws House near the village of Heiton, and on 5 November factor Andrew Frame received a letter addressed 'To Lady Grisell Baillie at Mallerston'.

You are hereby ordered forthwith to repair to Our Secretary's office at Kelso and make payment of the Cess or Land tax of your Lands lying in the County of Berwick And this our Order you are to obey under the pain of Military Execution Given at Kelso the fifth day of November 1745 By His Highness's Command Sic Subscribitur J Murray

(Ironically, Grisie's brother-in-law, Sir John Murray of Broughton, was secretary to Prince Charles.) The accounts, in Grisie's handwriting, show that Frame complied with the threatening request, 'Demanded by Secretary John Murray under pain of Military execution & payd to the Rebels Cess for Melerstain, Nenthorn, Butterdean & Foulden for Sep'r 1745 £15:9:8 Frame reveals that at the same time he had received another demand addressed to Grisell, 'requiring 6 bagage horses to be sent in to Kelso that night under the pain of military execution – accordingly 5 men & horses from Mellerstain toun, the Mill & mains went to Kelso (the 6th who should have gone hid himself out of the way) one whereof made his escape after the second days march, The other 4 went the length of Brampton [nine miles east of Carlisle] where one of them got his leave to come off, and the remaining three got away without leave – all of them returned home safe man and horse.' Not so fortunate were the crew of HMS *Fox* which was wrecked in a storm on 14 November just off Tyninghame Sands, with the loss of over 200 lives, as reported in a letter by May Menzies. No lives were lost at Mellerstain, but on 30 November Andrew Frame catalogues losses of possessions suffered by Grisell's tenants. Six people had had a horse taken from them, others had lost 'several pieces of beef', 'two stones of meal and some children's clothes', 'a bigg coat together with a web coarse linen and several mans shirts', 'a sadle, a whip, two or three cheeses & a couple of rasors'. 'The highlanders shot about ten sheep belonging to Alexander Trotter…Alex[ande]r Foord in Mainberry had several of his wife's head cloaths [caps or headdresses] taken away by some of the highland wives'. In a previous letter to Frame, Grisell must have said she thought the terrible events were a judgement from God, and Frame agrees. 'I am satisfied your L[adyshi]p hath a very Just view of the present troubles on the land as a Judgment inflicted for the punishment of our Iniquitys…I pray the Lord may preserve Mr Hamilton [grandson Charles] and cover his head in the day of battel'. Grisell's own horses at Mellerstain had been scattered to outlying places for safety, and her accounts show the expense of their keep. 'With horses abroad time of the Rebelion £1'.

The Jacobite army had continued its progress southwards and captured Carlisle Castle on 14-15 November, without huge resistance from the garrison, and Charles Hamilton, now 18, was among the troops sent to try to recapture it. Writing to his aunt Grisie on 1 January 1746, he says, 'our canon is at last come up and last Saturday they began to play upon the Town & fired all that day and the next upon the Castle, which brought down a good deal of the wall; and on Sunday we threw into the town some cohorns, [small mortars for throwing grenades] play things which did not go well down with them, so they thought proper to hang out their white flag and surrender the town. Tuesday morning the Duke [of Cumberland] went into the town; all the Rebels were put in the church, I believe between 3 or 4 hunderd, I never saw such a pack of shabby dogs in all my life, there was none but old men and children, I should be vastly sorry to be kill'd by such scoundrels'. The 'last Saturday' mentioned by Charles was Grisell's 80th birthday and presumably in connection with this he says, 'I drunk my Grand-Mama's health in flip [a heated mixture of beer, rum and sugar] and milke pounch [milk, brandy, sugar and vanilla]'.

Writing in London on 2 April 1746 to daughter Rachy who is taking the waters in Bath, Grisell writes the kind of letter she has always written, jumping from minutiae of family life in one sentence to matters of national importance in the next. She complains that none of her household knows how to cook macaroni, and asks Rachy to get Ruth to send instructions, that Lord and Lady Stanhope and Bishop Burnet's family had arrived the other evening at almost 9 o'clock, so all that could be offered them for supper was 'a barrel of oysters and what was in the house', that the Bishop of Hereford had fallen down dead yesterday, and that Lord Archbald Hamilton had fallen off his horse and broken his arm. Of Rachy's elder daughter Grisie, Lady Stanhope, Grisell says, 'L. Sten has been very sick this two days & spewing again but very well otherwise.' Young Grisie is now six months pregnant, giving Grisell the anticipation of becoming a great-grandmother. Having retreated from the north of England, the focus of the Jacobite insurrection has shifted to the Highlands where, says Grisell, 'there is four companys of L[or]d Lauderdale's men taken by the Rebals', and she is glad that her grandson's regiment is out of harm's way. 'I'm sory poor Charly must leave Chest[er] but hapy he gos not to Scotland'.

The Battle of Culloden had taken place on 16 April but Grisie, writing to her sister Rachy in Bath almost a fortnight

later on 29 April, laments that she has no news of it other than
what is in the newspapers, and adds 'There has been great sla[u]
ghter, thank God there is so few on our side. I wish it coud have
been ended w[ithou]t loss any where.' Now a respectable widow,
not a reprehensible separated woman, Grisie's presence at court
on a regular basis is obviously acceptable as she continues, 'I
have don nothing but go to Court', though she gives no detail
of what her role there might be. George II's court at this time
was a lacklustre affair since the death of his Queen Caroline
in 1737, and seemingly dominated by his warring mistresses.
Grisie reports on her mother's health, giving us a glimpse of
Grisell's life in London as a very elderly lady by the standards
of the day, being 'kept an eye on' by her family. 'Mama is quite
another creatur than she has been for several months...L[ad]y
Stair woud have me go home with her from Court, but I said
I did not care to leave Mama. She beg'd me to bring her wc
I did, we was very merry L[or]d Stair seemed very well and
rejoiced to see Mama we came home as soon as we din[e]d.
yesterday befor dinner she walked in the Queens walk wt the
dutches, they set me down at Whitehall then the dut [duchess]
came and played at Bag: [backgammon] wt her till diner time'.
Grisie also casts light on the contrasting habits of Grisell's two
eldest grandsons. 'Geo[rge] (Plate 29) never leaves her when
I am out. L[or]d H[addington] we see not often, he was last
night at a Ball at Churchills & is not yet up.' In an undated
letter to Rachy, possibly enclosed in Grisie's letter above, Grisell
tells of receiving news of Culloden by 'ane express come today.
The Rebells is intirely routed, the Prince gone westward with
only Sullivan & Sherredain his secretary Perth & his brother
are both gone off & not held Loch[i]ell has both his legs shot
off'. Perhaps hinting that young people's dress often meets with
the disapproval of their elders, she advises her daughter 'Pray
let not Rachel appear like a scrub'. (Rachel, Grisell's youngest

grandchild, is now 16). She concludes with 'services to all friends & to Nash [Richard 'Beau' Nash, master of ceremonies at Bath]'.

Probably at some time after the move to London in 1744, Grisell's likeness (Plate 30) was drawn in coloured chalks by family friend Allan Ramsay, also resident in London and who had already painted a double portrait of grandchildren Charles and Rachel in 1740 (Plate 31). Ramsay captured Grisell's forceful personality, but made no attempt to flatter, showing us a sharp-featured old woman in a close-fitting cap. At this period also, a set of small wax portrait reliefs were made by Isaac Gosset, a renowned wax modeller. They depict Grisell's wider family, and include a posthumous portrait of George Baillie. The reliefs were possibly commissioned while the family were all gathered at Grisell's house for granddaughter Grisie's marriage in July 1745, though they do not appear in Grisie's accounts until 1747, and comprise Grisell herself and George Baillie, Grisie, Rachy, Tamie, granddaughter Rachel, granddaughter Grisie and her new husband Philip Stanhope, and also Philip Dormer Stanhope, a cousin of young Grisie's husband, all shown in profile.

The accounts of Sundry Expenses for 1746, in Grisie's handwriting, begin with, 'For carriage of a trunk with Child bed linnin & all necessars in the munth for Lady Stanhope from Mellerstain £1:5s6d.' On 24 June 1746, granddaughter Grisie's son was born, making Grisell a proud great-grandmother, and she was asked to be Godmother at his christening. The infant was named Philip, and bore the title Viscount Mahon. The accounts continue, 'For my dear Mother standing God Mother at Philip Stanhope Lord Mahon's Christening, born June 24th £10.' A dissenting minister, Mr. Crookshanks, was paid two guineas for performing the ceremony, and the baby was lavishly dressed in a cloak made from five yards of scarlet padesoy [corded silk] costing £2:7s6d, with another £2:4s for lining and wadding it and attaching the four yards of silver lace. The child's outfit was completed with a velvet cap and feather costing 16s6d. It is likely that servants, particularly nurses, expected generous 'drink money' at important events such as christenings, and tips amounted to £2:6s6d in London, and £4 'at Chevening Lord Stanhops Country house'.

In the list of servants' wages for those left 'holding the fort' at Mellerstain, some of the same surnames crop up year after year, with the local population pleased to have a regular, if small, income and, in the case of the indoor servants, a roof over their head and three meals a day. Central London, however, was full of households employing a large number of servants, so choice of employment was great and Grisie notes, in a summary of servants employed 1745-7, money paid out 'to ten bad Cooks while at London'. Four butlers come and go in the space of four months, the next one, John Coyn, though designated 'bad' lasts eight months, and his successor Charles Wilkison a year and ten months, described by Grisie as 'clever but careless'. Two footmen are mentioned by name, George Landroff and John Bentley, with Landroff even earning the accolade 'good' in Grisie's estimation. One of the footmen's tasks was to answer the door, and it presumably fell to them also to write down the names of the various callers, and the Albemarle Street visitors' book commencing at 9 November 1746 still exists. The book is no grand leather-bound volume signed by the visitors themselves, but consists of a number of foolscap sheets of paper folded lengthways with a couple of stitches to hold them together. As well as the names of the visitors, many of them titled, it was also noted whether they 'Came' in person, or 'Sent' a servant with a message or enquiry. On 9 November twelve visitors 'Came', namely Lady Irwin, the Bishop of Landaff, Justice [Sir Thomas] Burnet, Lady Rich, Mrs. Carr, Docter Pringle, Lady Bath, Lady

Williams, Mrs. Cleland, Mr. Mitchel, Mrs. Walkinshaw and Lady Lessleys (all as spelled by the servant), and Lady Sharlet Edwind 'Sent'. The only member of the household ever singled out as recipient of a visitor is Tamie, Lord Haddington, and his visitors neither 'Came' nor 'Sent' but 'Cald for', as in 'Mr [David] Garick cald for Lord Hadinton' on 12 November. In the five weeks' duration of the book some names appear only once, others numerous times and of these latter some, Lord and Lady Findlater, the Earl and Countess of Rothes and several members of the Leslie family, are Lord Binning's relatives. Others, Mrs. Walkinshaw, Lady Archbald Hamilton, Lady Charlotte Edwin and Lady Anne Irwin, are known to have had positions at court, and a number were long-standing family friends: the Earl and Countess of Carlisle and their daughter Lady Mary Howard, the Duke and Duchess of Montrose and Molly Lepell, Lady Hervey. One frequent visitor otherwise not known to be part of Grisell's social circle is the Bishop of Llandaff, John Gilbert, who was sometimes accompanied by his wife and daughter.

The majority of visitors up to 17 November 1746 'Came' rather than 'Sent', but after this date the number of people sending a servant greatly outnumbers those who came in person, suggesting that at least one person in the household was ill, necessitating enquiries after their health, and restricting visits, though it seems that it was probably Grisie or Rachy who was unwell, rather than their mother. At the beginning of December on a small scrap of paper Grisell wrote the date '1 Dcmr 1746', and 'To the whole sums received since the 24th Septr 1744 3710...4'. This was later annotated by Grisie, 'of Little use, but keept because it is amongst the last things my dear Mother writ', as the first of December was the day Grisell fell ill. The next day, Doctor Shaw was summoned, and given a fee of two guineas, on 3 December and again on 4 December both Doctor Shaw and Doctor Pringle attended at a combined cost of eight guineas, and on 5 December Dr. Ward earned one guinea, and 'Coomcross', an apothecary, was paid £3:16s6d 'for twice blooding & his bill', but all to no avail as early on the morning of 6 December Grisell died, just three weeks short of her 81st birthday.

Realising her end was near, Grisell's last days were tinged with regret for the continued estrangement of her nephews Hugh, 3rd Earl of Marchmont, and his twin brother Alexander, as recounted by Lady Murray in the Memoirs. 'As we sat by her bed, and hoped she was asleep, we heard her earnestly praying: amongst other things, she said, "Lord, forgive the two brothers their injustice to me, and give them a sight of their sin and folly". When she was begged to lie quiet, and not disturb herself with those unworthy of it, "My dear," said she "remember they are my dear brother's sons".'

Lady Murray wrote, 'Two days before she died, we were all in the room: she said, "My dears, read the last chapter of the Proverbs; you know what it is." To have her grandsons happily married, lay near her heart.' Verses 10-31 of the last chapter of Proverbs begin with, 'Who can find a virtuous woman, for her price is far above rubies', and Lady Murray goes on to say, 'I think it a very strong picture of herself; and if any deserved to have it said of them, she does. The next day, she called me; gave directions about some few things; said she wished to be carried home to lie by my father, but that perhaps it might be too much trouble and inconvenience to us at that season, therefore left it to me to do as I pleased; but that, in a black purse in her cabinet, I would find sufficient money to do it, which she had kept by her, for that use, that whenever it happened, it might not straiten us. She added, "I have now no more to say or do;" tenderly embraced me, and laid down her head upon the pillow, and spoke little after that'.

Grisell's final hours were also described by Doctor Pringle

[later Sir John Pringle of Stichill] in a letter to his sister Margaret, Lady Hall. 'Lady Grisel Baillie died this morning after a few days illness, which begun with a cold & ended with a total suppression of urine. She had her senses visibly till within a few hours of her death & probably till she expired tho' she did not speak for about 12 hours before. Her family had the satisfaction to have Mr Baillie [George] come from the Country & to be seen & spoke to by her just before she ceased to take any notice of things about her. She herself had the last comfort of having all her children round her & serving her with that affection & concern she deserved of them'. In 1738, even before George Baillie's death, Grisell had written, 'I wish, if it please God, he may bring us home to dy in our own country amongst our friend[s] at the same time if we make a happy end, as I trust in Gods mercy we shall its no matter where it be'.

In the four days preceding Grisell's death no fewer than 44 families or individuals had sent enquiries, and callers in person who were not family members included Samuel Torriano, Lady Mary Howard, Mrs. Walkinshaw, the Bishop of Llandaff and the Countess of Strafford, Lady Anne Campbell, whose great-grandfather the 9th Earl of Argyll had been an associate of Grisell's father Sir Patrick in the dangerous days of the 1680s. For the last couple of years expenses from Grisell's cash books had been transferred to the Day Book or Journal by Grisie, and a mundane bill for street lighting, 'For Lamps lighted 27 weeks at 18d per week 2 lamps £2:0s6d' is followed by 'For blooding me the last artickle in my dear Mothers book 10s6d'. Grisie then writes: 'For the Expence of my dear Mothers sickness and funeral, the most sorrowfull ever happened to me, never to be forgot'. Most of the sums spent on 6 December are the expected funeral items, 'For a coffin lind with lead covered with black cloth etc £10, For hat bands, gloves, serchers, porters etc £1:12s6d' and 'For 4 y[ar]ds fine flannel and a burial sheet

£1:13s', but, more unusually, Grisie must have sent immediately to a sculptor's studio for someone to come and make a death mask of her mother: 'For taking a mold in Plaster of Paris £1:5s'. The mould having been taken, no undertaker was sent for, as Lady Murray explains in the Memoirs. 'My sister, who had been long ill, was carried out of her bed to attend her; but we were both almost incapable of doing the last duties to her; but *that* Lady Stanhope supplied, with the same tender dutifulness she had ever behaved to her; and with a fortitude uncommon at her age, stretched and dressed her in the manner she had always directed; which was in her ordinary night clothes, and then rolled in a sheet; all which she did, without letting another hand touch her; for which, and her tender care and concern for her mother and me, I doubt not God will reward her by the dutifulness of her own child. My mother had always expressed a dislike of the method in London, of delivering over to the undertakers for funerals, any one that died, to be ordered by them as they thought proper; therefore we were desirous that none such should come about her, or touch her; nor was she ever left by some of her family, till they saw the lead coffin soldered down. Though it rent the heart to be witness to it, we were all there, to see the last thing done that was in our power.'

The account books also contain some detail of Grisell's last journey to Mellerstain. 'For a Herse & 7 horses to Mellerstain 34 days [17 days each way] £52:15s, for feeding a sadle horse £3:18s10d, for turnpicks [road tolls], watching, crossing Tweed & guide £4:4s9d.' The coffin would probably have been transferred to a ferry to cross the Tweed at Coldstream, while the hearse and horses crossed at the ford, as another 16 years would pass before Grisell's grandson George Baillie was the chief mover of the committee formed to have a bridge built there. 'For the diet of two servants going and coming £9:14s' suggests that Grisell's corpse was accompanied only by servants and not by any family member, but perhaps her grandsons made their way to Mellerstain separately by coach. Although the burial was not taking place in the parish of St George's, Hanover Square, £1:17s still had to be paid 'For burial dews the Parroach of St Georges'.

On one sheet of paper, rapidly scrawled in two different hands, are two draft letters of intimation, to be sent out to friends and acquaintances. The first reads, 'London Dc 6 It is with the utmost affiction [sic] I write this to inform you that it pleased God to take my Grand=Mama from us this morning after a few days illness, you knew her worth so must be sensible of our loss. We are all better than could be expected. I am...'. The second is more curt, perhaps intended for people who had a more distant relationship with Grisell's family. 'I think it proper to inform you that it pleased God to take from us this morning at two o'clock my Grand Mother Lady Grisel to the great affliction of our whole family. I am...' Few words were wasted, but a large number of letters would have to be sent out, so George and Tamie's pens would have been scratching for many hours.

No doubt a less formal letter was sent to Mellerstain, but it had not reached there by 9 December, when factor Andrew Frame addresses a letter to Grisell, defending his account-keeping, which Grisell has expressed 'surprise' at in late November, assuring her that although he has not written up all the rental accounts, his collection of rents is up to date. When the news of Grisell's death finally reached Mellerstain, it probably fell to May Menzies to organize the funeral catering for the few gentlemen who had been bidden to the funeral, as well as Grisell's own tenants on the estate. She may have been assisted by Mrs. Mowbray, George Baillie's niece Rachel Dundas, who had been part of Grisell's household in her youth and was now so again since being widowed. It had been decided that it was most fitting to hold the funeral on Christmas Day, always celebrated as Grisell's birthday. The draft copy of a letter written by George or Tamie reads, 'The sixth of this month died my GrandMother Lady Grisell Baillie the favour of your Company at her house at Mellerstain the 25 to attend her funeral to her burying place there will very much oblige S:r Your most humble servant… Dec'r 9 1746'. Andrew Frame's cash book states, 'Paid to William Young Beddal [beadle] in Earlstoun for digging My Lady's Grave and bringing the Mortcloath etc £1', and 'Distribute to the begging poor present at Lady Grisel Baillies funerals £3:14s6d'; Grisie's own accounts reveal a further £5 given to the fund for the poor which was administered by the parish. Unlike George Baillie's funeral eight years previously, we have no details of the refreshments offered to mourners, Grisie simply noting, 'For expenses at the burial beside wine etc £6:18s'.

As it was Earlston's beadle who dug the grave and supplied the mortcloth, [a cloth, often black velvet, used to cover the coffin] it can be assumed that the minister of Earlston, John Gowdie (junior) conducted the funeral service at the Monument, when Grisell was laid in the earth of her beloved Mellerstain, beside George Baillie as she had wished. George Baillie had extended the estate about 1731 by purchasing the lands of Smailholm, and a funeral sermon was given there on 28 December, presumably by Alexander Duncan, the minister of Smailholm. He gave a résumé of Grisell's early life 'when all methods were used to enslave us again to Popery and arbitrary power', and points out Grisell's helpfulness to George Baillie, contrasting her with 'the common Run of Lady of high Birth who when their husbands are employed abroad are taken up wth finery & Cards & Company at home', suggesting that he didn't know Grisell very well as she was able to enjoy all those implicitly sinful things as well as working ceaselessly in the service of her family. The minister directly addresses his congregation, reminding them of Grisell's charity. 'She was a constant help to the poor and the needy; of which the poor of this place are proofs: You will remember how seasonably ofttimes she hath relieved you: the two last Scarce Seasons, when she was absent, she did send you a liberal Supply.' Towards the end of his lengthy eulogy, he says, 'I am sensible this Character is so uncommon & that I myself ly under so many obligations of gratitude & affection that I might justly be suspected of flattery; If I could not appeal to many living witnesses of the truth of what I have said'.

After Grisell's death, the household remained in London well into 1747, perhaps seeking diversions to console them for their loss. Grisell's granddaughter Rachel is distracted by 'a Maskerad, an Oratorio, plays' costing £2:14s6d, and viewing the 'lunaticks' at the Royal Bethlem Hospital in Moorfields seemed to have as much entertainment value as seeing the menagerie at the Tower of London: 'For a party to the Tower, Bedlam and Greenwich our own family & Mr Mitchells £2:11s6d'. Possibly the visit to Greenwich included the Royal Observatory as someone is indulged with 'a Reflecting Teliscop from Oliver Crowe 12 inches long', its price as well as its purpose being astronomical at £7:17s6d. The bookseller's bill at £11:10s6d featured numerous volumes on history, the arts, religion, law and poetry as well as paper and pens, and also included 19 shillings 'For printing 500 of my dear Mother's Epitaphs'. Grisie also wanted to have her sister Rachy immortalised for posterity at this significant moment in the family's history by commissioning Thomas Bardwell to paint her portrait in June, Rachy shown wearing a widow's veil and reading from the Bible. Bardwell's price was a modest four guineas, but Allan Ramsay could command a total of 21 guineas for the two portraits of Tamie and George commissioned shortly afterwards, both wearing 'van Dyck dress', George touchingly holding up a miniature of his beloved grandmother.

In July the household sets out northwards, aiming initially

for Wooler Haughhead and its healing goat whey, an expedition organized numerous times by Grisell herself, and Grisie lists 'Expences of our journey from London to Wooler haugh head in 12 days Lady Binning, her 3 children Mr Williamson and I six servants and eliven horses Jully 18th'. The '3 children' are presumably Rachel, George and Tamie, as Charles will be with his regiment and Grisie, Lady Stanhope with her husband and baby son at Chevening or London. Bringing the horses to London from Mellerstain with three servants had cost over £64. Household goods weighing 28 stone were sent to Newcastle by wagon at 3s6d per stone, and thence to Mellerstain, but 33 barrels of goods were sent by sea to Leith, at three shillings per barrel, then on to Dunbar, accompanied by '5 servants, 4 dogs and a catt', their ship unfortunately being wind bound at Harwich for nine days.

Finally, on 25 August 1747 the family arrives back at Mellerstain, giving Grisie and Rachy the first opportunity to visit their mother's grave, eight months after her burial. The monument, though finished in terms of the building of its walls, doors and gates before George Baillie was buried there in August 1738, still lacked inscriptions other than the general one:

BUILT BY GEORGE BAILLIE OF JERVISWOOD
AND LADY GRISELL BAILLIE
A.D.1736
The pious parents rear'd this hallowed place,
A monument for them, and for their race.
Descendants, be it your successive cares,
That no degenerate dust ere mix with their's.

In November 1747, included in 'Mr Roubillac Statuary in London his acc[oun]t' are '2 plates of Marble for the Monument containing 40 foot at 6 sh: a foot £12' followed with 'By ingraving of inscriptions on these plates of 2844 letters at 2d a letter £23:14s'. Louis-François Roubiliac is unlikely to have carved the lettering for the Monument himself, leaving that to an assistant, but certainly carved the marble bust of Grisell still on display at Mellerstain (Plate 32), probably working from the 'mold in Plaster of Paris' taken on the morning of her death, the bust costing £31:10s and 'a pedistel for it with an inscription' a further two guineas. Grisie herself also sat to Roubiliac for a marble bust, his studio in St Martin's Lane being only a mile from her lodgings in Albemarle Street. Grisie's bust also cost £31:10s with two guineas for the socle. Terracotta busts at 10 guineas each of Grisie and her mother were sent to Tyninghame, and plaster of Paris busts at two guineas each were cast from moulds made from these, the moulds remaining with Roubiliac.

George Baillie's inscription on the Monument is a 60-line Latin text composed by Walter Harte, one of George and Tamie's tutors at St Mary Hall in Oxford. Grisell's epitaph is 40 lines in English, written by Judge Sir Thomas Burnet, youngest son of George Baillie's cousin Bishop Burnet.

HERE LIETH

The Right Honourable LADY GRISELL BAILLIE

Wife of GEORGE BAILLIE of Jerviswood, Esq.

Eldest daughter

Of the Right Honourable PATRICK, Earl of Marchmont;

A pattern to her sex, and an honour to her country.

She excelled in the characters of a daughter, a wife, a mother.

While an infant,

At the hazard of her own, she preserved her father's life;

Who, under the rigorous persecution of arbitrary power,

Sought refuge in the close confinement of a tomb,

Where he was nightly supplied with necessaries, conveyed by
her,
With a caution far above her years,
A courage almost above her sex;
A real instance of the so much celebrated Roman charity.
She was a shining example of conjugal affection,
That knew no dissension, felt no decline,
During almost a fifty year's union;
The dissolution of which she survived from duty, not choice.
Her conduct, as a parent,
Was amiable, exemplary, successful,
To a degree not well to be expressed,
Without mixing the praises of the dead with those of the
living;
Who desire that all praise, but of her, should be silent.
At different times she managed the affairs
Of her father, her husband, her family, her relations,
With unwearied application, with happy economy,
As distant from avarice as from prodigality.
Christian piety, love of her country,
Zeal for her friends, compassion for her enemies,
Cheerfulness of spirit, pleasantness of conversation,
Dignity of mind,
Good breeding, good humour, good sense,
Were the daily ornaments of an useful life,
Protracted by Providence to an uncommon length,
For the benefit of all who fell within the sphere of her
benevolence.
Full of years, and of good works,
She died on the 6th day of December 1746,
Near the end of her 81st year,
And was buried on her birth-day, the 25th of that month.

Judge Burnet's eulogistic epitaph is in the language of its time, somewhat over-blown to modern ears. Perhaps Grisell might have preferred to be remembered using the last seven verses of Proverbs, in the mellifluous language of the King James Bible:

> *Strength and honour are her clothing; and she shall rejoice in time to come.*
>
> *She openeth her mouth with wisdom; and in her tongue is the law of kindness.*
>
> *She looketh well to the ways of her household, and eateth not the bread of idleness.*
>
> *Her children arise up, and call her blessed; her husband also, and he praiseth her.*
>
> *Many daughters have done virtuously, but thou excellest them all.*
>
> *Favour is deceitful, and beauty is vain: but a woman that praiseth the LORD, she shall be praised.*
>
> *Give her the fruit of her hands; and let her own works praise her in the gates.*

APPENDIX 1

Were na my hearts licht

Lady Grisell Baillie

There was an a May, and she lo'ed na Men:
She bigged her bonny Bow'r down in yon Glen;
But now she cries, dale and a-well-a-day,
Come down the green Gate and come here away.

When bonny young Johnny came over the Sea,
He said he saw nathing so bonny as me,
He haight me baith Rings and mony bra things,
And were na my Hearts light, I wad die.

He had a wee Titty that lo'ed na' me,
Because I was twice as bonny as she;
She rais'd sick a Pother twixt him and his Mother
That were na my Hearts light I wad die.

The Day it was set, and the Bridal to be;
The Wife took a Dwalm and lay doon to die,
She main'd and she grain'd out of Dollor and Pain,
Till he vow'd he ne'er wou'd see me again.

His Kin was for ane of a higher Degree
Said, what had he do with the Likes of me?
Appose I was bonny, I was na for Johnny;
And were na my Hearts light, I wad die.

They said, I had neither Cow nor Calf,
Nor drops of Drink runs through the Drawf;
Nor Pickles of Meal runs through the Mill-Eye;
And were na my Hearts light, I wad die.

The Maiden she was baith wylie and slye,
She spy'd me as I came o'er the Lee;
And then she ran in, and made sick a Din;
Believe your ain Een, an ye trow na me.

His Bonnet stood ay fu' round on his Brow,
His auld ane lookt ay as well as his new;
But now he lets't gang ony Gate it will hing,
And casts himsell down on the Corn-Bing.

And now he gaes drooping about the Dykes,
And a' he dow do is to hund the Tykes;
The live-lang Night he ne'er bows his Eye:
And were na my Hearts light, I wad die.

But young for thee as I ha' been,
We shou'd ha' been galloping down in yon Green;
And linking out o'er yon lilly white Lee;
And wow gin I were young for thee.

O, the ewe-buchtin's bonnie

Words: Lady Grisell Baillie

O, the ewe-bucht-in's bo-nnie. baith e'e-ning and morn, When our

blithe shep-herds play on the bog-reed and horn; While we'remilk ing, they're lil - ting, baith

pleas-ant and clear, But my heart's like to break when I think on my dear. O the

shep herds take pleas-ure to blow. on the horn__ To raise up their flocks o' sheep

soon__ i' the morn; On the bonn - ie green banks they feed

pleas - ant and free, But a - las, my dear heart, all my sigh-ing's for thee!

APPENDIX 2

ANCESTRY OF RACHEL BAILLIE

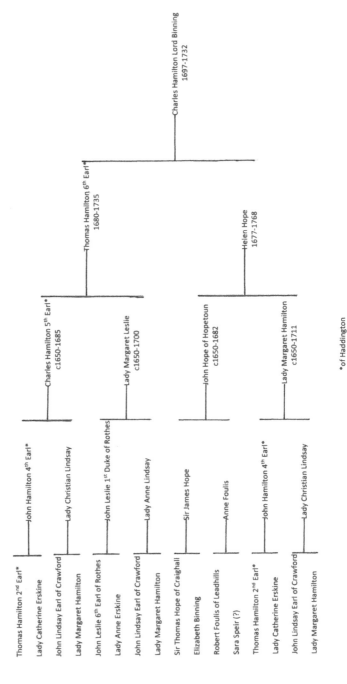

Thomas Hamilton 2ⁿᵈ Earl*

Lady Catherine Erskine

John Lindsay Earl of Crawford

Lady Margaret Hamilton

John Leslie 6ᵗʰ Earl of Rothes

Lady Anne Erskine

John Lindsay Earl of Crawford

Lady Margaret Hamilton

Sir Thomas Hope of Craighall

Elizabeth Binning

Robert Foulis of Leadhills

Sara Speir (?)

Thomas Hamilton 2ⁿᵈ Earl*

Lady Catherine Erskine

John Lindsay Earl of Crawford

Lady Margaret Hamilton

John Hamilton 4ᵗʰ Earl*

Lady Christian Lindsay

John Leslie 1ˢᵗ Duke of Rothes

Lady Anne Lindsay

Sir James Hope

Anne Foulis

John Hamilton 4ᵗʰ Earl*

Lady Christian Lindsay

Charles Hamilton 5ᵗʰ Earl*
c1650-1685

Lady Margaret Leslie
c1650-1700

John Hope of Hopetoun
c1650-1682

Lady Margaret Hamilton
c1650-1711

Thomas Hamilton 6ᵗʰ Earl*
1680-1735

Helen Hope
1677-1768

Charles Hamilton Lord Binning
1697-1732

* of Haddington

254

APPENDIX 3
ANCESTRY OF CHARLES HAMILTON

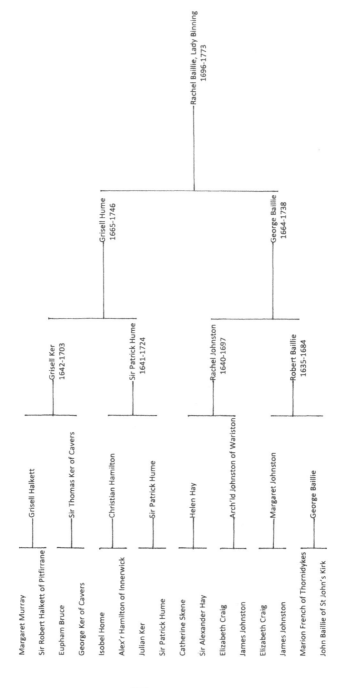

Margaret Murray
Sir Robert Halkett of Pitfirrane

Eupham Bruce
George Ker of Cavers

Isobel Home
Alex'r Hamilton of Innerwick

Julian Ker
Sir Patrick Hume

Catherine Skene
Sir Alexander Hay

Elizabeth Craig
James Johnston

Elizabeth Craig
James Johnston

Marion French of Thornidykes
John Baillie of St John's Kirk

Grisell Halkett

Sir Thomas Ker of Cavers

Christian Hamilton

Sir Patrick Hume

Helen Hay

Arch'ld Johnston of Wariston

Margaret Johnston

George Baillie

Grisell Ker
1642-1703

Sir Patrick Hume
1641-1724

Rachel Johnston
1640-1697

Robert Baillie
1635-1684

Grisell Hume
1665-1746

George Baillie
1664-1738

Rachel Baillie, Lady Binning
1696-1773

255

APPENDIX 4

Children of Sir Patrick Hume and Grisell Ker married 29th January 1659/60

1. Daughter March 1661 – died soon
2. Son 1662 – died soon
3. Christian 30.6.1663 died 18.10.1664
4. Patrick 11.11.1664 died 25.11.1709
5. **Grisell** 24.12.1665 died 6.12.1746
6. Thomas 29.4.1667 died 15.12 1668
7. Christian 4.5.1668 died c.11.11.1688
8. Robert 9.7.1669 died 1692
9. Julianne 9.11.1670 – died soon
10. Thomas 15.6.1672 – died soon
11. Julian 16.8.1673 died after 1724
12. Alexander (Sandy) 1.1.1675 died 27.2.1740
13. Daughter miscarried August 1675
14. Andrew 19.7.1676 died 16.3.1730
15. Anne 4.11.1677 died 24.1.1699
16. Son miscarried September 1678
17. ?Elizabeth (Tibbie) Died c. May1686
18. George 4.1.1682 died before 1685
19. Jean 27.3.1683 died 10.12.1751
20. Child miscarried at The Hague September 1688

Children of George Baillie and Grisell Hume married 17th September 1691

1. Grisell 26.10.1692 died 6.6.1759
2. Robert 23.1.1694 died 28.2.1696
3. Rachel 23.2.1696 died 24.3.1773

Children of Charles Hamilton, Lord Binning and Rachel Baillie married 24th July 1717

1. Grisell 6.4.1719 died 28.12.1811
2. Thomas 23.10.1720 died 19.5.1794
3. George 24.6.1723 died 16.4.1797
4. Helen 8.10.1724 died before 1730
5. Charles 6.10.1725 died before 1727
6. John 20.10.1726 died 1730
7. Charles James 3.10.1727 died 28.9.1806
8. Rachel died 20.10.1797

General Index

(Immediate family members and most servants
are not indexed as they occur too frequently.)